2 Practice Tests for the
SAT®

The Staff of The Princeton Review

PrincetonReview.com

Penguin
Random
House

The Princeton Review
110 East 42nd Street, 7th Floor
New York, NY 10017
Email: editorialsupport@review.com

Published in the United States by Penguin Random House LLC, New York, and in Canada by Random House of Canada, a division of Penguin Random House Ltd., Toronto.

ISBN: 978-0-375-97795-4

The material in this book was previously published in *10 Practice Tests for the SAT*, 2019 Edition, a trade paperback published by Random House LLC in 2018.

Editorial
Rob Franek, Editor-in-Chief
Casey Cornelius, Chief Product Officer
Mary Beth Garrick, Executive Director of Production
Craig Patches, Production Design Manager
Selena Coppock, Managing Editor
Meave Shelton, Senior Editor
Colleen Day, Editor
Sarah Litt, Editor
Aaron Riccio, Editor
Orion McBean, Associate Editor

Penguin Random House Publishing Team
Tom Russell, VP, Publisher
Alison Stoltzfus, Publishing Director
Amanda Yee, Associate Managing Editor
Ellen Reed, Production Manager
Suzanne Lee, Designer

Editor: Aaron Riccio
Production Editor: Kathy Carter
Production Artist: Deborah A. Weber

Printed in the United States of America.

10 9 8 7 6 5 4 3 2 1

First Edition

Acknowledgments

The Princeton Review would like to recognize Sara Kuperstein, Kathy Carter, and Deborah Weber for their swift and attentive work on this title.

Special thanks to Adam Robinson, who conceived of and perfected the Joe Bloggs approach to standardized tests, and many of the other successful techniques used by The Princeton Review.

Contents

Get More (Free) Content

1 Go to **PrincetonReview.com/cracking.**

2 Enter the following ISBN for your book: 9780375977954.

3 Answer a few simple questions to set up an exclusive Princeton Review account. (If you already have one, you can just log in.)

4 Click the "Student Tools" button, also found under "My Account" from the top toolbar. You're all set to access your bonus content!

Need to report a **technical** issue?

Contact
TPRStudentTech@review.com
and provide:

- your full name
- email address used to register the book
- full book title and ISBN
- computer OS (Mac/PC) and browser (Firefox, Safari, etc.)

Need to report a potential **content** issue?

Contact
EditorialSupport@review.com.
Include:

- full title of the book
- ISBN
- page number

Once you've registered, you can...

- Take a full-length practice SAT and/or ACT

- Get valuable advice about the college application process, including tips for writing a great essay and where to apply for financial aid

- If you're still choosing between colleges, use our searchable rankings of *The Best 384 Colleges* to find out more information about your dream school

- Check to see if there have been any corrections or updates to this edition

- Download additional bubble sheets and score conversion tables, and even score your test online

- Get our take on any recent or pending updates to the SAT

Chapter 1
What You Need to Know for the SAT

GENERAL INFORMATION ABOUT THE SAT

Let's take a moment to discuss some SAT facts. Some of them may surprise you.

Who Writes the SAT?

Even though colleges and universities make wide use of the SAT, they're not the ones who write the test. That's the job of Educational Testing Service (ETS), a nonprofit company that writes tests for college and graduate school admissions, and the College Board, the organization that decides how the tests will be administered and used.

They've changed the SAT twice in the last fifteen years, and they've admitted that students can and should prepare for the test, which means that the test *can* be beaten, and as they say, practice helps to make perfect.

What's on the SAT?

The SAT is 3 hours long, or 3 hours and 50 minutes long if you choose to take the "optional" essay. It includes four tests (and the essay).

- Reading Test: 65 minutes, 52 questions
- 10-minute break
- Writing and Language Test: 35 minutes, 44 questions
- Math Test (No Calculator): 25 minutes, 20 questions
- 5-minute break
- Math Test (Calculator): 55 minutes, 38 questions
- 2-minute break
- Essay: 50 minutes, 1 prompt

Wait, *Who* Writes This Test?
You may be surprised to learn that the people who write SAT test questions are NOT necessarily teachers or college professors. The people who write the SAT are professional test writers, not superhuman geniuses, so you can beat them at their own game.

"Optional" Is as Optional Does
Though the SAT refers to the essay as optional, there are some colleges that may require it. Before planning your test-day strategy, make sure you've researched each of the colleges you plan on applying to, and take the essay only if you have to.

With the exception of the open-ended essay prompt and a few grid-in problems in the math section, everything else is multiple-choice, with four options for each question. Here's a brief rundown of what to expect.

Reading Test

Your score on the Evidence-Based Reading and Writing section of the SAT comprises your scores on the Reading Test and the Writing and Language Test. The Reading Test is 65 minutes long and consists of 52 questions, all of which are passage-based and multiple-choice. Passages may be paired with informational graphics, such as charts or graphs, and there will also be a series of questions based on a pair of passages. The selected passages will be from previously published works in the areas of world literature, history/social studies, and science. Questions based on science passages may ask you to analyze data or hypotheses, or to read graphs, while questions about literature passages will concentrate more on literary concepts like theme, mood, and characterization. The main goal is to measure your ability to both understand words in context and find and analyze evidence.

Writing and Language Test

The Writing and Language Test is 35 minutes long and consists of 44 questions, which are also multiple-choice and based on several passages. However, instead of asking you to analyze a passage, questions will ask you to proofread and edit the passage. That means you'll have to correct grammar and word choice and make larger changes to the organization or content of the passage.

Math Test

You'll have a total of 80 minutes to complete the Math Test, which, as we mentioned earlier, is divided into two sections. The No-Calculator portion is 25 minutes, and has 20 questions, while the Calculator portion is 55 minutes, with 38 questions. Most questions are multiple-choice, but there are also handfuls of student-produced response questions, which are also known as grid-ins. (Instead of choosing from four answer choices, you'll have to work through a problem and then enter your answer on your answer sheet by bubbling in the appropriate numbers.) Exactly 13 of the 58 math questions will be grid-ins.

Optional Essay

Unlike other essays you may have seen on standardized tests, this one does not require you to write about a personal experience or to argue for or against a position. Instead, you'll have to read a short passage and explain how the author effectively builds his or her argument. The test writers want to see how you comprehend an idea and demonstrate that understanding in writing, using evidence from that author's text.

The Experimental Section

The College Board is not straightforward with whether there will be an experimental section on the SAT and, if so, whether any of the questions within it will actually count toward your score. One vital consideration is that only students who do not take the optional essay might find themselves facing down this fifth section. Therefore, in order to better prepare those students who may see this optional section, the second test in this book includes a bonus experimental section before the essay. You would never have to take both the essay and an experimental section on the SAT, so choose one or the other. We just want you to be prepared. This way, you can be more familiar with the test structure if in fact you are one of the "lucky" ones.

One final twist: while we know, at least as of the printing of this book, that the experimental section is 20 minutes long, we also know that this section can be on reading, writing, or math. Resist the urge to peek at which one we've included. As with both tests in this book, you want to emulate testing conditions as closely as possible, and in this case, you're also making sure you're ready to deal with potential testing fatigue. You've got this!

Scoring on the SAT

The SAT is scored on a scale of 400–1600 and also introduces a series of cross-test scores and subscores that analyze various proficiencies. Here's the breakdown:

- **Total score (1):** The sum of the two section scores (Evidence-Based Reading and Writing and Math), ranging from 400 to 1600
- **Section scores (2):** Evidence-Based Reading and Writing, ranging from 200 to 800; Math, also ranging from 200 to 800
- **Test scores (3):** Reading Test, Writing and Language Test, Math Test, each of which is scored on a scale from 10 to 40
- **Cross-test scores (2):** Each is scored on a scale from 10 to 40 and based on selected questions from the three tests (Reading, Writing and Language, Math):
  1) Analysis in History/Social Studies
  2) Analysis in Science
- **Subscores (7):** Each of the following receives a score from 1 to 15:
  1) Command of Evidence (Reading; Writing and Language)
  2) Words in Context (Reading; Writing and Language)
  3) Expression of Ideas (Writing and Language)

A Note on Essay Scoring

If you choose to write the essay, you will be graded by two readers in three areas: Reading, Writing, and Analysis. You will be scored on a 2- to 8-point scale for each of the three areas.

4) Standard English Conventions (Writing and Language)
5) Heart of Algebra (Math)
6) Problem Solving and Data Analysis (Math)
7) Passport to Advanced Math (Math)

Scoring Tricks

You will not be penalized for wrong answers on the SAT. This means that you should always guess, even if this means choosing an answer at random. With only four answers to choose from, your odds of getting a right answer are decent, and only get better if you use Process of Elimination (POE) to eliminate an answer choice or two.

Because time is at a premium on the test, don't be shy about bubbling in a guess on a question that you don't fully understand so that you can move on to questions that you feel more confident you can answer correctly (and quickly). That said, try to indicate which questions you've done this on so that if you have time left at the end of a test, you can return to those tricky questions and try to get a few extra points.

WHEN IS THE SAT GIVEN?

The SAT schedule for the school year is posted on the College Board website at www.collegeboard.org. There are two different ways to sign up for the test. You can either sign up online by going to www.collegeboard.org and clicking on the SAT hyperlink, or sign up through the mail with an SAT registration booklet, which may be available at your school guidance counselor's office.

Try to sign up for the SAT as soon as you know when you'll be taking the test. If you wait until the last minute to sign up, there may not be any open spots in the testing centers that are closest to you.

If you require any special accommodations while taking the test (including, but not limited to, extra time or assistance), www.collegeboard.org has information about applying for those. Make sure to apply early; we recommend doing so six months before you plan to take the test.

Stay on Schedule
Although you may take the SAT any time starting freshman year, most students take it for the first time in the spring of their junior year and possibly retake it in the fall of their senior year. In addition, you may also need to take SAT subject tests (some competitive colleges require or recommend them), so don't leave everything to the last minute. You can't take SAT and SAT Subject Tests on the same day. Sit down and plan a schedule.

Chapter 2
Practice Test 1

Reading Test

65 MINUTES, 52 QUESTIONS

Turn to Section 1 of your answer sheet to answer the questions in this section.

Questions 1–10 are based on the following passage.

This passage is excerpted from Robert Louis Stevenson, *Treasure Island,* originally published in 1883. The narrator and his parents own an inn on the English coast.

The stranger kept hanging about just inside the inn door, peering round the corner like a cat waiting for a mouse. Once I stepped out myself into the road, but
Line he immediately called me back, and as I did not obey
5 quick enough for his fancy, a most horrible change came over his tallowy face, and he ordered me in with an oath that made me jump. As soon as I was back again he returned to his former manner, half fawning, half sneering, patted me on the shoulder, told me I
10 was a good boy and he had taken quite a fancy to me. "I have a son of my own," said he, "as like you as two blocks, and he's all the pride of my 'art. But the great thing for boys is discipline, sonny—discipline. Now, if you had sailed along of Bill, you wouldn't have stood
15 there to be spoke to twice—not you. That was never Bill's way, nor the way of sich as sailed with him. And here, sure enough, is my mate Bill, with a spy-glass under his arm, bless his old 'art, to be sure. You and me'll just go back into the parlour, sonny, and get
20 behind the door, and we'll give Bill a little surprise—bless his 'art, I say again."

So saying, the stranger backed along with me into the parlour and put me behind him in the corner so that we were both hidden by the open door. I was very
25 uneasy and alarmed, as you may fancy, and it rather added to my fears to observe that the stranger was certainly frightened himself. He cleared the hilt of his cutlass and loosened the blade in the sheath; and all the time we were waiting there he kept swallowing as if
30 he felt what we used to call a lump in the throat.

At last in strode the captain, slammed the door behind him, without looking to the right or left, and marched straight across the room to where his breakfast awaited him.
35 "Bill," said the stranger in a voice that I thought he had tried to make bold and big.

The captain spun round on his heel and fronted us; all the brown had gone out of his face, and even his nose was blue; he had the look of a man who sees a
40 ghost, or the evil one, or something worse, if anything can be; and upon my word, I felt sorry to see him all in a moment turn so old and sick.

"Come, Bill, you know me; you know an old shipmate, Bill, surely," said the stranger.
45 The captain made a sort of gasp.

"Black Dog!" said he.

"And who else?" returned the other, getting more at his ease. "Black Dog as ever was, come for to see his old shipmate Billy, at the Admiral Benbow Inn. Ah,
50 Bill, Bill, we have seen a sight of times, us two, since I lost them two talons," holding up his mutilated hand.

"Now, look here," said the captain; "you've run me down; here I am; well, then, speak up; what is it?"

"That's you, Bill," returned Black Dog, "you're
55 in the right of it, Billy. I'll have a glass of rum from this dear child here, as I've took such a liking to; and we'll sit down, if you please, and talk square, like old shipmates."

CONTINUE ➡

When I returned with the rum, they were already
60 seated on either side of the captain's breakfast-table—
Black Dog next to the door and sitting sideways so
as to have one eye on his old shipmate and one, as I
thought, on his retreat.

He bade me go and leave the door wide open.
65 "None of your keyholes for me, sonny," he said; and I
left them together and retired into the bar.

For a long time, though I certainly did my best to
listen, I could hear nothing but a low gattling; but at
last the voices began to grow higher, and I could pick
70 up a word or two, mostly oaths, from the captain.

"No, no, no, no; and an end of it!" he cried once.
And again, "If it comes to swinging, swing all, say I."

1

Which choice is the best synopsis of what happens in
the passage?

A) Two characters make a plan to surprise a third
   character.

B) One character shows another character how to
   properly behave in a parlour.

C) One character unpleasantly surprises another
   character with an unexpected reunion.

D) Two characters reminisce about their time
   together on a ship.

2

Which choice best describes the developmental
pattern of the passage?

A) A detailed analysis of an enthusiastic encounter

B) An inaccurate dictation of a notable conference

C) An apprehensive account of a contentious meeting

D) A dismissive description of an important
   homecoming

3

As it is used in line 5 and line 10, "fancy" most nearly
means

A) elaboration.

B) impatience.

C) imagination.

D) preference.

4

Which emotion does the narrator most sense from
the stranger regarding his imminent meeting with the
captain?

A) The stranger is fearful about the captain's reaction
   to seeing him.

B) The stranger is overjoyed to reunite with the
   captain.

C) The stranger is worried the captain won't
   remember him.

D) The stranger is concerned the captain will be more
   interested in his breakfast than in conversation.

5

Which choice provides the best evidence for the
answer to the previous questions?

A) Lines 24–27 ("I was . . . himself")

B) Lines 31–34 ("At last . . . him")

C) Lines 43–44 ("Come, Bill . . . stranger")

D) Line 71 ("No, no, . . . once")

6

In the passage, the stranger addresses the narrator
with

A) respect but not friendliness.

B) violence but not anger.

C) disgust but not hatred.

D) affection but not trust.

CONTINUE →

7

The main purpose of the first paragraph is to

A) introduce a character.

B) criticize a belief.

C) describe a relationship.

D) investigate a discrepancy.

8

As it is used in line 51, "talons" most nearly means

A) weapons.

B) claws.

C) fingers.

D) hooks.

9

Why does the narrator describe the captain's face as something from which "all the brown had gone out of" (line 38)?

A) The captain has grown pale after being on land so long.

B) The captain has washed his face before the meal.

C) The captain has become ill during his walk.

D) The captain has gone pale with fright.

10

Which choice provides the best evidence for the answer to the previous question?

A) Lines 22–24 ("So saying . . . door")

B) Lines 39–42 ("he had . . . sick")

C) Lines 52–53 ("Now, look . . . is it")

D) Lines 59–63 ("When I . . . retreat")

CONTINUE

Questions 11–21 are based on the following passage and supplementary material.

This passage is adapted from Russell W. Belk, "It's the Thought that Counts." © 1976 by University of Illinois at Urbana-Champaign.

The phenomenon of selecting an object or service "X" to present as a gift to person "Y" on occasion "Z" is a unique and important act of consumer behavior.
Line Not only must the gift giver attempt to infer the
5 recipient's tastes, needs, desires, and reactions, the gift selection may also be affected by the information which it would appear to convey about the giver and the giver-recipient relationship. The ancient practice of gift-giving is still pervasive and significant in modern
10 cultures. For instance, Lowes, Turner, and Willis (1971) cite a series of British Gallup Polls from 1963-1967, in which it was found that over 90 percent of the adult population did some Christmas gift-giving each year. Another limited sample of middle and upper
15 income families in Montreal, Caron and Ward (1975) found that third- and fifth-grade children received an average of between five and six gifts for Christmas. Both because of its prevalence and because of its strong interpersonal meanings, gift-giving offers a potentially
20 rich area for consumer behavioral explanation.
      Gift-giving has been treated from a variety of related theoretical perspectives, focusing primarily on the functions and effects of giving. The preeminent theoretical analysis of the gift-giving process is an essay
25 by French anthropologist-sociologist Marcell Mauss (1923). Based on his examination of gift-giving among numerous primitive, remote, or ancient societies, Mauss concluded that gift-giving is a self-perpetuating system of reciprocity. More specifically, Mauss outlined
30 three types of obligations, which perpetuate gift-giving:
      1. The obligation to give,
      2. The obligation to receive,
      3. The obligation to repay.
The obligation to give may be based on moral
35 or religious imperatives, the need to recognize and maintain a status hierarchy, the need to establish or maintain peaceful relations, or simply the expectation of reciprocal giving. These motives, which do not admit purely selfless giving, become institutionalized
40 in a society so that under appropriate conditions an individual is socially obligated to give. Receiving is seen as similarly obligatory, and avoiding or refusing

gifts is construed as an unfriendly or even hostile act. Mauss noted however that there is a certain tension
45 created in receiving a gift since acceptance is an implicit recognition of dependence on the giver. This tension may then be reduced by fulfilling the third obligation, the obligation to repay. Failure to repay or failure to repay adequately results in a loss of status
50 and self-esteem. Adequate or overly adequate repayment, on the other hand, creates an obligation to repay on the part of the original giver, and the cycle is reinitiated.
      Schwartz (1967) noted that beyond the functions
55 served by the general process of gift exchange, the characteristics of the gift itself also act as a powerful statement of the giver's perception of the recipient. He also suggested that acceptance of a particular gift constitutes an acknowledgment and acceptance of the
60 identity that the gift is seen to imply. Among children this may lead to lasting changes in self-perceptions, but presumably gifts have less influence on the self-concept of an adult.
      Nevertheless, the importance of this symbolic
65 function of gift selection appears clear enough in a gift shop's recent advertisement, which asks, "Do you want your gifts to tell someone how creative you are, how thoughtful you are, or just how big your Christmas bonus was? Do you buy with a specific
70 price or a specific personality in mind?" While the answers to such basic questions about gift selection may be personally evident, the underlying behavioral questions have not been addressed by empirical research.
75   There can be little doubt that gift-giving is a pervasive experience in human life and consumer behavior. Despite the additional variables which gift-giving introduces to conceptions of consumer behavior (e.g., characteristics of the recipient, gifter-
80 receiver similarity, nature of the occasion), the present findings suggest that preference for cognitive balance is a concept which can go far toward explaining gift selection and evaluation.

CONTINUE ▶

GIFT-GIVING AS COMMUNICATION

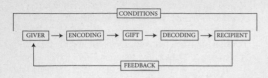

11

The author most likely uses the examples in lines 4–17 of the passage ("Not only . . . Christmas") to highlight the

A) recent increase in consumerism around Christmas time.

B) discrepancies in gift-giving between ancient and modern times.

C) apprehension between gift-givers and receivers.

D) pervasiveness of gift-giving on special occasions.

12

In line 20, the word "rich" most nearly means

A) opulent.

B) embellished.

C) fertile.

D) saccharine.

13

The author indicates that the self-perpetuating system of reciprocity

A) is a form of communication between gift-giver and recipient.

B) functions as a form of status hierarchy.

C) can wreak havoc on a child's concept of him- or herself.

D) requires equal participation in a relationship.

14

Which choice provides the best evidence for the answer to the previous question?

A) Lines 5–8 ("the gift . . . relationship")

B) Lines 34–38 ("The obligation . . . giving")

C) Lines 50–53 ("Adequate or . . . reinitiated")

D) Lines 60–63 ("Among children . . . adult")

15

Schwartz, mentioned in paragraph 4 (lines 54–63), would likely describe the process of gift exchange as

A) stressful.

B) unnerving.

C) intentional.

D) symbolic.

16

The fourth paragraph (lines 54–63) indicates that the acceptance of a gift may be

A) considerate.

B) influential.

C) authoritative.

D) immutable.

17

Which choice provides the best evidence for the answer to the previous question?

A) Lines 58–60 ("He also . . . imply")

B) Lines 60–63 ("Among children . . . adult")

C) Lines 66–69 ("Do you . . . was")

D) Lines 75–77 ("There can . . . behavior")

CONTINUE ➤

18

As it is used in line 65, "function" most nearly means

A) purpose.

B) tradition.

C) occasion.

D) occupation.

19

The author refers to a gift shop's recent advertisement (lines 65–66) in order to

A) question a former claim.

B) offer a motive.

C) introduce a counter explanation.

D) support an argument.

20

The graph and the passage offer evidence that the communication process of gift-giving predicts that a gift will demonstrate

A) the receiver's self-concept.

B) the amount the gift-giver spent.

C) encoded meaning.

D) the thoughtfulness of the gift-giver.

21

The author would likely attribute the encoding and decoding phases of communication as represented in the graph to

A) an emerging form of conditional approval.

B) an inability to communicate effectively.

C) an increasing amount of pressure on gift-giving.

D) a component of implicit evaluation.

CONTINUE →

Questions 22–31 are based on the following passage and supplementary material.

This passage is adapted from Nils Ekholm, "On the Variations of the Climate of the Geological and Historical Past and Their Causes." © 1901 by *Quarterly Journal of the Royal Meteorological Society*. Ekholm's studies are based on new mathematical calculations that show discrepancies among earlier scientists' findings in the study of historical changes in climate.

The atmosphere plays a very important part of a double character as to the temperature at the earth's surface. Firstly, the atmosphere may act like the glass of
Line a green-house, letting through the light rays of the sun
5 relatively easily, and absorbing a great part of the dark rays emitted from the ground, and it thereby may raise the mean temperature of the earth's surface. Secondly, the atmosphere acts as a heat store placed between the relatively warm ground and the cold space, and thereby
10 lessens in a high degree the annual, diurnal, and local variations of the temperature.

There are two qualities of the atmosphere that produce these effects. The one is that the temperature of the atmosphere generally decreases with the height
15 above the ground or the sea-level, owing partly to the dynamical heating of descending air currents and the dynamical cooling of ascending ones, as is explained in the mechanical theory of heat. The other is that the atmosphere, absorbing but little of the
20 insolation and most of the radiation from the ground, receives a considerable part of its heat store from the ground by means of radiation, contact, convection, and conduction, whereas the earth's surface is heated principally by direct radiation from the sun through
25 the transparent air.

It follows from this that the radiation from the earth into space does not go on directly from the ground, but on average from a layer of the atmosphere having a considerable height above sea-level. The
30 height of that layer depends on the thermal quality of the atmosphere, and will vary with that quality. The greater is the absorbing power of the air for heat rays emitted from the ground, the higher will that layer be. But the higher the layer, the lower is its temperature
35 relatively to that of the ground; and as the radiation from the layer into space is the less lower its temperature is, it follows that the ground will be hotter the higher the radiating layer is.

Now if we are able to calculate or estimate how
40 much the mean temperature that layer is lower than the mean temperature of the ground, we may apply Table I for calculating the mean temperature of the ground, as soon as we know by direct measurements the quantity of solar heat absorbed by the ground.
45 Owing to the clouds and dust floating in the atmosphere, this heat is probably only about a third of that derived by using Langley's solar constant; and is thus about 360 calories per square centimeter during twenty-four hours. This gives, by means of Table I,
50 a temperature of −31°C to the radiating layer. But, according to Arrhenius's estimate, this is at a height of about 7600 meters; and assuming a corresponding decrease of 0.6°C per 100 meters, we find its temperature to be 46°C lower than that of the ground,
55 and thus the mean temperature of the ground equal to 15°C, as it is according to observations.

The table shows the loss of heat by radiation into space from a perfectly black body of the temperature t^o centigrade. In gram-calories per square centimeter per
60 24 hours at 7600 meters.

t	Loss of Heat	t	Loss of Heat	t	Loss of Heat
100	2023	20	770	−60	215
80	1624	0	581	−80	145
60	1285	−20	428	−100	94
40	1003	−40	308	−120	57

22

A student claims that over half of solar radiation influences the ground temperature on the earth's surface. Which of the following statements in the passage contradicts the student's claim?

A) Lines 3–7 ("Firstly, the . . . surface")

B) Lines 13–18 ("The one . . . heat")

C) Lines 45–49 ("Owing to . . . hours")

D) Lines 49–50 ("This gives . . . layer")

CONTINUE ➤

23

In the first paragraph (lines 1–11), what does the author claim is the atmosphere's importance to the temperature of the earth's surface?

A) The trapping of all hot air and energy from the sun

B) Controlling the heat energy that is admitted and released

C) The enclosure of all the earth's heat-producing mechanisms

D) The free passage of heat energy to and from the surface

24

The author uses the word "green-house" in line 4 to indicate that

A) the heat on the ground and in the atmosphere of the earth is provided exclusively by solar radiation.

B) most of the heat in the atmosphere comes from radiation from the ground.

C) the agricultural and botanical sectors of the economy are those most affected by climate fluctuations.

D) solar heat enters the atmosphere relatively unobstructed but the same does not apply as it leaves.

25

Based on the passage, the author's statement "the earth's surface is heated principally by direct radiation from the sun through the transparent air" (lines 23–25) implies that

A) when the sun is obscured by clouds the ground is heated principally by other sources of energy.

B) heat generated independently by the ground and by the sun is held in the atmosphere and released as cool air.

C) the heat from the sun that warms the ground must be partially absorbed by the earth's atmosphere.

D) the solar heat reflected back from the earth does not account for all the heat in the atmosphere.

26

The author's use of the words "if," "may," and "as soon as" in lines 39–43 functions mainly to

A) provide definitive evidence that the author's mathematical calculations predict the span of global warming with accuracy.

B) demonstrate that many of the author's conclusions rely on both observable and non-observable factors.

C) support the hypothesis that ground temperatures are warmer than higher temperatures.

D) warn against the indiscretion of earlier scientists who made incorrect claims with insufficient evidence.

27

The author's main purpose in noting the observations of ground temperature is to

A) indicate that the mathematical calculations given in this paragraph correspond to data recorded by others.

B) show the limitations of mathematical formulas in providing precise measurements of observable phenomena.

C) provide an example of one place in which the global temperature has risen because of human activity.

D) underline the importance of mathematical calculations in determining the influence of solar radiation.

28

Based on the table and passage, which choice gives the correct temperature on the ground when the loss of heat is approximately 300 gram-calories per square centimeter for 24 hours?

A) 40°C

B) 6°C

C) –6°C

D) –40°C

CONTINUE

29

Do the data in the table support the author's claim regarding the atmosphere as a heat store?

A) Yes, because at each given temperature, as the temperature decreases, the heat loss decreases as well but by larger and larger intervals.

B) Yes, because at each given temperature, as the temperature decreases, the heat loss decreases as well but by smaller and smaller intervals.

C) No, because at each given temperature, as the temperature decreases, the heat loss fluctuates according to an irregular pattern and series of intervals.

D) No, because at each given temperature, as the temperature decreases, the heat loss increases by larger and larger intervals.

30

According to the table, which of the following pairs of heat-loss values at different temperatures provide evidence in support of the answer to the previous question?

A) 2023 to 1624 and 2023 to 57

B) 1003 to 581 and 581 to 94

C) 1003 to 770 and 770 to 581

D) 308 to 94 and 581 to 57

31

Based on the passage and the table, does the temperature of the atmosphere of the earth stay the same or does it vary with distance from the earth, and which statement made by the authors is most consistent with this data?

A) The same; "Firstly, the . . . surface" (lines 3–7)

B) The same; "It follows . . . sea-level" (lines 26–29)

C) It varies; "Now if . . . ground" (lines 39–44)

D) It varies; "But, according . . . observations" (lines 50–56)

CONTINUE

Questions 32–41 are based on the following passage.

This passage is adapted from Frederick Douglass's speech "On Women's Suffrage" delivered in 1888 to a gathering of women's suffrage activists.

Mrs. President, Ladies and Gentlemen:— I come to this platform with unusual diffidence. Although I have long been identified with the Woman's Suffrage
Line movement, and have often spoken in its favor, I am
5 somewhat at a loss to know what to say on this really great and uncommon occasion, where so much has been said.

When I look around on this assembly, and see the many able and eloquent women, full of the subject,
10 ready to speak, and who only need the opportunity to impress this audience with their views and thrill them with "thoughts that breathe and words that burn," I do not feel like taking up more than a very small space of your time and attention, and shall not.
15 I would not, even now, presume to speak, but for the circumstance of my early connection with the cause, and of having been called upon to do so by one whose voice in this Council we all gladly obey. Men have very little business here as speakers, anyhow;
20 and if they come here at all they should take back benches and wrap themselves in silence. For this is an International Council, not of men, but of women, and woman should have all the say in it. This is her day in court. I do not mean to exalt the intellect of woman
25 above man's; but I have heard many men speak on this subject, some of them the most eloquent to be found anywhere in the country; and I believe no man, however gifted with thought and speech, can voice the wrongs and present the demands of women with
30 the skill and effect, with the power and authority of woman herself. The man struck is the man to cry out. Woman knows and feels her wrongs as man cannot know and feel them, and she also knows as well as he can know, what measures are needed to redress them.
35 I grant all the claims at this point. She is her own best representative. We can neither speak for her, nor vote for her, nor act for her, nor be responsible for her; and the thing for men to do in the premises is just to get out of her way and give her the fullest opportunity
40 to exercise all the powers inherent in her individual personality, and allow her to do it as she herself shall elect to exercise them. Her right to be and to do is as full, complete and perfect as the right of any man on earth. I say of her, as I say of the colored people, "Give
45 her fair play, and hands off." There was a time when, perhaps, we men could help a little. It was when this woman suffrage cause was in its cradle, when it was not big enough to go alone, when it had to be taken in the arms of its mother from Seneca Falls, N.Y., to
50 Rochester, N.Y., for baptism. I then went along with it and offered my services to help it, for then it needed help; but now it can afford to dispense with me and all of my sex. Then its friends were few—now its friends are many. Then it was wrapped in obscurity—now it is
55 lifted in sight of the whole civilized world, and people of all lands and languages give it their hearty support. Truly the change is vast and wonderful.

There may be some well-meaning people in this audience who have never attended a woman suffrage
60 convention, never heard a woman suffrage speech, never read a woman suffrage newspaper, and they may be surprised that those who speak here do not argue the question. It may be kind to tell them that our cause has passed beyond the period of arguing. The demand
65 of the hour is not argument, but assertion, firm and inflexible assertion, assertion which has more than the force of an argument. If there is any argument to be made, it must be made by opponents, not by the friends of woman suffrage. Let those who want
70 argument examine the ground upon which they base their claim to the right to vote. They will find that there is not one reason, not one consideration, which they can urge in support of man's claim to vote, which does not equally support the right of woman to vote.

32

The main purpose of the passage is to

A) qualify the credentials of a speaker.

B) provide support for the suffrage movement.

C) argue for the equal rights of women.

D) compare the sufferings of women to those of African-Americans.

CONTINUE

33

The central claim of the passage is that

A) women should have the floor at this assembly.

B) men should act for women in this movement.

C) women and men have the same justification for voting.

D) the suffrage movement should be less obscure.

34

Douglass uses the word "cause" throughout the passage mainly to

A) clarify his early connection to the suffrage movement.

B) explain why the suffrage movement deserves support.

C) compare the suffrage movement to a baby in a cradle.

D) describe the suffrage movement.

35

According to the passage, Douglass

A) wants to give a great speech, because he has been identified with the suffrage movement.

B) is hesitant to speak, even though he has been identified with the suffrage movement.

C) does not want to speak, though he has been identified with the suffrage movement.

D) is hesitant to give a lengthy speech, since he has been identified with the suffrage movement.

36

Douglass indicates that men

A) should not be speakers in such a movement.

B) should not take too much time and attention.

C) should primarily listen at such a gathering.

D) should voice the wrongs of women publicly.

37

Which choice provides the best evidence for the answer to the previous question?

A) Lines 8–14 ("When I . . . not")

B) Lines 15–18 ("I would . . . obey")

C) Lines 18–21 ("Men have . . . silence")

D) Lines 24–31 ("I do . . . herself")

38

Douglass characterizes the "demands of women" in line 29 as related to injuries that

A) women can best describe and suggest solutions for.

B) men should speak about more eloquently.

C) the civilized world should support heartily.

D) men and women should both be responsible for.

39

Which choice provides the best evidence for the answer to the previous question?

A) Lines 25–27 ("but I . . . country")

B) Lines 32–34 ("Woman knows . . . them")

C) Lines 42–44 ("Her right . . . earth")

D) Lines 45–46 ("There was . . . little")

CONTINUE

40

Which choice most closely captures the meaning of the figurative "cradle" referred to in line 47?

A) Nest

B) Rock

C) Hold

D) Beginnings

41

The surprise referred to in lines 58–74 mainly serves to emphasize how

A) some attendees may have expected different sorts of speeches.

B) male attendees may have expected more arguments than assertions.

C) audience members may not have expected speeches on women's suffrage.

D) speakers may have presented unexpected arguments for the right to vote.

CONTINUE

Questions 42–52 are based on the following passages.

Passage 1 is adapted from Michael B. McElroy and Xi Li, "Fracking's Future." © 2013 by *Harvard Monthly*. Passage 2 is adapted from Natural Resources Defense Council, "Unchecked Fracking Threatens Health, Water Supplies." © 2015.

Passage 1

Supplies of natural gas now economically recoverable from shale in the United States could accommodate the country's domestic demand for natural gas at current levels of consumption for more
5   than a hundred years: an economic and strategic boon, and, at least in the near term, an important stepping-stone toward lower-carbon, greener energy.

The first step in extracting gas from shale involves drilling vertically to reach the shale layer, typically a
10 kilometer or more below the surface. Drilling then continues horizontally, extending a kilometer or more from the vertical shaft, and the vertical and horizontal components of the well are lined with steel casing, cemented in place. The horizontal extension of the
15 casing is then perforated, using explosives; thereafter, water, carrying sand and proprietary chemicals, is injected into the well at high pressure. The water encounters the shale through the perforations, generating a series of small fractures in the rock (hence
20 the nickname, "fracking"); the sand in the water keeps the cracks open, while the chemicals enhance release of gas from the shale. The injected water flows back up to the surface when the pressure in the well is released following completion of the fracking procedure. Then
25 the well starts to produce natural gas.

As many as 25 fracture stages (per horizontal leg) may be involved in preparing a single site for production, each requiring injection of more than 400,000 gallons of water—a possible total of more than
30 10 million gallons before the well is fully operational. A portion of the injected water flows back to the surface, heavily contaminated with the fracking chemicals and others it has absorbed from the shale. Depending on the local geology, this "return water" may also include
35 radioactive elements.

Drillers developing a well must take exceptional care to minimize contact between the wellbore and the surrounding aquifer—often the source of nearby residents' fresh water. Serious problems have arisen
40 in the past from failures to isolate the drilling liquids, including cases where well water used for drinking became so contaminated that human and animal health was threatened. It is essential that monitoring be in place to ensure the continuing integrity of the seal
45 isolating the well from the aquifer even *after* the well has been fully exploited and abandoned.

Passage 2

The oil and gas industry is rapidly expanding production across the nation, as new technology makes it easier to extract oil or gas from previously
50 inaccessible sites. Over the last decade, the industry has drilled hundreds of thousands of new wells all across the country. These wells are accompanied by massive new infrastructure to move, process, and deliver oil and gas, together bringing full-scale
55 industrialization to often previously rural landscapes.

The sector's growth is spurred by the use of hydraulic fracturing, or fracking, in which often-dangerous chemicals are mixed with large quantities of water (or other base fluid) and sand and injected
60 into wells at extremely high pressure. Unconventional development using advanced fracking methods poses threats to water, air, land, and the health of communities. Studies have shown dangerous levels of toxic air pollution near fracking sites; and oil and
65 gas extraction have caused smog in rural areas at levels worse than downtown Los Angeles. Oil and gas production have been linked to increased risk of cancer and birth defects in neighboring areas; as well as to a risk of increased seismic activity.
70 Constant massive truck traffic associated with large-scale development disrupts communities and creates significant hazards. The millions of gallons of water used in fracking operations not only strain water resources, but end up as vast amounts of contaminated
75 wastewater. Fracking has been reported as a suspect in polluted drinking water around the country. And methane—a potent climate change pollutant—leaks rampantly throughout the extraction, processing, and distribution of oil and gas.
80 Weak safeguards and inadequate oversight have allowed oil and gas producers to run roughshod over communities across the country with their extraction and production activities for too long, resulting in

CONTINUE →

contaminated water supplies, dangerous air pollution,
85 destroyed streams, and devastated landscapes. Our
state and federal leaders have failed to hold them to
account, leaving the American people unprotected.
Many companies don't play by the few rules that do
exist; and industry has used its political power at every
90 turn to gain exemptions from environmental laws
designed to protect our air and water.

42

In lines 26–30, the author of Passage 1 mentions the
number of gallons of water primarily to

A) warn of the inevitable dangers of industrial
fracking in small communities.

B) show the variety of ways that natural gas and oil
can be extracted from shale.

C) expand upon the idea that fracking uses only a few
basic elements.

D) establish the size and scope of the industrial
equipment required for fracking.

43

The author of Passage 1 indicates that fracking could
have which positive effect?

A) It could support small, local economies that do
not have other sources of income.

B) It could alter the way scientists understand the
shale layer of the Earth.

C) It could provide resources that meet the needs of
contemporary consumers.

D) It could lower the price that large-scale industrial
firms pay for natural gas.

44

Which choice provides the best evidence for the
answer to the previous question?

A) Lines 1–5 ("Supplies of . . . years")

B) Lines 17–22 ("The water . . . shale")

C) Lines 22–25 ("The injected . . . gas")

D) Lines 30–35 ("A portion . . . elements")

45

What function does the discussion of the aquifer in
lines 36–46 serve in Passage 1?

A) It outlines one significant risk involved in the
process described in earlier paragraphs.

B) It addresses and disputes the concerns of those
whose attitude toward fracking is cautious.

C) It extends a discussion of a significant term that
begins in the previous paragraph.

D) It presents an unexpected new finding that
undermines industry arguments for a certain
practice.

46

As used in line 44, "integrity" most nearly means

A) morality.

B) impermeability.

C) moisture.

D) confidence.

47

The central claim of Passage 2 is that fracking mines
useful resources but

A) the wells that have been built are not sufficiently
productive to justify all the cost.

B) some experts believe that natural gas can be
acquired just as easily from other sources.

C) it may lead some industry executives to believe
that they can mine resources from any place they
choose.

D) it is currently not sufficiently regulated in a way
that is safe for local populations.

CONTINUE

48

As used in line 81, "roughshod" most nearly means

A) productive.

B) rapid.

C) unregulated.

D) industrial.

49

Which statement best describes the relationship between the passages?

A) Passage 2 undermines the optimistic confidence of the author of Passage 1.

B) Passage 2 expands upon some of the concerns expressed less explicitly in Passage 1.

C) Passage 2 argues for certain regulations of which the author of Passage 1 does not approve.

D) Passage 2 describes the process discussed in Passage 1 but does so with more detail and statistics.

50

The author of Passage 2 would most likely respond to the discussion of drillers in lines 36–46, Passage 1, by claiming that these drillers

A) cite their successes in having grown the mining industry throughout the country.

B) often come from small towns themselves and are not likely to abuse the land.

C) have already caused irreparable harm to the American landscape.

D) can be difficult to contact when their work is conducted so far underground.

51

Which choice provides the best evidence for the answer to the previous question?

A) Lines 47–52 ("The oil . . . country")

B) Lines 56–60 ("The sector's . . . pressure")

C) Lines 66–72 ("Oil and . . . hazards")

D) Lines 80–85 ("Weak safeguards . . . landscapes")

52

Which point about the potential effects of fracking is implicit in Passage 2 and explicit in Passage 1?

A) The pollution caused by fracking can affect both the water and the air.

B) The process of fracking requires the use of many billions of gallons of water.

C) The process can contaminate drinking water and thus harm both animals and humans.

D) The economic costs of preparing wells can often cost more than the profits gained from mining.

STOP

If you finish before time is called, you may check your work on this section only. Do not turn to any other section in the test.

No Test Material On This Page

Writing and Language Test

35 MINUTES, 44 QUESTIONS

Turn to Section 2 of your answer sheet to answer the questions in this section.

DIRECTIONS

Each passage below is accompanied by a number of questions. For some questions, you will consider how the passage might be revised to improve the expression of ideas. For other questions, you will consider how the passage might be edited to correct errors in sentence structure, usage, or punctuation. A passage or a question may be accompanied by one or more graphics (such as a table or graph) that you will consider as you make revising and editing decisions.

Some questions will direct you to an underlined portion of a passage. Other questions will direct you to a location in a passage or ask you to think about the passage as a whole.

After reading each passage, choose the answer to each question that most effectively improves the quality of writing in the passage or that makes the passage conform to the conventions of standard written English. Many questions include a "NO CHANGE" option. Choose that option if you think the best choice is to leave the relevant portion of the passage as it is.

Questions 1–11 are based on the following passage.

A Horse of a Different Doctor

Although medical science has made huge bounds in understanding many parts of the body, the brain remains a kind of mystery. A heart attack, for instance, is much easier to identify and prevent than a brain stroke. And mental illness aside, **1** the variety of neurological disorders can make specific brain diagnoses complicated and often unreliable. As a result, the therapeutic resources available to neurologists and those with neurological disorders must necessarily be as vast and diverse as the patient base itself. Disciplines like art therapy, aromatherapy, and horticultural therapy have begun to gain some traction in the popular imagination. Some fields, however, are still awaiting **2** the okay from the people, although their achievements and successes are just as significant. One such field is that of hippotherapy.

1

A) NO CHANGE
B) the variety of different kinds of neurological disorders
C) the differing variety of disorders in neurology
D) disorders that show a variety of differences

2

A) NO CHANGE
B) broader public acceptance
C) something elusive from the public
D) a public to give the thumbs up

CONTINUE ➡

Hippotherapy positions itself at the intersection of physical, occupational, and speech therapy. In this discipline, the characteristic movements of a horse (*hippo-* in Greek) **3** is used to build a foundation for improvements in human neurological functions and sensory processing. Its main difference from therapeutic horseback riding is that hippotherapy uses the movement of the horse as a way to treat a specific ailment. **4** Thus, it is more concerned with learning a skill set and establishing a bond between rider and horse.

3

A) NO CHANGE
B) has been used
C) are used
D) used

4

At this point, the writer is considering adding the following sentence.

> Therapeutic horseback riding teaches riding skills and is more concerned with emotional and behavioral disabilities.

Should the writer make this addition here?

A) Yes, because it makes the argument that hippotherapy is the more effective of the two disciplines.

B) Yes, because it further clarifies the difference between the two disciplines discussed in this paragraph.

C) No, because it undermines the point the author is trying to make about the validity of hippotherapy.

D) No, because a discussion of therapeutic horseback riding has no place in this particular paragraph.

CONTINUE

[1] Many fields use the basic tenets of hippotherapy, but they each provide a unique spin on the practice. [2] Physical therapists may incorporate hippotherapy to manage a variety of disabilities and, hopefully, cure diseases. [3] Occupational therapists use many of the same features of the horse's movement, but they **5** are similarly plagued by the lack of laboratory support. [4] The research on the effectiveness of hippotherapy is still in the early stages of development, but therapists in a variety of fields, even including speech and language pathology, regularly achieve success with this technique and **6** eagerly to recommended it to their patients. [5] As the name suggests, these therapists are concerned mainly with the movement of the horse as it relates to physical aspects such as balance, posture, and strengthening the core. **7**

The American Hippotherapy Association can provide certification for those wishing to work in the discipline. Physical therapists, occupational therapists, and speech-language pathologists must have practiced for at least three years and had 100 hours of hippotherapy practice before they can sit for the Hippotherapy Clinical Specialty Certification Exam, and the certification lasts for five years. Because the discipline is relatively **8** new, certified, hippotherapists have stringent requirements for staying current on the research within the field.

5

Which choice provides a supporting example that reinforces the main point of the sentence?

A) NO CHANGE

B) use the therapy to develop the cognitive and fine motor skills.

C) work on different maladies and different parts of the body.

D) have a whole different set of requirements and backgrounds.

6

A) NO CHANGE

B) eager recommending of

C) eagerly recommending

D) eagerly recommend

7

To make this paragraph most logical, sentence 5 should be placed

A) where it is now.

B) before sentence 3.

C) before sentence 4.

D) at the beginning of the paragraph.

8

A) NO CHANGE

B) new, certified

C) new, and certified

D) new; certified

CONTINUE ➜

Just as medical science is constantly evolving, **9** so are its alternatives. Hippotherapy may seem a bit out of the ordinary, but if it provides effective relief or treatment for people in pain, the skeptics **10** between doctors and researchers will not hesitate to embrace it. **11** Becoming a hippotherapist is pretty hard, as evidenced by all those hours one has to spend keeping up with the literature.

9

A) NO CHANGE
B) so too are its alternatives.
C) its alternatives also are.
D) its alternatives are, too.

10

A) NO CHANGE
B) above
C) within
D) among

11

The writer wants a concluding sentence that restates the main argument of the passage. Which choice best accomplishes that goal?

A) NO CHANGE

B) Hippotherapy has positioned itself at the crossroads of many disciplines, and it may just be the practice to provide relief in ways the other therapies have not done yet.

C) Many people used bloodletting and radiation regularly before the medical establishment showed how unsafe these practices were.

D) It makes you wonder whether the medical profession is ready for such a crazy discovery.

CONTINUE ➔

Questions 12–22 are based on the following passage and supplementary material.

The Call of the Wilderness

The way science textbooks teach about different ecosystems [12] elicit responses primarily from our visual and tactile senses. We have all seen pictures of the silent sands of the desert and can almost feel the heat radiating from the sands. We all know the ballet of fish and marine life coursing through the vast ocean. Some recent studies, however, have expanded our ideas about these ecosystems by incorporating another one of our senses: sound.

[13] It was Marco Polo who crossed the desert on his way to China, he described the sound he heard as "a variety of musical instruments." Researchers now understand that the curious sound that Polo heard, that odd confluence of pipe organ and [14] cello, probably resulted from the wind blowing across the sand dunes. In a study conducted in the deserts of California, scientists found that the "singing" dunes had dry, tightly-packed layers of sand, with dry sand on top of layers of damp sand. This variation creates an effect similar to that of a musical [15] instrument, a tonal quality coming from the trapping and release of certain frequencies.

12
A) NO CHANGE
B) elicits responses
C) illicit responses
D) illicits responses

13
A) NO CHANGE
B) Marco Polo crossed the desert
C) They called him Marco Polo, he who crossed the desert
D) As Marco Polo crossed the desert

14
A) NO CHANGE
B) cello;
C) cello—
D) cello: it has

15
A) NO CHANGE
B) instrument; a tonal quality coming from the trapping and release of certain frequencies.
C) instrument, a tonal quality that is said to be coming from the trapping and release of certain frequencies.
D) instrument, this quality comes from the trapping and release of certain frequencies.

CONTINUE ➤

16 From among the world's countless ecosystems and throughout that world, the ocean, too, has recently been given a kind of "voice." Although Jacques Cousteau referred to this body of water as *le monde du silence*—"the silent world"—recent research has shown the ocean to be anything but silent. University of Washington biologist Kate Stafford has, for the past five years, recorded sounds in the deep waters of the Bering Strait. **17** For Stafford, sound provides advantage that sight cannot: one can continue to record sound at night or underneath ice cover, and the challenges of deep-sea sound-recording are not nearly as problematic as those of deep-sea diving.

16

Which choice most smoothly and effectively introduces the writer's discussion of the sounds of the ocean in this paragraph?

A) NO CHANGE

B) Ecosystems are filled with sound, and one such sound in one such ecosystem is the "voice" of the ocean.

C) Another place that has recently been given a kind of "voice" is the ocean.

D) DELETE the underlined sentence.

17

At this point, the writer is considering adding the following sentence.

> If you go far enough from the coast, the only sounds you will hear are those of distant ships passing in the night.

Should the writer make this addition here?

A) Yes, because it creates a poetic image that complements the main idea of the paragraph.

B) Yes, because it supports the main idea of the passage as a whole.

C) No, because it undermines the argument made by the scientist described in this paragraph.

D) No, because it would be more appropriately placed at the beginning of the paragraph.

CONTINUE ➡

According to Stafford's research, one of the most interesting aspects of the sound of the ocean is [18] its unwillingness to [19] not act so weird. Stafford's team found incredible inconsistencies among the sounds at any particular time of year. This may help to explain the [20] clear direct relationship in whale migrations between 2012-2013 and previous seasons. Recent data shows that it is not at all abnormal for nearly 40 whales to migrate on a single day when, on average, [21] only 14 whales would migrate on that same day. This gives some hint to how marine animals are and will be adapting to climate change in the future. It seems that those with the most flexibility will be those who are least affected.

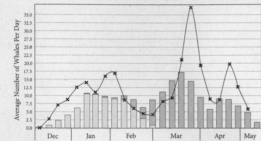

This Season, Compared to the Averages of the Last Ten Seasons

Key
☐ Southbound Whales
☐ Northbound Whales

18

A) NO CHANGE
B) it's
C) their
D) they're

19

A) NO CHANGE
B) follow any discernible patterns.
C) chill out and be normal for a second.
D) play nice with others.

20

Which choice offers the most accurate interpretation of the data in the chart?
A) NO CHANGE
B) definable inverse relationship
C) absolute confluence
D) notable inconsistency

21

Which choice offers an accurate interpretation of the data in the chart?
A) NO CHANGE
B) most whales would typically migrate in the summer months.
C) many more whales migrate southward every single day.
D) over half that number migrate every day in the coldest winter months.

CONTINUE ➤

The work that Stafford and others are doing adds another dimension to how we understand different ecosystems. Sound may clarify the processes of these ecosystems in ways that were not available to researchers before. **22**

22

The writer wants a conclusion that points toward the role that sound might play in future research into different ecosystems. Which choice results in the passage having the most appropriate concluding sentence?

A) NO CHANGE

B) This is not, of course, to say that no research has ever been done on sound before; that would be an overstatement.

C) Researchers may have missed this sound component, but you have to hand it to them for covering the other parts as thoroughly as they have.

D) The vividness of soundscapes is nowhere more evident than in the experiences of the blind, who can use sound in much the way that sighted people use sight.

CONTINUE

Questions 23–33 are based on the following passage.

Roosevelt's 100 Days

    In the 1932 presidential election, up-and-comer Franklin D. Roosevelt 23 won— in a landslide over the incumbent Herbert Hoover, who had done little to avert the crisis that would become known as the Great Depression. 24 And Hoover took office in 1929, the unemployment rate was a mere 3.2%. By 1932, that rate had skyrocketed to 25%.

    25 Roosevelt took office with a clear mandate for action. Even so, no one was quite ready for the legislative whirlwind that would follow. This period became known as Roosevelt's "100 Days." Roosevelt's first action came on March 5, 1933, when an executive order shut down all the nation's banks. At that time, he sent government workers to inspect each bank, 26 although determining which banks would be safe and sustainable to reopen. Four days later, the banks reopened and started business anew.

23

A) NO CHANGE
B) won;
C) won,
D) won

24

A) NO CHANGE
B) Because
C) When
D) DELETE the underlined portion and begin the sentence with a capital letter.

25

Which choice most effectively sets up the paragraph?

A) NO CHANGE
B) Politics could move a bit more quickly in those days.
C) That unemployment rate is remarkably low.
D) Hoover had given up all hope of ending the Depression.

26

A) NO CHANGE
B) for
C) thereby
D) whereupon

CONTINUE ➡

Roosevelt's main goal was to lift the country from depression and to get the **27** economy operating again. In the 100 days, Roosevelt established programs to aid the poor, such as the $500 million Federal Emergency Relief Association. The Civilian Conservation Corps was established to give unemployed men six-month job assignments on environmental projects, such as national parks. In agricultural regions, Roosevelt sought to control supply as a way to level **28** with demand, and certain projects were geared toward electrifying until-then remote regions. The Tennessee Valley Authority brought dams to the non-coastal southern states, **29** including Tennessee itself, of course, but also the northern parts of Alabama and Mississippi.

27

Which choice provides the most specific information on the areas that Roosevelt hoped to stimulate?

A) NO CHANGE

B) industrial and agricultural sectors

C) whole thing

D) money flowing and the economy

28

A) NO CHANGE

B) on

C) off

D) to

29

Which choice gives an additional supporting detail that emphasizes the importance of the TVA in Roosevelt's larger economic project?

A) NO CHANGE

B) taking account of the fact that farming is difficult without a reliable large body of water.

C) establishing not only more reliable sources of water and work but electricity for millions of Americans.

D) one of many impressive public-works projects completed throughout Roosevelt's tenure.

CONTINUE

Many of the programs, including the Tennessee Valley Authority, continue to exist to this day. Roosevelt's 100 Days were unique in that they not only jumpstarted the American economy at a time when a stimulus was most needed but also laid the groundwork for programs that could persist into the **30** future, past their own moment. Indeed, Roosevelt's "New Deal" remains new even though, at this point, **31** it's more than eighty years old.

Still, Roosevelt's 100 Days remain the subject of controversy. In Roosevelt's day, there was widespread criticism from those who thought government should play a smaller rather than a larger role in **32** people's day-to-day lives. For many others, Roosevelt's government interventions are a model for how governments should aid citizens in times of need. **33** Clearly, Roosevelt's unadulterated successes would seem odd in an era of political wrangling characterized by gridlock rather than swift action.

30

A) NO CHANGE

B) future.

C) future, which is to say after the present.

D) future, many years beyond when they were created.

31

A) NO CHANGE

B) its

C) they're

D) there

32

A) NO CHANGE

B) peoples'

C) peoples

D) peoples's

33

The writer wants to conclude the paragraph effectively without dismissing the debate described in this paragraph. Which choice best accomplishes this goal?

A) NO CHANGE

B) Unfortunately, even Roosevelt's obvious failures can

C) In either case, Roosevelt's achievements in the first 100 Days of his presidency

D) All of the things described above could accomplish this goal.

CONTINUE ➤

Questions 34–44 are based on the following passage.

Setsuko Hara: In and Out of the Tokyo Spotlight

One of the [34] hammiest board-treaders in the history of Japanese cinema was also one of the most mysterious. Setsuko Hara died in September 2015 at the age of 95, and while she is remembered as perhaps the most formidable actress in Japan's long cinematic tradition, no one had seen her in anything since the 1960s. The actress went into seclusion after the death of her longtime collaborator, the director Yasujiro Ozu.

Hara's first acting role came when she was only 15. The Japanese film industry had divided loyalties at the time, [35] despite its obvious debt to American cinema amid the increasing international tensions with the United States and others that would lead to World War II. Hara's first film, a German-Japanese production called *The Daughter of the Samurai* (1937), emerged among these tensions [36] using as it did the conventions of the American melodrama to promote an early version of what would become Axis propaganda. After her success in this film, Hara became one of the faces of the Japanese propaganda effort during the Second World War.

34
A) NO CHANGE
B) most exquisite thespians
C) most emotive of histrionists
D) greatest actresses

35
A) NO CHANGE
B) as evidenced by
C) contrasting with
D) enabled by

36
The writer is considering the deleting the underlined portion (ending the sentence with a period). Should the writer make this deletion?

A) Yes, because the information is provided in the previous sentence.

B) Yes, because the underlined portion undermines the paragraph's description of the Axis propaganda effort.

C) No, because the underlined portion gives a specific example of how the Axis powers conducted their propaganda campaign.

D) No, because the underlined portion provides information that clarifies an idea central to this paragraph.

CONTINUE

After Japan's defeat in the war, however, Hara's career changed significantly. Directors and audiences discovered her incredible talent acting in quieter dramas. The masterpieces in this mode were Ozu's *Late Spring* (1949) and *Tokyo Story* (1953), in which Hara plays a woman who is torn between the demands of various family members, who in turn **37** represented different generational expectations. Hara could reveal incredible emotion through subtle, almost imperceptible facial expressions and voice modulations. **38** Moreover, her compelling and unique beauty kept screen audiences eagerly engaged.

The subtle conflicts in *Late Spring* capture Hara's particular **39** style of acting in films. Even in the 1940s, Hollywood films were characterized by grand conflicts and even grander emotions. The films of Ozu's late period, especially his collaborations with Hara, however, worked with a much smaller canvas, usually with very few sets, limiting the scenes to a character's **40** office kitchen, living room, or garden. In *Late Spring*, Hara's character

37
A) NO CHANGE
B) would represent
C) had represented
D) represent

38
A) NO CHANGE
B) In sum,
C) Nevertheless,
D) Meanwhile,

39
A) NO CHANGE
B) acting style.
C) acting methods that were unique to her.
D) acting style in film and presumably in the theater.

40
A) NO CHANGE
B) office, kitchen, living,
C) office, kitchen, living
D) office, kitchen living,

CONTINUE

Noriko is twenty-seven years old and has not married. Against the [41] council of her friends and family, she has instead chosen to care for her aging widowed father. The conflict and plot are that simple, [42] and Ozu's cinematography and Hara's expressive face show that sometimes the simplest and smallest domestic conflicts can have profound implications.

[1] Hara never formally announced her retirement, though she made her last film in 1963. [2] Rumors have always circulated about Hara's mysterious disappearance from the screen, and viewers' many theories show [43] their grief at having lost such a bright star. [3] Some believe that she had been going blind and did not want to do so in the public eye. [4] In either case, Hara left an indelible mark on the shape of world cinema. [5] Especially in a moment when all cinematic achievement seems to point toward bigger and louder, Setsuko Hara provides the important reminder that smaller and quieter can be just as powerful. [44]

41

A) NO CHANGE
B) council from
C) counsel with
D) counsel of

42

A) NO CHANGE
B) for
C) so
D) yet

43

A) NO CHANGE
B) one's
C) his
D) your

44

The writer plans to add the following sentence to this paragraph.

> Others believe that her grief over Ozu's death in 1963 kept her from returning to the cinema.

To make this paragraph most logical, the sentence should be placed

A) after sentence 2.
B) after sentence 3.
C) after sentence 4.
D) after sentence 5.

STOP
**If you finish before time is called, you may check your work on this section only.
Do not turn to any other section in the test.**

Math Test – No Calculator

25 MINUTES, 20 QUESTIONS

Turn to Section 3 of your answer sheet to answer the questions in this section.

DIRECTIONS

For questions 1–15, solve each problem, choose the best answer from the choices provided, and fill in the corresponding circle on your answer sheet. **For questions 16–20,** solve the problem and enter your answer in the grid on the answer sheet. Please refer to the directions before question 16 on how to enter your answers in the grid. You may use any available space in your test booklet for scratch work.

NOTES

1. The use of a calculator **is not permitted**.
2. All variables and expressions used represent real numbers unless otherwise indicated.
3. Figures provided in this test are drawn to scale unless otherwise indicated.
4. All figures lie in a plane unless otherwise indicated.
5. Unless otherwise indicated, the domain of a given function f is the set of all real numbers x for which $f(x)$ is a real number.

REFERENCE

$A = \pi r^2$
$C = 2\pi r$

$A = \ell w$

$A = \frac{1}{2} bh$

$c^2 = a^2 + b^2$

Special Right Triangles

$V = \ell wh$

$V = \pi r^2 h$

$V = \frac{4}{3}\pi r^3$

$V = \frac{1}{3}\pi r^2 h$

$V = \frac{1}{3}\ell wh$

The number of degrees of arc in a circle is 360.
The number of radians of arc in a circle is 2π.
The sum of the measures in degrees of the angles of a triangle is 180.

CONTINUE

1

An editor is paid $25 an hour to edit 3 essays and an additional $50 bonus when the edits on all three essays are completed. If the edits on the essays are completed, what expression could be used to determine how much the editor earned?

A) $50y + 25$, where y is the number of hours

B) $25y + 50$, where y is the number of hours

C) $y(25 + 2) + 3$, where y is the number of essays

D) $50y + (25 + 2)$, where y is the number of essays

2

$$(-mn^2 + 2n^2 - 6m^2n) + (2mn^2 - 2n^2 + 3m^2n)$$

The expression above is equivalent to which of the following?

A) $mn^2 + 4n^2 - 9m^2n$

B) $mn^2 - 3m^2n$

C) $3mn^2 - 4n^2$

D) $3m^2n - mn^2$

3

$$\frac{1}{12}x - \frac{1}{12}y = 13$$
$$\frac{1}{3}x - \frac{1}{6}y = 20$$

Which ordered pair (x, y) satisfies the equations above?

A) $(-35, 190)$

B) $(-36, -192)$

C) $(168, 25)$

D) $\left(\dfrac{752}{5}, \dfrac{304}{5}\right)$

4

Kelly is a salesperson at a shoe store, where she must sell a pre-set number of pairs of shoes each month. At the end of each workday, the number of pairs of shoes that she has left to sell that month is given by the equation $S = 300 - 15x$, where S is the number of pairs of shoes Kelly still needs to sell and x is the number of days she has worked that month. What is the meaning of the number 300 in this equation?

A) Kelly must sell 300 pairs of shoes per week.

B) Kelly must sell 300 pairs of shoes per day.

C) Kelly will sell the pairs of shoes in 300 days.

D) Kelly must sell 300 pairs of shoes each month.

CONTINUE

5

A certain amusement park sells half-day passes and all-day passes. The amusement park charges $40 for a half-day pass and $80 for an all-day pass. The amusement park sold a total of 70 passes one day for $4,600. How many all-day passes did the amusement park sell?

A) 25

B) 35

C) 45

D) 60

7

Which of the following must be true if $\dfrac{t + u}{t} = \dfrac{12}{11}$?

A) $\dfrac{u}{t} = \dfrac{1}{11}$

B) $\dfrac{u}{t} = \dfrac{23}{11}$

C) $\dfrac{t - u}{t} = \dfrac{1}{11}$

D) $\dfrac{t + 2u}{t} = -\dfrac{8}{11}$

6

$$5x^2 + 7x - 6 = 0$$

If a and b are two solutions to the equation above and $a < b$, which of the following is the value of $b - a$?

A) $\dfrac{3}{5}$

B) $\dfrac{6}{5}$

C) $\dfrac{8}{5}$

D) $\dfrac{13}{5}$

8

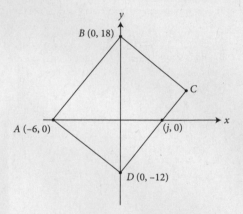

Parallelogram $ABCD$ is shown in the xy-plane above. What is the value of j ?

A) 15

B) 12

C) 4

D) 3

CONTINUE

9

$$x = \frac{y(y-3)}{2}$$

The number of diagonals, x, that can be drawn within a polygon depends on the number of sides, y, of the polygon according to the formula above. If a polygon has at least 7 diagonals, what is the least number of sides it can have?

A) 7

B) 6

C) 5

D) 4

10

The value of a car decreases $500 for every 1,000 miles it is driven. The current value of the car is $23,000, and the car is driven an average of 10,000 miles per year. What will be the value of the car, in dollars, at a point in time y years from now?

A) $23,000 – $5,000$y$

B) $23,000 – 500y$

C) $23,000 – 0.02y$

D) $23,000 – 0.0002y$

11

$$7x - cy = 10$$
$$5x + 2y = 8$$

In the system of equations above, x and y are variables and c is a constant. What must the value of c be if the system of equations has no solution?

A) $\dfrac{14}{5}$

B) $\dfrac{27}{25}$

C) $-\dfrac{27}{25}$

D) $-\dfrac{14}{5}$

12

Which of the following complex numbers is equal to $\dfrac{4 - 7i}{6 + 3i}$? (Note: $i = \sqrt{-1}$)

A) $\dfrac{1}{15} + \dfrac{6i}{5}$

B) $\dfrac{1}{15} - \dfrac{6i}{5}$

C) $\dfrac{2}{3} - \dfrac{7i}{3}$

D) $\dfrac{2}{3} + \dfrac{7i}{3}$

CONTINUE

13

$$g(x) = 2(x^2 + 14x + 7) - 7(x + c)$$

In the polynomial $g(x)$ defined above, c is a constant. If $g(x)$ is divisible by x, what is the value of c ?

A) −2

B) 0

C) 2

D) 5

14

If $3r - s = 10$, then which of the following is equivalent to $\dfrac{27^r}{3^s}$?

A) 27^2

B) 9^4

C) 3^{10}

D) The value cannot be determined from the information given.

15

Which of the following is equivalent to $\dfrac{4n + 9}{n - 5}$?

A) $4 + \dfrac{29}{n - 5}$

B) $4 + \dfrac{9}{n - 5}$

C) $4 - \dfrac{9}{5}$

D) $-\dfrac{4 + 9}{5}$

CONTINUE

DIRECTIONS

For questions 16–20, solve the problem and enter your answer in the grid, as described below, on the answer sheet.

1. Although not required, it is suggested that you write your answer in the boxes at the top of the columns to help you fill in the circles accurately. You will receive credit only if the circles are filled in correctly.
2. Mark no more than one circle in any column.
3. No question has a negative answer.
4. Some problems may have more than one correct answer. In such cases, grid only one answer.
5. **Mixed numbers** such as $3\frac{1}{2}$ must be gridded as 3.5 or 7/2. (If 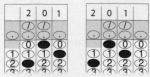 is entered into the grid, it will be interpreted as $\frac{31}{2}$, not as $3\frac{1}{2}$.)
6. **Decimal Answers:** If you obtain a decimal answer with more digits than the grid can accommodate, it may be either rounded or truncated, but it must fill the entire grid.

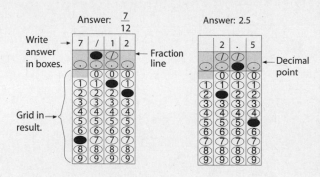

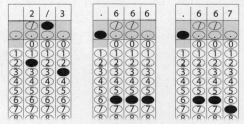

Acceptable ways to grid $\frac{2}{3}$ are:

Answer: 201 – either position is correct

NOTE: You may start your answers in any column, space permitting. Columns you don't need to use should be left blank.

CONTINUE

16

For what value of x is $37 = \dfrac{x}{20} - 3$?

18

If $a \neq 0$, what is the value of $\dfrac{9(5a)^2}{(3a)^2}$?

17

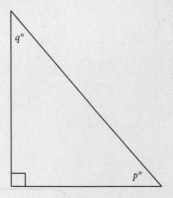

In the triangle above, the cosine of $p°$ is 0.8. What is the sine of $q°$?

CONTINUE →

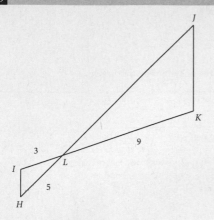

Segment HJ intersects segment IK at L in the figure above. If $\overline{HI} \parallel \overline{JK}$, what is the length of segment HJ ?

What is the value of y if $z = 5\sqrt{3}$ and $3z = \sqrt{3y}$?

STOP

If you finish before time is called, you may check your work on this section only.
Do not turn to any other section in the test.

Math Test – Calculator

55 MINUTES, 38 QUESTIONS

Turn to Section 4 of your answer sheet to answer the questions in this section.

For questions 1–30, solve each problem, choose the best answer from the choices provided, and fill in the corresponding circle on your answer sheet. **For questions 31–38**, solve the problem and enter your answer in the grid on the answer sheet. Please refer to the directions before question 31 on how to enter your answers in the grid. You may use any available space in your test booklet for scratch work.

1. The use of a calculator **is permitted**.
2. All variables and expressions used represent real numbers unless otherwise indicated.
3. Figures provided in this test are drawn to scale unless otherwise indicated.
4. All figures lie in a plane unless otherwise indicated.
5. Unless otherwise indicated, the domain of a given function f is the set of all real numbers x for which $f(x)$ is a real number.

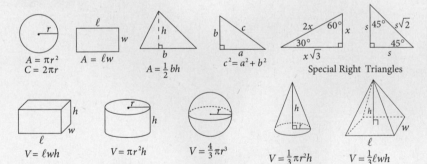

$$A = \pi r^2$$
$$C = 2\pi r$$

$$A = \ell w$$

$$A = \frac{1}{2}bh$$

$$c^2 = a^2 + b^2$$

Special Right Triangles

$$V = \ell wh$$

$$V = \pi r^2 h$$

$$V = \frac{4}{3}\pi r^3$$

$$V = \frac{1}{3}\pi r^2 h$$

$$V = \frac{1}{3}\ell wh$$

The number of degrees of arc in a circle is 360.
The number of radians of arc in a circle is 2π.
The sum of the measures in degrees of the angles of a triangle is 180.

CONTINUE ➡

1

David has a mobile data plan for which the monthly fee is $20.00 and the data usage fee is $2.50 per gigabyte. Which of the following functions expresses David's cost, in dollars, for a month in which he uses g gigabytes of data?

A) $f(g) = 22.50g$

B) $f(g) = 20g + 2.50$

C) $f(g) = 20 + 250g$

D) $f(g) = 20 + 2.50g$

2

Annual Profits

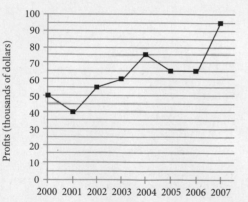

The line graph above shows the annual profit of a particular clothing store from 2000 to 2007. According to the graph, what was the greatest change (in absolute value) in the annual profit between two consecutive years?

A) $25,000

B) $30,000

C) $35,000

D) $40,000

3

In order to qualify for a fitness competition, a person must be able to complete 30 pull-ups in one minute. Jim can currently do 14 pull-ups in one minute and believes that he can increase that amount by 7 pull-ups each year. Which of the following represents the number of pull-ups that Jim believes he will be able to complete in one minute y years from now?

A) $7y + 14$

B) $7y + 30$

C) $14y + 7$

D) $14 - 7y$

4

$$v = 17 + 2.5t$$

A constantly-accelerating particle is moving in a straight line. After t seconds, the particle is moving at a velocity of v, in meters per second, as shown in the equation above. What is t when v is 67 ?

A) 184.5

B) 67

C) 33.6

D) 20

CONTINUE

5

When function h is graphed in the xy-plane, it has x-intercepts at -4, 2, and 4. Which of the following could define h ?

A) $h(x) = (x - 4)(x - 2)(x + 4)$

B) $h(x) = (x - 4)(x + 2)(x + 4)$

C) $h(x) = (x - 4)^2(x + 2)$

D) $h(x) = (x + 2)(x + 4)^2$

6

When three times a number n is added to 9, the result is 3. What is the result when 4 times n is added to 14 ?

A) -2

B) 3

C) 6

D) 22

7

A coffee shop is filling coffee cups from an industrial urn that contains 64 gallons of coffee. At most, how many 16-ounce cups of coffee can be filled from the urn? (1 gallon = 128 ounces)

A) 4

B) 512

C) $1,024$

D) $2,048$

8

What is the slope of the line in the xy-plane that passes through the points $\left(5, \dfrac{8}{3}\right)$ and $\left(1, -\dfrac{1}{3}\right)$?

A) -2

B) $-\dfrac{4}{3}$

C) $\dfrac{3}{4}$

D) 2

CONTINUE

9

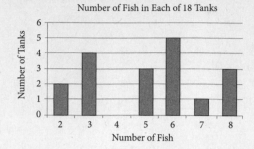

Number of Fish in Each of 18 Tanks

Based on the histogram above, which of the following is closest to the average (arithmetic mean) number of fish per tank?

A) 5

B) 6

C) 7

D) 8

10

A telephone survey was conducted in order to determine if people in City C are more likely to work 9-to-5 office jobs than other jobs. The research team called 5,000 random people between 12 P.M. to 4 P.M. on a Thursday. Of the 5,000 people called, 3,000 did not answer, and 250 refused to participate. Which of the following was the biggest flaw in the design of the survey?

A) The time the survey was taken

B) Population size

C) Sample size

D) The fact that the survey was done by telephone

11

If the function p has exactly four distinct roots, which of the following could represent the complete graph of $y = p(x)$ in the xy-plane?

A)

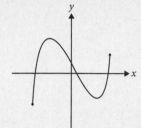

B)

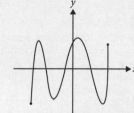

C)

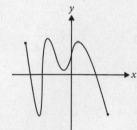

D)

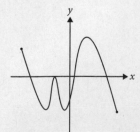

CONTINUE

12

One morning in a particular restaurant, 85 percent of the customers ordered the brunch special. Which of the following could be the total number of customers in the restaurant that morning?

A) 40

B) 42

C) 44

D) 48

13

$$d = -8t^2 + vt + h$$

The equation above gives the distance, d, in meters, a projectile is above the ground t seconds after it is released with an initial velocity of v meters per second from an initial height of h meters. Which of the following gives v in terms of d, t, and h ?

A) $v = \dfrac{d - h}{t} + 8t$

B) $v = \dfrac{d + h}{t} - 8t$

C) $v = \dfrac{d - h + 8}{t}$

D) $v = d + h - 8t$

14

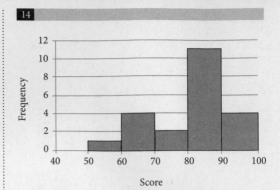

The histogram above shows the distribution of the scores of 22 students on a recent biology test. Which of the following could be the median score of the 22 students represented in the histogram?

A) 68

B) 71

C) 77

D) 84

CONTINUE

Questions 15-17 refer to the following information.

A survey of 130 randomly selected workers in a particular metropolitan area was conducted to gather information about average daily commute times. The data are shown in the table below.

	Commutes by public transit	Does not commute by public transit	Total
Less than 1 hour	22	46	68
At least 1 hour	29	33	62
Total	51	79	130

15

Which of the following is closest to the percent of those surveyed who commute using public transit?

A) 65%

B) 46%

C) 39%

D) 32%

16

In 2014, the population of the metropolitan area from the survey was about 13 million. If the survey results were used to estimate information about commute times throughout the metropolitan area, which of the following is the best estimate for the number of individuals who used public transit and had an average daily commute of at least one hour?

A) 290,000

B) 2,200,000

C) 2,900,000

D) 6,200,000

17

Based on the data, how many times more likely is it for a person with a commute of less than 1 hour NOT to commute by public transit than it is for a person with a commute of at least one hour NOT to commute by public transit? (Round the answer to the nearest hundredth.)

A) 1.39 times as likely

B) 1.27 times as likely

C) 0.78 times as likely

D) 0.72 times as likely

CONTINUE

In order to determine the effect that caffeinated beverage C would have on sleep, researchers conducted a study. From a large population of people without sleep disorders, 500 subjects were randomly selected. Half the subjects were randomly selected to consume beverage C and the rest did not consume beverage C. The results of the study showed that the subjects who consumed beverage C slept less than those who did not consume beverage C. Based on the design and results of the study, which of the following statements is the best conclusion?

A) Beverage C will cause more loss in sleep than all other caffeinated beverages.

B) Beverage C will cause a substantial loss in sleep.

C) Beverage C is likely to reduce the amount of sleep of people without sleep disorders.

D) Beverage C will reduce sleep of anyone who consumes it.

19

The sum of four numbers is 1,764. One of the numbers, n, is 40% more than the sum of the other three numbers. What is the value of n ?

A)   287

B)   735

C)   1,029

D)   1,260

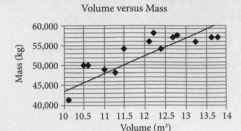

Volume versus Mass

Selin weighs 14 different objects of similar density. The scatterplot shown above shows the volume of each object and the corresponding weight of each object. The line of best fit for the data is shown above. For the object that had a volume of 11.5 m³, the actual mass was about how many kilograms more than the mass predicted by the line of best fit?

A)   1,000

B)   2,000

C)   3,000

D)   4,000

CONTINUE →

21

Jessica owns a store that sells only laptops and tablets. Last week, her store sold 90 laptops and 210 tablets. This week, the sales, in number of units, of laptops increased by 50 percent, and the sales, in number of units, of tablets increased by 30 percent. By what percentage did total sales, in units, in Jessica's store increase?

A) 20 percent

B) 25 percent

C) 36 percent

D) 80 percent

22

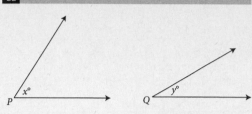

Note: Figures not drawn to scale

For acute angles P and Q shown above, $\cos(x°) = \sin(y°)$. If $x = 3c - 23$ and $y = 7c - 42$, what is the value of c ?

A) 24.5

B) 15.5

C)   9.0

D)   6.0

CONTINUE

23

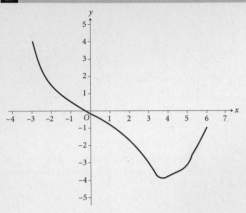

What is the maximum value of the function graphed in the *xy*-plane above, for $-3 \leq x \leq 6$?

A) 4

B) 5

C) 6

D) ∞

24

Matthew constructs a fence around a patch of grass in his backyard. The patch has a width that is 8 feet more than 4 times the length. What is the perimeter of the fence if Matthew's patch of grass has an area of 5,472 square feet?

A) 364 feet

B) 376 feet

C) 396 feet

D) 400 feet

25

In the *xy*-plane, the line determined by the points $(c, 3)$ and $(27, c)$ intersects the origin. Which of the following could be the value of c ?

A) 0

B) 3

C) 6

D) 9

26

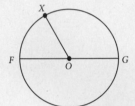

In the circle above, the length of arc $\overparen{FXG}$ is 14π. If $\overline{FG}$ is a chord that passes through the circle's center, O, what is the length of the segment $\overline{XO}$?

A)   7

B) 14

C) 28

D) 56

CONTINUE

27

Let p and q be numbers such that $-|p| < q < |p|$. Which of the following must be true?

I. $p > 0$

II. $|p| > -q$

III. $p > |q|$

A) I only

B) II only

C) II and III only

D) I, II, and III only

28

A rectangular container with a base that measures 10 feet by 10 feet is filled with jelly beans. The container is divided into regions each with the same height as the container and a square base with sides that measure 1 foot each. Sherman randomly selects ten of these regions and counts the number of blue jelly beans in each region. The results are shown in the table below.

Region	Blue Jelly Beans	Region	Blue Jelly Beans
I	20	VI	22
II	21	VII	25
III	27	VIII	24
IV	31	IX	28
V	19	X	23

Which of the following is a reasonable approximation of the number of blue jelly beans in the entire container?

A) 25,000

B) 2,500

C) 250

D) 25

CONTINUE

29

Product Type	Flavor	
	Frozen Yogurt	Ice Cream
Vanilla		
Chocolate		
Total	32	152

The incomplete table above shows the sales for a particular sweet shop by product and flavor. There were 4 times as many vanilla ice creams sold as vanilla frozen yogurts, and there were 6 times as many chocolate ice creams sold as chocolate frozen yogurts. If there were a total of 32 frozen yogurts and 152 ice creams sold, and no flavors other than vanilla and chocolate were available, which of the following is closest to the probability that a randomly selected ice cream sold was vanilla?

A) 0.250

B) 0.435

C) 0.526

D) 0.667

30

$$\begin{cases} y \geq x \\ 3y < 2x - 3 \end{cases}$$

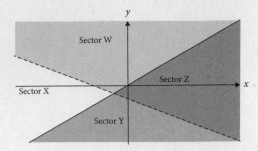

A system of inequalities is graphed above. Which sector or sectors on the graph could represent all of the solutions to the system shown?

A) Sectors Y and Z

B) Sectors W and Y

C) Sector W

D) Sector X

CONTINUE

DIRECTIONS

For questions 31–38, solve the problem and enter your answer in the grid, as described below, on the answer sheet.

1. Although not required, it is suggested that you write your answer in the boxes at the top of the columns to help you fill in the circles accurately. You will receive credit only if the circles are filled in correctly.

2. Mark no more than one circle in any column.

3. No question has a negative answer.

4. Some problems may have more than one correct answer. In such cases, grid only one answer.

5. **Mixed numbers** such as $3\frac{1}{2}$ must be gridded as 3.5 or 7/2. (If is entered into the grid, it will be interpreted as $\frac{31}{2}$, not as $3\frac{1}{2}$.)

6. **Decimal Answers:** If you obtain a decimal answer with more digits than the grid can accommodate, it may be either rounded or truncated, but it must fill the entire grid.

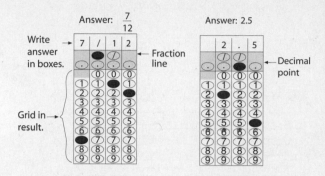

Acceptable ways to grid $\frac{2}{3}$ are:

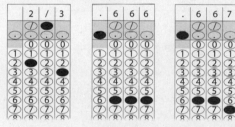

Answer: 201 – either position is correct

NOTE: You may start your answers in any column, space permitting. Columns you don't need to use should be left blank.

31

At a certain food truck, hamburgers are sold for $5 each and hot dogs are $3 each. If Martina buys one hamburger and h hot dogs and spends at least $20 and no more than $25, what is one possible value of h?

32

Number of States in 14 Federal Nations			
Nation	States	Nation	States
Australia	6	Micronesia	4
Austria	9	Nigeria	36
Brazil	26	Saint Kitts and Nevis	2
Germany	16	South Sudan	10
India	29	Sudan	17
Malaysia	13	United States	50
Mexico	31	Venezuela	23

The table above lists the number of states in each of the 14 federal nations that have subdivisions called states. According to the table, what is the mean number of states of these nations? (Round your answer to the nearest tenth.)

33

In the xy-plane, the point $(-2, 6)$ lies on the graph of the function $g(x) = 2x^2 + kx + 18$. What is the value of k?

34

In a certain college dormitory, 108 students are assigned dorm rooms. The dormitory has 26 dorm rooms, each of which is assigned 3 or 5 students. How many of the dorm rooms will be assigned 3 students?

CONTINUE

35

Population of Town A
Each Decade from 1910 to 2000

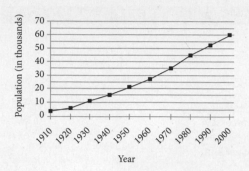

According to the figure shown above, the population of Town A in 1970 was what fraction of the population of Town A in 2000 ?

36

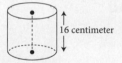

16 centimeter

A wooden block is in the shape of the right circular cylinder shown above. If the volume of the wooden block is 64π cubic centimeters, what is the <u>diameter</u> of the base of the cylinder, in centimeters?

Questions 37 and 38 refer to the following information.

$\omega^2 = \omega_0^2 + 2\alpha\theta$ (angular position – angular velocity)

$\omega = \omega_0 + \alpha t$ (time – angular velocity)

$\theta = \omega_0 t + \dfrac{1}{2}\alpha t^2$ (time – angular position)

A carousel is rotating at an angular velocity of 90 degrees per second. The instant a particular point on the carousel reaches angular position $\theta = 0°$, the carousel operator flips a switch, causing the carousel at a constant angular acceleration to slow down and eventually change direction. The equations above describe the constant-acceleration motion of the carousel, where ω_0 represents the initial angular velocity, ω is the angular velocity as it travels, θ is the angular position of the particular point on the carousel, t is the time since the switch was flipped, and α is the constant angular acceleration ($-12.6°/s^2$).

37

To the nearest degree, at what angular position will the carousel change direction?

38

To the nearest second, how long will it take the carousel to come to a complete stop before it changes direction?

STOP

**If you finish before time is called, you may check your work on this section only.
Do not turn to any other section in the test.**

SAT Essay

DIRECTIONS

The essay gives you an opportunity to show how effectively you can read and comprehend a passage and write an essay analyzing the passage. In your essay you should demonstrate that you have read the passage carefully, present a clear and logical analysis, and use language precisely.

Your essay must be written on the lines provided in your answer sheet booklet; except for the planning page of the answer booklet, you will receive no other paper on which to write. You will have enough space if you write on every line, avoid wide margins, and keep your handwriting to a reasonable size. Remember that people who are not familiar with your handwriting will read what you write. Try to write or print so that what you are writing is legible to those readers.

You have <u>50 minutes</u> to read the passage and write an essay in response to the prompt provided inside this booklet.

REMINDER

— Do not write your essay in this booklet. Only what you write on the lined pages of your answer booklet will be evaluated.

— An off-topic essay will not be evaluated.

CONTINUE ➡

As you read the passage below, consider how Jimmy Carter uses

- evidence, such as facts or examples, to support claims.
- reasoning to develop ideas and to connect claims and evidence.
- stylistic or persuasive elements, such as word choice or appeals to emotion, to add power to the ideas expressed.

Adapted from Jimmy Carter, "The President's Proposed Energy Policy." The speech was televised and was delivered on April 18, 1977.

1 Tonight I want to have an unpleasant talk with you about a problem unprecedented in our history. With the exception of preventing war, this is the greatest challenge our country will face during our lifetimes. The energy crisis has not yet overwhelmed us, but it will if we do not act quickly. It is a problem we will not solve in the next few years, and it is likely to get progressively worse through the rest of this century. We must not be selfish or timid if we hope to have a decent world for our children and grandchildren.

2 We simply must balance our demand for energy with our rapidly shrinking resources. By acting now, we can control our future instead of letting the future control us.

3 Two days from now, I will present my energy proposals to the Congress. Its members will be my partners and they have already given me a great deal of valuable advice. Many of these proposals will be unpopular. Some will cause you to put up with inconveniences and to make sacrifices. The most important thing about these proposals is that the alternative may be a national catastrophe. Further delay can affect our strength and our power as a nation.

4 Our decision about energy will test the character of the American people and the ability of the President and the Congress to govern. This difficult effort will be the "moral equivalent of war"—except that we will be uniting our efforts to build and not destroy. I know that some of you may doubt that we face real energy shortages. The 1973 gasoline lines are gone, and our homes are warm again. But our energy problem is worse tonight than it was in 1973 or a few weeks ago in the dead of winter. It is worse because more waste has occurred, and more time has passed by without our planning for the future. And it will get worse every day until we act.

5 The oil and natural gas we rely on for 75 percent of our energy are running out. In spite of increased effort, domestic production has been dropping steadily at about six percent a year. Imports have doubled in the last five years. Our nation's independence of economic and political action is becoming increasingly constrained. Unless profound changes are made to lower oil consumption, we now believe that early in the 1980s the world will be demanding more oil than it can produce.

CONTINUE ➡

6   The world now uses about 60 million barrels of oil a day and demand increases each year about five percent. This means that, just to stay even, we need the production of a new Texas every year, an Alaskan North Slope every nine months, or a new Saudi Arabia every three years. Obviously, this cannot continue.

7   We must look back in history to understand our energy problem. Twice in the last several hundred years there has been a transition in the way people use energy. The first was about 200 years ago, away from wood—which had provided about 90 percent of all fuel—to coal, which was more efficient. This change became the basis of the Industrial Revolution. The second change took place in this century, with the growing use of oil and natural gas. They were more convenient and cheaper than coal, and the supply seemed to be almost without limit. They made possible the age of automobile and airplane travel. Nearly everyone who is alive today grew up during this age and we have never known anything different.

8   Because we are now running out of gas and oil, we must prepare quickly for a third change, to strict conservation and to the use of coal and permanent renewable energy sources, like solar power.

9   …Other generations of Americans have faced and mastered great challenges. I have faith that meeting this challenge will make our own lives even richer. If you will join me so that we can work together with patriotism and courage, we will again prove that our great nation can lead the world into an age of peace, independence, and freedom.

Write an essay in which you explain how Jimmy Carter builds an argument to convince his audience to support his proposed energy policy. In your essay, analyze how Carter uses one or more of the features listed in the box above (or features of your own choice) to strengthen the logic and persuasiveness of his argument. Be sure that your analysis focuses on the most relevant features of the passage.

Your essay should not explain whether you agree with Carter's claims, but rather explain how Carter builds an argument to persuade his audience.

END OF TEST

DO NOT RETURN TO A PREVIOUS SECTION.

Completely darken bubbles with a No. 2 pencil. If you make a mistake, be sure to erase mark completely. Erase all stray marks.

1.
YOUR NAME: _____
(Print)   Last   First   M.I.

SIGNATURE: _____ DATE: __ / __ / __

HOME ADDRESS: _____
(Print)   Number and Street

_____
        City   State   Zip Code

PHONE NO.: _____
(Print)

IMPORTANT: Please fill in these boxes exactly as shown on the back cover of your test book.

2. TEST FORM

6. DATE OF BIRTH

Month	Day	Year
○ JAN		
○ FEB	⓪⓪	⓪⓪
○ MAR	①①	①①
○ APR	②②	②②
○ MAY	③③	③③
○ JUN	④	④④
○ JUL	⑤	⑤⑤
○ AUG	⑥	⑥⑥
○ SEP	⑦	⑦⑦
○ OCT	⑧	⑧⑧
○ NOV	⑨	⑨⑨
○ DEC		

3. TEST CODE

4. REGISTRATION NUMBER

7. SEX
○ MALE
○ FEMALE

The **Princeton Review®**

5. YOUR NAME

First 4 letters of last name | FIRST INIT | MID INIT

Ⓐ Ⓑ Ⓒ Ⓓ Ⓔ Ⓕ Ⓖ Ⓗ Ⓘ Ⓙ Ⓚ Ⓛ Ⓜ Ⓝ Ⓞ Ⓟ Ⓠ Ⓡ Ⓢ Ⓣ Ⓤ Ⓥ Ⓦ Ⓧ Ⓨ Ⓩ

Test ❶ Start with number 1 for each new section.
If a section has fewer questions than answer spaces, leave the extra answer spaces blank.

Section 1—Reading

1. Ⓐ Ⓑ Ⓒ Ⓓ
2. Ⓐ Ⓑ Ⓒ Ⓓ
3. Ⓐ Ⓑ Ⓒ Ⓓ
4. Ⓐ Ⓑ Ⓒ Ⓓ
5. Ⓐ Ⓑ Ⓒ Ⓓ
6. Ⓐ Ⓑ Ⓒ Ⓓ
7. Ⓐ Ⓑ Ⓒ Ⓓ
8. Ⓐ Ⓑ Ⓒ Ⓓ
9. Ⓐ Ⓑ Ⓒ Ⓓ
10. Ⓐ Ⓑ Ⓒ Ⓓ
11. Ⓐ Ⓑ Ⓒ Ⓓ
12. Ⓐ Ⓑ Ⓒ Ⓓ
13. Ⓐ Ⓑ Ⓒ Ⓓ
14. Ⓐ Ⓑ Ⓒ Ⓓ
15. Ⓐ Ⓑ Ⓒ Ⓓ
16. Ⓐ Ⓑ Ⓒ Ⓓ
17. Ⓐ Ⓑ Ⓒ Ⓓ
18. Ⓐ Ⓑ Ⓒ Ⓓ
19. Ⓐ Ⓑ Ⓒ Ⓓ
20. Ⓐ Ⓑ Ⓒ Ⓓ
21. Ⓐ Ⓑ Ⓒ Ⓓ
22. Ⓐ Ⓑ Ⓒ Ⓓ
23. Ⓐ Ⓑ Ⓒ Ⓓ
24. Ⓐ Ⓑ Ⓒ Ⓓ
25. Ⓐ Ⓑ Ⓒ Ⓓ
26. Ⓐ Ⓑ Ⓒ Ⓓ
27. Ⓐ Ⓑ Ⓒ Ⓓ
28. Ⓐ Ⓑ Ⓒ Ⓓ
29. Ⓐ Ⓑ Ⓒ Ⓓ
30. Ⓐ Ⓑ Ⓒ Ⓓ
31. Ⓐ Ⓑ Ⓒ Ⓓ
32. Ⓐ Ⓑ Ⓒ Ⓓ
33. Ⓐ Ⓑ Ⓒ Ⓓ
34. Ⓐ Ⓑ Ⓒ Ⓓ
35. Ⓐ Ⓑ Ⓒ Ⓓ
36. Ⓐ Ⓑ Ⓒ Ⓓ
37. Ⓐ Ⓑ Ⓒ Ⓓ
38. Ⓐ Ⓑ Ⓒ Ⓓ
39. Ⓐ Ⓑ Ⓒ Ⓓ
40. Ⓐ Ⓑ Ⓒ Ⓓ
41. Ⓐ Ⓑ Ⓒ Ⓓ
42. Ⓐ Ⓑ Ⓒ Ⓓ
43. Ⓐ Ⓑ Ⓒ Ⓓ
44. Ⓐ Ⓑ Ⓒ Ⓓ
45. Ⓐ Ⓑ Ⓒ Ⓓ
46. Ⓐ Ⓑ Ⓒ Ⓓ
47. Ⓐ Ⓑ Ⓒ Ⓓ
48. Ⓐ Ⓑ Ⓒ Ⓓ
49. Ⓐ Ⓑ Ⓒ Ⓓ
50. Ⓐ Ⓑ Ⓒ Ⓓ
51. Ⓐ Ⓑ Ⓒ Ⓓ
52. Ⓐ Ⓑ Ⓒ Ⓓ

Section 2—Writing and Language Skills

1. Ⓐ Ⓑ Ⓒ Ⓓ
2. Ⓐ Ⓑ Ⓒ Ⓓ
3. Ⓐ Ⓑ Ⓒ Ⓓ
4. Ⓐ Ⓑ Ⓒ Ⓓ
5. Ⓐ Ⓑ Ⓒ Ⓓ
6. Ⓐ Ⓑ Ⓒ Ⓓ
7. Ⓐ Ⓑ Ⓒ Ⓓ
8. Ⓐ Ⓑ Ⓒ Ⓓ
9. Ⓐ Ⓑ Ⓒ Ⓓ
10. Ⓐ Ⓑ Ⓒ Ⓓ
11. Ⓐ Ⓑ Ⓒ Ⓓ
12. Ⓐ Ⓑ Ⓒ Ⓓ
13. Ⓐ Ⓑ Ⓒ Ⓓ
14. Ⓐ Ⓑ Ⓒ Ⓓ
15. Ⓐ Ⓑ Ⓒ Ⓓ
16. Ⓐ Ⓑ Ⓒ Ⓓ
17. Ⓐ Ⓑ Ⓒ Ⓓ
18. Ⓐ Ⓑ Ⓒ Ⓓ
19. Ⓐ Ⓑ Ⓒ Ⓓ
20. Ⓐ Ⓑ Ⓒ Ⓓ
21. Ⓐ Ⓑ Ⓒ Ⓓ
22. Ⓐ Ⓑ Ⓒ Ⓓ
23. Ⓐ Ⓑ Ⓒ Ⓓ
24. Ⓐ Ⓑ Ⓒ Ⓓ
25. Ⓐ Ⓑ Ⓒ Ⓓ
26. Ⓐ Ⓑ Ⓒ Ⓓ
27. Ⓐ Ⓑ Ⓒ Ⓓ
28. Ⓐ Ⓑ Ⓒ Ⓓ
29. Ⓐ Ⓑ Ⓒ Ⓓ
30. Ⓐ Ⓑ Ⓒ Ⓓ
31. Ⓐ Ⓑ Ⓒ Ⓓ
32. Ⓐ Ⓑ Ⓒ Ⓓ
33. Ⓐ Ⓑ Ⓒ Ⓓ
34. Ⓐ Ⓑ Ⓒ Ⓓ
35. Ⓐ Ⓑ Ⓒ Ⓓ
36. Ⓐ Ⓑ Ⓒ Ⓓ
37. Ⓐ Ⓑ Ⓒ Ⓓ
38. Ⓐ Ⓑ Ⓒ Ⓓ
39. Ⓐ Ⓑ Ⓒ Ⓓ
40. Ⓐ Ⓑ Ⓒ Ⓓ
41. Ⓐ Ⓑ Ⓒ Ⓓ
42. Ⓐ Ⓑ Ⓒ Ⓓ
43. Ⓐ Ⓑ Ⓒ Ⓓ
44. Ⓐ Ⓑ Ⓒ Ⓓ

Completely darken bubbles with a No. 2 pencil. If you make a mistake, be sure to erase mark completely. Erase all stray marks.

Test ❶ Start with number 1 for each new section.
If a section has fewer questions than answer spaces, leave the extra answer spaces blank.

Section 3—Mathematics: No Calculator

Section 4—Mathematics: Calculator

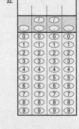

Chapter 3
Practice Test 1:
Answers and
Explanations

PRACTICE TEST 1 ANSWER KEY

	Section 1: Reading				Section 2: Writing & Language				Section 3: Math (No Calculator)				Section 4 : Math (Calculator)		
1.	C	27.	A	1.	A	23.	D	1.	B	11.	D	1.	D	20.	D
2.	C	28.	B	2.	B	24.	C	2.	B	12.	B	2.	B	21.	C
3.	D	29.	B	3.	C	25.	A	3.	B	13.	C	3.	A	22.	B
4.	A	30.	C	4.	B	26.	C	4.	D	14.	C	4.	D	23.	A
5.	A	31.	D	5.	B	27.	B	5.	C	15.	A	5.	A	24.	B
6.	D	32.	B	6.	D	28.	C	6.	D	16.	800	6.	C	25.	D
7.	A	33.	A	7.	B	29.	C	7.	A			7.	B	26.	B
8.	C	34.	D	8.	B	30.	B	8.	C	17.	$\frac{8}{10}$,	8.	C	27.	B
9.	D	35.	B	9.	B	31.	A	9.	B		$\frac{4}{5}$,	9.	A	28.	B
10.	B	36.	C	10.	D	32.	A	10.	A		or	10.	A	29.	C
11.	D	37.	C	11.	B	33.	C				0.8	11.	D	30.	D
12.	C	38.	A	12.	B	34.	D			18.	25	12.	A	31.	5
13.	A	39.	B	13.	D	35.	B			19.	20	13.	A		or 6
14.	A	40.	D	14.	A	36.	D			20.	225	14.	D	32.	19.4
15.	D	41.	A	15.	A	37.	D					15.	C	33.	10
16.	B	42.	D	16.	C	38.	A					16.	C	34.	11
17.	A	43.	C	17.	C	39.	B					17.	B		
18.	A	44.	A	18.	A	40.	C					18.	C	35.	$\frac{7}{12}$
19.	D	45.	A	19.	B	41.	D					19.	C	36.	4
20.	C	46.	B	20.	D	42.	D							37.	321
21.	D	47.	D	21.	A	43.	A							38.	7
22.	C	48.	C	22.	A	44.	B								
23.	B	49.	B												
24.	D	50.	C												
25.	D	51.	D												
26.	B	52.	C												

For self-scoring assessment tables, please turn to page 213.

PRACTICE TEST 1 EXPLANATIONS

Section 1: Reading

1. **C** This is a general question about what happens in the passage as a whole. Leave it until the end of the questions because it will be easier to answer once all the specific questions for this passage have been answered. This passage is about a stranger showing up unexpectedly for an unhappy reunion with a former shipmate. Choice (A) might initially look attractive because the narrator and the stranger do hide and then surprise the captain, but there is no *plan* to surprise the captain. Eliminate (A). Choice (B) has nothing to do with the passage and can be eliminated. Choice (C) is a solid paraphrase of the prediction, so keep it. Choice (D) does mention two characters sharing time on a ship, but the passage does not indicate that the two men were reminiscing at all. Choice (C) is the correct answer.

2. **C** This is a general question that will be best answered after all of the more detail-oriented questions. Look at the second part of each answer choice. The *encounter* in the passage is not *enthusiastic*, so (A) can be eliminated. There is no *conference*, so (B) can also be eliminated. Choice (C) looks good because the narrator was worried, and the stranger and the captain fought, so keep (C). There is no *homecoming*, so eliminate (D). Choice (C) is the correct answer.

3. **D** This is a Vocab-in-Context question, so go back to the text, find the word *fancy* in lines 5 and 10, and cross it out. Replace it with another word that makes sense in the sentence based on the context of the passage. In the first case, the narrator says that he didn't step back inside *quick enough for his fancy*. *Fancy* could be replaced with *liking*. See if that also makes sense in the second occurrence. The stranger tells the narrator that he's *taken quite a fancy* to him because the narrator reminds him of his own son, or *the pride of [his] 'art*. *Liking* definitely fits in that context as well. Choices (A) and (C) can be eliminated immediately. Choice (B) might appear to match the context of the first occurrence of *fancy*, but *impatience* has nothing to do with the prediction of *liking*, so (B) can be eliminated. *Preference* means *liking*. Choice (D) is the correct answer.

4. **A** This question asks about the narrator's sense of the stranger's emotions regarding the coming meeting between him and the captain. Find evidence in the text to predict how the stranger feels about seeing the captain. In the second paragraph, there is plenty of evidence to predict that the stranger feels very bad about the upcoming meeting. The narrator is *uneasy and alarmed*, and he notices that the stranger is *certainly frightened himself*. The narrator goes on to say that the stranger readies his weapon and keeps *swallowing as if he felt…a lump in the throat*. The stranger is definitely not *overjoyed*, so eliminate (B). Choice (D) has nothing to do with the passage, so eliminate it. Choices (A) and (C) both have negative emotions, but the evidence in the text shows the stranger is clearly fearful, not just worried the captain won't recognize him. Choice (A) is the correct answer.

5.	**A**	This is a best evidence question, so simply refer to the lines used to predict the answer to the previous question. Choice (A) is the correct answer.

6.	**D**	This question asks about how the narrator is addressed by the stranger, so look for evidence in the text to predict what the answer might be. In the text used to answer previous questions, the stranger tells the narrator he has *taken a fancy* to him, but in that same paragraph the stranger swears at the boy *with an oath that made [him] jump*. Eliminate (A) because, while the stranger does address the narrator with friendliness at one point, he never addresses him with respect. Choice (B) is reversed—the stranger does address the boy with anger but he's never violent to him. Choice (C) does not match the prediction. *Affection* in (D) looks good, and later the stranger shows that he does not trust the narrator when he sends him for rum but tells him to leave the door open. Choice (D) is the correct answer.

7.	**A**	In order to determine the purpose of the first paragraph, simply look to see what's happening in that paragraph. Throughout the paragraph, the narrator creates a picture of the stranger, from how he looks to how he acts. Choice (A) is the correct answer.

8.	**C**	This is a Vocab-in-Context question, so go back to the text, find the word *talons* in line 51, and cross it out. Replace it with another word that makes sense in the sentence based on the context of the passage. Black Dog says he's lost two talons, and then he holds up *his mutilated hand. Talons* must mean *fingers*. Choice (C) is the correct answer.

9.	**D**	This question asks why the narrator uses a particular phrase (*all the brown had gone out of his face*), so go back to the text to see what's happening around that phrase. The narrator uses the phrase to describe the captain's reaction to seeing the stranger. Black Dog surprises the captain, who *spun round on his heel...he had the look of a man who sees a ghost, or the evil one, or something worse, if anything can be; and upon my word, I felt sorry to see him all in a moment turn so old and sick.* The narrator uses the phrase to show that the captain is reacting badly to the surprise of seeing Black Dog. Choice (A) does not match that prediction, so it can be eliminated. Choice (B) might be true, but isn't supported by the text. Choice (C) doesn't have any support in the text, either, so it can be eliminated. Choice (D) is a clear paraphrase of the prediction and is the correct answer.

10.	**B**	This is a best evidence question, so simply refer to the lines used to predict the answer to the previous question. Choice (B) is the correct answer.

11.	**D**	This question asks why the author mentions certain examples. Use the line reference to find the correct window and look for the claim the examples are meant to illustrate. The examples of gift giving are both recent and about Christmas, but they are offered to show that *the ancient practice of gift-giving is still pervasive and significant in modern cultures*. Eliminate (A), as there's no mention of a *recent increase*. Eliminate (B) and (C), since neither *discrepancies* nor *apprehension* is mentioned. Choice (D) matches the prediction and is the correct answer.

12.   **C**   This is a Vocab-in-Context question, so go back to the text, find the word *rich* in line 20, and cross it out. Replace it with another word that makes sense in the sentence based on the context of the passage. In this case, *rich* refers to the plethora of information that might help to explain consumer behavior. Choices (A) and (B) are actual definitions of the word *rich*, but they don't make sense based on the context. Both of these answers can be eliminated. Choice (C) could work, because when something is *fertile* it is *abundantly productive,* which fits the context of the passage. Choice (D) might connect with the idea of foods that are rich, but that doesn't make sense in this context. Eliminate (D), leaving (C) as the correct answer.

13.   **A**   This question asks about the *self-perpetuating system of reciprocity.* Notice that the following question is a best evidence question, so Q13 and Q14 can be answered in tandem. Look at the answers choices for Q14 first. Choice (14A) suggests that gift-giving conveys information, which supports (13A). Draw a line connecting those two answers. Choice (14B) deals specifically with the *obligation to give,* and (14C) deals with *repayment*—both refer only to part of the system of reciprocity, and neither supports an answer choice in Q13, so both can be eliminated. Choice (14D) might appear to support (13C), but the lines do not support the idea of wreaking *havoc,* so the relationship is weak. Eliminate (14D). Without any support from Q14, (13B), (13C), and (13D) can be eliminated. That leaves (13A) and (14A) as the correct answers.

14.   **A**   (See explanation above.)

15.   **D**   This question asks how Schwartz would view the gift-exchange process. The fourth paragraph presents Schwartz's insights about a gift's ability to reflect *the giver's perception of the recipient* and the implicit acceptance of that perception when a receiver accepts a gift. This point about the process matches well with (D), *symbolic.* Though it may be true that such a process could be *stressful* or *unnerving,* no evidence is given that Schwartz considers it to be so. Thus, (A) and (B) can be eliminated. While some givers and receivers may act *intentional[ly],* there's no evidence that the process always operates that way, so (C) can be eliminated. The best answer is (D).

16.   **B**   This question asks what the passage says about *the acceptance of a gift.* The fourth paragraph states that accepting a gift constitutes acceptance of the implied identity the gift conveys and that *this may lead to changes in self-perceptions.* The correct answer must have something to do with *a lot of power.* This prediction matches well with (B), *influential.* Eliminate (A), as there's no discussion of the idea that accepting a gift is *considerate.* Eliminate (C) because there is no indication that accepting a gift is *authoritative.* Choice (D) can be eliminated as well because, while accepting a gift may have influence on the recipient, there no evidence that it's *immutable.* Choice (B) is the best answer.

17.   **A**   This is a specific paired set with Q16, so simply look at the lines used to predict the answer to the previous question. Choice (A) is the correct answer.

18.   **A**   This is a Vocab-in-Context question, so go back to the text, find the word *function* in line 65, and cross it out. Replace it with another word that makes sense in the sentence based on the context of the passage. In this case, *function* refers to the purpose of gift selection, which supports (A). The *nevertheless* at the beginning of the sentence shows a continuation from the previous paragraph. The focus of the previous paragraph was how gift-giving *does* something, not *when* the gifts are given. Therefore, *function* in this context does not have to do with an event. Choices (B) and (C) can be eliminated. Choice (D), *occupation*, does not fit the context of the sentence. Choice (A) is the correct response.

19.   **D**   This question asks why the author mentions *a gift shop's recent advertisement*. Use the line reference to find the window and read for context. Here, the line reference points to the fourth paragraph and to the quoted advertisement. The ad does not question any prior claims or counter any explanations, eliminating (A) and (C). Choice (B) can be eliminated because the advertisement does not *offer a motive* for a certain behavior. The ad supports what was said in paragraph 3, making (D) the correct choice.

20.   **C**   The question asks about information in both the passage and the graph. Use the passage and the graph to answer it. The recipient's self-concept is not included in the graph, nor is the amount of money the giver spent, eliminating (A) and (B). Choice (D) does not work because the thoughtfulness is not measured by the graph. Rather, the graph shows the implicit communication between the gift-giver and recipient, and the passage supports this information in the last paragraph. Therefore, (C) is correct.

21.   **D**   This question asks about the author's thoughts on the graph. For graph-related questions, look at the graph and see what is also supported by the passage. The graph shows the various steps of communication and evaluation in the gift-giving process, as mentioned in the last lines of the passage. *Conditional approval* is not mentioned, making (A) incorrect. While (B) mentions communication, it does not state that parties cannot *communicate effectively*. Similarly, while (C) might be true, it is not supported by the passage, and therefore is incorrect. Choice (D) is supported by the graph and the last lines of the passage and therefore is the correct choice.

22.   **C**   This question asks for a piece of information that *contradicts* the student's claim that *over half of solar radiation influences the ground temperature*. Use the line references given in each of the answer choices to check. Choice (A) refers to a situation in which the atmosphere is *letting through the light rays of the sun relatively easily*, which would confirm rather than contradict the student's claim and should therefore be eliminated. Choice (B) mentions *the temperature of the atmosphere* but does not address solar radiation or ground temperature, so this answer can be eliminated. Choice (C) should be kept because it specifically contradicts the student's claim with these lines: *Owing to the clouds and dust floating in the atmosphere, this heat is probably only about a third of that derived by using Langley's solar constant.* In other words, the *clouds and dust floating in the atmosphere* block the sun's full energy. Choice (D) refers only to the table, not to

the conceptual information regarding the sun's radiation, so it too can be eliminated. Choice (C) is the correct answer.

23. **B**   This question asks about the importance of the atmosphere as it influences the temperature of the earth. Use the given line reference to find the window. The relevant information is here: *the atmosphere may act like the glass of a green-house, letting through the light rays of the sun relatively easily, and absorbing a great part of the dark rays emitted from the ground, and it thereby may raise the mean temperature of the earth's surface.* A second purpose is cited here: *the atmosphere acts as a heat store placed between the relatively warm ground and the cold space, and thereby lessens in a high degree the annual, diurnal, and local variations of the temperature.* In other words, the atmosphere plays a crucial role in allowing certain heat in and trapping that heat so it influences ground temperature. Choice (A) is extreme in its use of the word *all*, particularly given that the text indicates that much of the heat is transferred back out of the atmosphere. Eliminate (A). Choice (B) should be kept because it captures the ideas from both quotations without overstating. Choice (C) can be eliminated because it neglects the role of solar radiation. Choice (D) can be eliminated because the words *free passage* are extreme—the passage indicates that the atmosphere absorbs *a great part of the dark rays emitted from the ground*. Choice (B) is the correct answer.

24. **D**   This question asks why the author uses the word *green-house* to describe the effects in this passage. Use the given line reference to find the window. The relevant information is here: *like the glass of a green-house, letting through the light rays of the sun relatively easily, and absorbing a great part of the dark rays emitted from the ground.* In other words, the atmosphere is like a greenhouse in that it lets in more heat than it lets out. Choice (A) may be partially true (though it is extreme in its use of the word *only*), but it does not match the prediction because it does not answer the question as to why the word *green-house* is used. Eliminate (A). Choice (B) can also be eliminated because it neglects the role of solar radiation entirely. Choice (C) is deceptive in that it applies the term *green-house* literally rather than figuratively. Eliminate (C). Choice (D) matches well with the prediction and captures both the idea of solar radiation and the atmosphere's role in absorbing it. Choice (D) is the correct answer.

25. **D**   This question asks which of the answers can be supported by the quoted statement and its surrounding context. Read the quotation carefully—the word *principally* indicates that most but not all of this energy comes from solar radiation. Choice (A) states a version of this, but there is no indication in the quotation or the passage that clouds block out solar radiation entirely, nor that ground heat does whatever heating solar energy cannot. Eliminate (A). Choice (B) correctly implies that heat can be generated by the sun and other sources, but this choice then goes on to state that the heat is held in the atmosphere and released as cool air, which is untrue. Eliminate (B). Choice (C) may seem plausible, but it overlooks the green-house effect described throughout this passage, which states that solar energy passes relatively unobstructed into the earth's atmosphere. Eliminate (C). Choice (D) takes proper account of the word *principally* by

stating that the heat in the atmosphere comes from the sun and other sources and that heat may be generated from non-solar sources. Choice (D) is thus the correct answer.

26. **B** This question asks why the author uses a few particular words in this context. The window is given by the line numbers in the passage. The cited lines read: *Now if we are able to calculate or estimate how much the mean temperature that layer is lower than the mean temperature of the ground, we may apply Table I for calculating the mean temperature of the ground, as soon as we know by direct measurements the quantity of solar heat absorbed by the ground.* The conditional language here implies that many factors must be considered as one calculates these values. Choice (A) overstates the confidence this language implies in the calculations, so this choice should be eliminated. Choice (B) is true, given the author's indication that the calculations will depend on mathematical formulas and constants in combination with some experimental observations. Choice (C) cannot be supported in the passage because it presumes the knowledge that the described calculations are setting out to find. Choice (D) identifies a harsh critique of earlier scientists where none is present in any part of the passage. Choice (D) can thus be eliminated. Choice (B) is the correct answer.

27. **A** This question asks why the author notes the observations of ground temperature. Using the chronology of previous questions, look for the lead words *observations* and *ground temperature* in the last paragraph. They appear in the last part of the last sentence: *assuming a corresponding decrease of 0.6°C per 100 meters, we find its temperature to be 46°C lower than that of the ground, and thus the mean temperature of the ground equal to 15°C, as it is according to observations.* Taken as a whole, the phrase *as it is according to observations* implies an agreement between the calculated data and the data observed by measurement. In this sense, the author cites the observations as a way to show the correctness of his calculations. Choice (A) captures the importance of the *observations*, so this answer should be kept. Choice (B) would undermine the importance of the mathematical calculations, when in fact the mention of *observations* is used to show the value of mathematical calculations. Eliminate (B). Choice (C) cites a contemporary theory of climate change, one that is not identified in the passage itself, so (C) should be eliminated. Choice (D) can be eliminated because it does not address the importance of the *observations* cited in the question. Choice (A) is the correct answer.

28. **B** This question asks for a combination of information from the table and passage. The relevant information in the passage is indicated by the data *1000 gram-calories per square centimeter for 24 hours*. This refers to the *Loss of Heat* columns in the chart, which are given in this unit. A *Loss of Heat* of 300 corresponds to a temperature of approximately −40°C. However, as the passage indicates, the figures given in the chart indicate the temperature at an elevation of *7600 meters*. Therefore, for the numbers given in the chart, *we find its temperature to be 46°C lower than that of the ground*. In other words, when the temperature on the chart is −40°C, the temperature on the ground must be approximately 6°C, or 46°C warmer, which corresponds with (B). Choices (A) and (D) pull the number directly from the chart but do not account for the information in the passage. Choice (C) confuses the negative signs. Choice (B) is the correct answer.

29.   **B**   This question asks whether the data from the chart support the author's claim regarding the atmosphere's *heat store*: *the atmosphere acts as a heat store placed between the relatively warm ground and the cold space*. This information is then expanded upon with the detail that *the higher the [atmospheric] layer, the lower is its temperature relatively to that of the ground*. Since this layer of atmosphere is located between the hot earth and cold space and the earth temperature gets colder with higher elevation, the loss of heat will be less as colder earth temperatures come nearer to space temperatures. Despite this technical explanation, this question can be answered with aggressive POE, particularly by looking at the given reasons rather than the "Yes" and "No" components of each answer. Choice (A) can be eliminated because it states that heat loss decreases at larger intervals at lower temperatures, which is not true. For each twenty-degree temperature interval, the heat-loss intervals shrink. In other words, whereas the heat loss at temperatures 100°C and 80°C goes down approximately 400, the heat loss at temperatures −100°C and −120°C goes down only 37. Choice (B) should be kept because it correctly establishes this relationship. Choices (C) and (D) can be eliminated because they cite incorrect relationships between temperature and loss of heat. Choice (B) is the correct answer.

30.   **C**   This question asks for a piece of information that will support the conclusion in the previous question. The correct answer to the previous question stated that *as the temperature decreases, the heat loss decreases as well but by smaller and smaller intervals*. This agrees with the information given in the chart. Choice (A) shows a widening gap between two heat-loss values, but it does not show the shrinking intervals mentioned in Q29. Eliminate (A). Choice (B) shows large intervals in heat-loss values, which make it difficult to form any conclusion. Eliminate (B). Choice (C) shows adjacent heat-loss values that decrease at smaller and smaller intervals, so keep this choice. Choice (D) shows decreasing values, but these are random and cannot be used to support a conclusion. Eliminate (D). The correct answer is (C).

31.   **D**   This question asks whether the temperature of the atmosphere varies relative to the distance from the ground. The chart does show variations in temperature, but it does not show variations in height. Therefore, the answer cannot be gleaned from the table alone and must be more explicitly stated within the passage. Choice (C) does hypothesize that temperatures may be different at the ground and at certain heights, but it does not offer conclusive proof and thus should be eliminated. Choice (D) offers conclusive proof of the relationship in the lines, *we find its temperature to be 46°C lower than that of the ground*. Choice (A) can be eliminated because it does not discuss different distances from the earth. Choice (B) can be eliminated for the same reason. Choice (D) is the correct answer.

32.   **B**   This question asks about the main purpose of the passage, or why this passage was composed. To answer it, ask why Douglass is speaking at this convention. He refers to his *early connection with the cause* as well as *having been called upon to do so by one whose voice in this Council we all gladly obey*. Now look for an answer choice that best fits these reasons. Choice (A) reflects a statement in paragraph 2 (*Men have very little business here as speakers, anyhow*), but does not fit this prediction. Choice (B) is consistent with the prediction. Choice (C) does not have

support in the passage, which explicitly states that *our cause has passed beyond the period of arguing*. Choice (D) reflects a statement in paragraph 2 (*I say of her, as I say of the colored people, "Give her fair play, and hands off"*), but does not fit this prediction. Choice (B) is the correct answer.

33.   **A**   This question asks for the central claim of the passage. To answer it, look for an answer choice that fits the most parts of the text, and eliminate answer choices that are true, but fit only part of the text. Choice (A) has support in paragraph 1 and several points of paragraph 2. Choice (B) contradicts the passage, which says that men *can neither speak for her, nor vote for her, nor act for her*. Choice (C) has support in the end of paragraph 3. Choice (D) slightly contradicts the passage, which indicates that the suffrage movement has become less obscure. It could be true that it should become less obscure still, but the passage doesn't say this, and so this cannot be the passage's central claim. Having eliminated (B) and (D), compare (A) and (C). Since (C) has less support, it is less likely to be the central claim; eliminate (C). Choice (A) is the correct answer.

34.   **D**   This question asks why Douglass uses the word *cause* throughout the passage. To answer it, find each time the word *cause* appears and take note of what Douglass is doing in each case. The first time, in paragraph 2, Douglass explains why he is speaking at this convention, and refers to his early connection to the cause. The second time, also in paragraph 2, he refers to the history of *this woman suffrage cause*. The third time, in paragraph 3, he refers to the convention of women and uses the phrase *our cause*. Putting these ideas together, it is clear that Douglass uses the word *cause* to refer to the women's suffrage movement. Now look for an answer choice that best fits this prediction, and eliminate answer choices that are either false, or true for only one instance of *cause*. (Remember, the question asks how Douglass uses the word *throughout* the passage.) Choice (A) could be true, since it refers to his early connection, but this better fits the first two uses of the word *cause*. Choice (B) goes beyond the scope of the passage: Douglass is not explaining why the movement deserves support; he assumes that it does, and that it is already clear to most people in attendance that it does. Eliminate (B). Choice (C) does not fit any of the uses of the word *cause*. Eliminate (C). Choice (D) could be true, since in each of the three uses of the word *cause* Douglass is referring to the suffrage movement. Now compare (A) and (D), and see that (A) kind of fits two out of three uses of the word, and that (D) completely fits three out of three uses of the word. Choice (D) is the correct answer.

35.   **B**   This question asks for something true about the passage. Notice that the first half of each answer choice addresses Douglass's speaking, and that the last half of each answer choice addresses his identification with the movement. Start by choosing the easier half and using POE. If that is the first half, begin by finding what the passage says about Douglass speaking. In paragraphs 1 and 2, Douglass indicates that he feels diffidence, that he is at a loss for words, and that men really have no business speaking here. Thus, (A) can be eliminated right away:

Douglass is not saying that he wants to give a great speech. Choice (C) also seems extreme, since he is in fact speaking. Eliminate (C). The first half of (B) and (D) are similar, and fit the text. Now look at the second half of (B) and (D). According to (B), he is hesitant to speak *even though* he is connected to the movement. That fits. According to (D), he is hesitant to speak *since* he is connected to the movement. This makes no sense. Eliminate (D). Choice (B) is the correct answer.

36.   **C**   This question is a excellent question for the Parallel POE strategy because it contains no line reference and no useful lead word. Douglass mentions *men* throughout the passage, so use the line references provided in the next question to help eliminate answer choices. Begin with (37A). Douglass says that he doesn't want to take *more than a very small space of... time and attention*. This could support (36B), so draw a line connecting those two answers. Choice (37B) talks about how he ended up speaking at the gathering, which doesn't support any of the answers from Q36. Eliminate (37B). Choice (37C) says that *men have very little business here as speakers* and that they should *take back benches and wrap themselves in silence*. This supports men *primarily listening*, so draw a line connecting this to (36C). Choice (37D) does not support any of the answers for Q36, so eliminate it. Without support from Q37, (36A) and (36D) can both be eliminated. Now compare the remaining pairs of (36B)/(37A) and (36C)/(37C). The question asks what Douglass indicates *about men*. While he does say that he doesn't want to take up much time, he's speaking specifically about himself and not men in general. The (36B)/(37A) pair can be eliminated. This leaves (36C)/(37C), which is consistent with the text and the question. The correct answers are (36C) and (37C).

37.   **C**   (See explanation above.)

38.   **A**   This question asks how the *demands of women* in line 29 are related to some kind of injuries. To answer it, find the phrase, and read a bit before and after to understand the context. Douglass says: *I believe no man, however gifted with thought and speech, can voice the wrongs and present the demands of women with the skill and effect, with the power and authority of woman herself.* He goes on to say that woman *knows and feels her wrongs as man cannot...* and *she is her own best representative.* Therefore, the demands of women are something that women can better speak about than men can. Look for an answer choice that fits this prediction. Choice (A) fits this prediction; keep it. Choice (B) can be eliminated because Douglass does not argue that the injuries are for men to speak about. Choice (C) can be eliminated because there is no evidence anywhere that the *world should support* injuries to women. Choice (D) may be true, but it doesn't fit the prediction. Choice (A) is the correct answer.

39.   **B**   This question asks for the best evidence to answer question 38. Look back at the lines used to predict the answer to the previous question. Lines 27–31 and 31–36 were used. Choice (B) is the correct answer.

40.   **D**   This question asks for the meaning of the word *cradle*, which the passage uses figuratively. Find the word in the passage, and read it in context: *It was when this woman suffrage cause*

was in its cradle, when it was not big enough to go alone, when it had to be taken in the arms of its mother from Seneca Falls, N.Y., to Rochester, N.Y., for baptism. Douglass is referring to the history of the movement, so the word *cradle* here means something like its early years. Choices (A), (B), and (C) have nothing to do with this prediction; eliminate them. Choice (D) fits this prediction exactly. Choice (D) is the correct answer.

41.   **A**   This question asks what the surprise referred to in lines 58–74 serves to emphasize. To do this, first find the word *surprise*, read it in context, and then determine what the author is trying to emphasize. Read the window: *There may be some…period of arguing.* Douglass says that some people attending were expecting arguments about women's suffrage, but were surprised to find no arguments. Look for an answer choice that fits this prediction. Choice (A) refers to *different sorts of speeches,* which could refer to *arguments* versus *no arguments.* Keep (A). Choice (B) may be attractive because of the reference to *more arguments than assertions,* but the text does not explicitly say what the gender of *some well-meaning people* is. Eliminate (B). Choice (C) can be eliminated. Although the phrase *may not have expected* might look good on its own, the answer as a whole clearly does not match the prediction. Choice (D) can be eliminated, because the arguments weren't *unexpected*. It was the lack of arguments that was surprising. Choice (A) is the correct answer.

42.   **D**   This question asks why the author mentions the number of gallons in discussing fracking. Use the given line reference to check: *As many as 25 fracture stages (per horizontal leg) may be involved in preparing a single site for production, each requiring injection of more than 400,000 gallons of water—a possible total of more than 10 million gallons before the well is fully operational.* Phrases like *as many as* and *more than* are there to draw attention to the size and scale of these numbers. Choice (A) can be eliminated because of the extreme language of the word *inevitable* and because it does not address the size of the fracking operation. Choice (B) can be eliminated because this passage discusses a single method, fracking, for extracting natural gas from shale. Choice (C) can be eliminated because while water might be described as a *basic element,* there is no indication that *only a few* of these basic elements are at play in fracking. Choice (D) should be kept because it reflects the passage's language of size and scale. Choice (D) is the correct answer.

43.   **C**   This question asks for some positive aspect of fracking in Passage 1. Notice that the following question is a best evidence question, so this question and Q44 can be answered in tandem. Look at the answers for Q44 first. The lines in (44A) mention that the natural gas from fracking can *accommodate the country's domestic demand for natural gas at current levels of consumption for more than a hundred years.* These lines match with (43C), which paraphrases that information. Connect these two answers. Next, consider the lines for (44B). These lines describe the way that high-pressure water is used to perforate the shale layer. The shale layer is mentioned in (43B), so those answers can be connected, though the connection is tentative. Next, consider the lines for (44C). These lines complete the description of how fracking extracts natural gas

from the shale layer, but the lines have no match in Q43, so (44C) can be eliminated. Next, consider the lines for (44D). These lines set up the discussion of water contamination and pollution in the next paragraph, but the lines have no match in Q43, so (44D) can be eliminated. Without any support from Q44, (43A) and (43D) can be eliminated. Consider the remaining pairs of answer choices in the context of the passage. The positive aspect of fracking is that it produces a lot of natural gas. Choices (43B) and (44B) can be eliminated because they do not contain this positive aspect. Choices (43C) and (44A) are the correct answers.

44. **A** (See explanation above.)

45. **A** This question asks why the author discusses the *aquifer* in the given lines. Use the line reference to find the window in which the *aquifer* is discussed. In the final paragraph of Passage 1, the aquifer is mentioned twice: *Drillers developing a well must take exceptional care to minimize contact between the wellbore and the surrounding aquifer—often the source of nearby residents' drinking water* and *It is essential that monitoring be in place to ensure the continuing integrity of the seal isolating the well from the aquifer even after the well has been fully exploited and abandoned.* In both sentences, the *aquifer* is mentioned as something that must be isolated and protected from the outflowing water used to frack. Choice (A) should be kept because it points to the *significant risk* that the aquifer could be contaminated. Choice (B) may address the concerns of those who worry about fracking, but it does not *dispute* those concerns, so (B) can be eliminated. Choice (C) can also be eliminated because the word *aquifer* does not appear before the final paragraph of Passage 1. Choice (D) can be eliminated because there is no indication that water contamination is a *new finding*. Choice (A) is the correct answer.

46. **B** This question asks for the meaning of the word *integrity* in this context. Remember the Vocab-in-Context strategy. Cross out the word, and use the surrounding context to fill in another word that makes sense based on the passage. Earlier sentences refer to the need to *minimize contact between the wellbore and the surrounding aquifer* and to *failures to isolate the drilling liquids.* The word in the blank should therefore mean something like "solidness," or any of a number of words that mean the opposite of "leakiness." Choice (A) does provide one definition of the word *integrity*, but that definition does not agree with the prediction based on the context above, so (A) can be eliminated. Choice (B) matches the prediction, so it should be kept. Choice (C) may be deceptive because this paragraph discusses water at such length, but the word *moisture* does not match the prediction and should be eliminated. Choice (D) provides another possible definition of the word *integrity*, but that definition does not match the context, so (D) can be eliminated. Choice (B) is the correct answer.

47. **D** This question asks for some aspect of Passage 2's main idea—something negative, as evidenced by the word *but* in the question. Because this question deals with Passage 2 as a whole, it is best to save it for later, after the more detail-oriented questions. The evidence appears throughout the passage—the first paragraph describes fracking's usefulness, but the remaining two paragraphs discuss its risks. The last paragraph is vicious in its criticism of *Weak safeguards*

and inadequate oversight. In short, the author of Passage 2 sees the potential value of fracking, but he does not consider it to be regulated in a way that protects local populations. Choice (A) does not address safety, only cost, so this answer can be eliminated. Choice (B) might be true, but it is not addressed in the passage, so it can be eliminated. Choice (C) is deceptive because while the author of Passage 2 does believe that industry executives flout the rules, there is no indication that these executives believe *they can mine resources from any place they choose.* This is extreme language that is not supported by the passage. Eliminate (C). Choice (D) effectively paraphrases the evidence presented in the passage, so it is the correct answer.

48.   **C**   This question asks for the meaning of the word *roughshod* in this context. Remember the Vocab-in-Context strategy. Cross out the word, and use the surrounding context to fill in another word that makes sense based on the passage. These lines continue the author's critique of industry leaders and overseers, who have created insufficient regulations and have been lax in enforcing the regulations that do exist. Therefore, the word in the blank should mean something like "without restriction" or "without care." Choice (A) could certainly describe the industries that have used fracking to generate a good deal of natural gas, but this does not match the prediction, so (A) can be eliminated. Choice (B) could also describe the industries that have quickly transformed certain rural landscapes, but this does not match with the prediction, so (B) can be eliminated. Choice (C) matches nicely with "without restriction" and "without care," so it should be kept. Choice (D) is deceptive because the sentence describes industrial processes, but the word in the blank should mean "without restriction," and (D) does not match. Choice (C) is the correct answer.

49.   **B**   This questions asks about the relationship between the two passages. This question should be done last because it asks about the main ideas of both passages. Passage 1 gives an overview of the process of fracking and hints at some of its dangers. Passage 2 is primarily concerned with these dangers and is less admiring of fracking's ability to extract natural resources. Choice (A) can be eliminated because Passage 1's author is not blind to the dangers of fracking and his attitude could not be described as *optimistic confidence.* Choice (B) should be kept because it offers a reasonable paraphrase of the relationship between the two passages. Choice (C) can be eliminated because there is no indication that the author of Passage 1 would disapprove of any particular regulations. Choice (D) can also be eliminated because Passage 2 is less concerned with the process of fracking than is Passage 1. Choice (B) is the correct answer.

50.   **C**   This question asks how the author of Passage 2 might respond to the referenced lines in Passage 1. The lines in Passage 1 discuss both the care that drillers must take to ensure that pollution does not occur and the risks associated with such pollution. Notice that the following question is a best evidence question, so this question and Q51 can be answered in tandem. Look at the answers in Q51 first. The lines in (51A) discuss the expansion of the mining industry. There is no match for this answer choice in Q50, so (51A) can be eliminated. Next, consider the lines for (51B), which continue the discussion of the proliferation of the practice of fracking. These lines match with (50A), which cites the mining industry's success and growth.

Connect these two answers. The lines for (51C) refer in a general way to increased industrial production, but they do not address the risks of drilling in particular. Choice (51C) can be eliminated because it does not match with any of the answers in Q50. Next, consider the lines for (51D). These lines match almost exactly with (50C), so these two answers should be connected. Without any support from Q51, (50B) and (50D) can be eliminated. Consider the remaining pairs of answer choices in the context of the passage. Passage 2's tone is overwhelmingly critical, so the author of Passage 2 is not likely to cite the successes of the mining industry in response to a claim about drillers' risks. Choices (50A) and (51B) can be eliminated because they are not sufficiently critical. Choices (50C) and (51D) are the correct answers.

51.   **D**   (See explanation above.)

52.   **C**   This question asks for something that is *implicit* (or implied) in Passage 2 and *explicit* (or stated outright) in Passage 1. Consider each answer separately and use POE. Choice (A) can be eliminated because Passage 2 explicitly states that fracking causes air and water pollution, and Passage 1 is concerned only with water pollution. Choice (B) can be eliminated because Passage 2 mentions the *millions of gallons of water used in fracking operations* but doesn't give any indication that it could also be *billions*. Passage 2 also focuses on the effects of fracking rather than the process. Choice (C) should be kept because Passage 2 addresses the effects of fracking on drinking water but does not specifically mention animals, whereas Passage 1 states explicitly, *Serious problems have arisen ... including cases where well water used for drinking became so contaminated that human and animal health was threatened.* Choice (D) can be eliminated because neither passage addresses the costs in setting up wells for drilling. Choice (C) is the correct answer.

Section 2: Writing and Language

1.   **A**   The words *variety* and *difference* mean roughly the same thing in this context, so having versions of both words in the same answer would be redundant. The best choice is therefore (A), which contains only the word *variety*.

2.   **B**   All choices express essentially the same idea, so choose the one that expresses that idea in a way that is consistent with the tone of the passage. Choices (A) and (D) are too informal and can be eliminated. Choice (C) is too vague in its mention of *something elusive*. This leaves (B), which expresses a definitive idea and does so in a way that is in keeping with the tone of the passage.

3.   **C**   The subject of the underlined verb is *movements*, which is plural and therefore requires a plural verb, thus eliminating (A) and (B). Choice (D) would not make sense in the context, because it changes the meaning, saying that the movements *used* to do something. Instead, they are being used to do something. Only (C) remains, which matches the rest of the paragraph with its tense and the subject of the sentence with the plural verb *are*.

4. **B** As the paragraph now stands, its last sentence contains an ambiguous pronoun. It is unclear whether the *it* at the beginning of the last sentence refers to *difference*, *therapeutic horseback riding*, *hippotherapy*, *way*, or *ailment*. The addition of the new sentence would clarify that pronoun, so the sentence should be inserted, thus eliminating (C) and (D). In addition, the sentence helps to further clarify the differences between *therapeutic horseback riding* and *hippotherapy*, making (B) the correct answer.

5. **B** The first and second sentences of this paragraph describe the different applications of hippotherapy within different disciplines, stating that many fields *use the basic tenets of hippotherapy, but they each provide a unique spin on the practice.* Choice (A) would not contribute a useful detail in this regard, and (C) and (D) do not actually offer any specific examples. Choice (B) is therefore the best of the available answer choices in that it describes the work of occupational therapists by providing a specific example.

6. **D** The underlined verb should be consistent with the other verb in this part of the sentence, *achieve*. This eliminates all choices except for (D), which contains the verb *recommend*, which is in the simple present and matches *achieve*.

7. **B** The clues in this sentence are the references to *therapists* who are concerned with *physical aspects*. The only other sentence that discusses physical therapists is sentence 2. Sentence 4 should therefore go after sentence 1 because it refers *back* to the physical therapists mentioned earlier in the paragraph. Therefore, the best answer is (B).

8. **B** Although the underlined portion makes it seem that *new* and *certified* are both adjectives modifying a single noun, in fact, *new* is the end of the previous idea and *certified* is the beginning of the next one. The first idea, *Because the discipline is relatively new*, is incomplete and introduces the second idea, so there should be a comma after the word *new*, eliminating (D). There is no reason to insert a pause in the phrase *certified hippotherapists*, so the best available answer is (B).

9. **B** The words *Just as* at the beginning of the sentence require the words *so too* to complete the idiom, in the same way that *neither* requires *nor* or *not only* requires *but also*. Given the necessity of the words *so* and *too*, (A), (C), and (D) can all be eliminated, leaving only (B).

10. **D** In this sentence, choose a word that establishes the relationship between the *skeptics* and the *doctors and researchers*. Choices (B) and (C) can be eliminated because the relationship they create is illogical. Choice (A) can also be eliminated because it implies a division between doctors and researchers, where none is stated in the passage. Only (D) remains, suggesting that the *skeptics* are those *among* the medical community at large.

11. **B** Read the question carefully. It asks for a choice that *restates the main argument of the passage*. The passage as a whole is about hippotherapy, so this should be in the answer, eliminating (C). Choice (D) undermines the passage's claim that hippotherapy is gaining in popularity. Choice (A) mentions hippotherapy, but it can be eliminated because it is too informal and cites only

a minor detail rather than the passage's central argument. Only (B) remains, as it fulfills the goal outlined in the question.

12. **B** The word *elicit* is a verb meaning "to evoke or draw out." The word *illicit* is an adjective meaning "illegal." In this case, nothing illegal is being described, and the underlined part of speech is a verb, so (C) and (D) can be eliminated. Then, the subject of the underlined verb is *way*, which is singular, and thus requires the singular verb *elicits*, as in (B).

13. **D** Choice (A) creates a comma splice because it separates two complete ideas—*It was Marco Polo who crossed the desert on his way to China* and *he described the sound he heard as "a variety of musical instruments"*—with only a comma. Choices (B) and (C) create the same mistake. Only (D) fixes the mistake by making the first part of the sentence incomplete.

14. **A** The word *cello* is the last word in the phrase *that odd confluence of pipe organ and cello*. As the comma before the word *that* indicates, this phrase is meant to be set off as unnecessary information. Therefore, in order to remain consistent with the non-underlined part of the sentence, the entire phrase should be set off with commas, as in (A).

15. **A** Choice (B) can be eliminated because it uses a semicolon to set off a complete idea from an incomplete idea, when a semicolon should be used to separate only complete ideas. Choice (D) can be eliminated because it contains two complete ideas but insufficient punctuation—only a comma, not a semicolon or a period. Choices (A) and (C) state the same idea, but (A) does so more concisely, so (A) is the better of the two answers.

16. **C** This paragraph shifts the focus from the desert to the ocean, so there must be a phrase or sentence at the beginning to signal that shift, thus eliminating (D). Choices (A) and (B) provide this transition, but they do so in wordy, awkward ways. Choice (C) is relatively simple, but it does not contain any less information that (A) and (B), and it fulfills the purpose outlined in the question.

17. **C** The passage as a whole is all about sound—the sound of the seemingly silent desert sands or the seemingly silent ocean. The passage is mainly concerned with showing that these, especially the ocean, are actually noisy places. The proposed sentence goes against that general argument, so the sentence should not be added to the passage at all, thus making (C) the most appropriate answer.

18. **A** The underlined pronoun refers back to the word *ocean*, which is singular. The plural pronouns given in (C) and (D) can therefore be eliminated. Then, the sentence is referring to the *ocean's unwillingness*, so the possessive form *its* should be used, not the contraction *it's*. The best answer is thus (A).

19. **B** All four answers express essentially the same idea, but (A), (C), and (D) do so in oddly informal language. Only (B) is in keeping with the general tone of the passage and is therefore the best answer.

20. **D** The line graph and the bar graph on the chart show almost no consistency with one another, so the choices that describe a consistent relationship—(A), (B), and (C)—can be eliminated. Only (D) accurately describes the chart.

21. **A** Because the trends in this chart are so erratic, it is crucial to work with only single data points. At the point in March described earlier in the sentence, when there were 40 whale sightings, the average was approximately 14. Choice (A) captures this relationship. Choice (B) is not supported in the chart because summer months are not shown. Choice (C) is false by any measure. Choice (D) suggests that over 20 whales migrate every day in some other months (whatever those coldest winter months are), a claim which is not substantiated by information in the chart.

22. **A** Read the question carefully. It asks for *a conclusion that points toward the role that sound might play in future research into different ecosystems*. In fact, the paragraph already contains this information, so there is no reason to add a new sentence. In order words, that goal can be fulfilled most directly and concisely with NO CHANGE to the passage.

23. **D** Punctuation should only be used when it has a clear and definite purpose. In this case, there is no need for any punctuation, so the best available option is to eliminate punctuation entirely, as (D) does.

24. **C** When given the option to DELETE the underlined portion, give it serious consideration. It is often correct. In this case, however, the underlined portion must be kept—without it, there is only a comma separating two complete ideas. This eliminates (D). This sentence and the next one create a sequence—from 1929 to 1932. Therefore, the best of the available answers will be a word that indicates time, as only (C), *When*, does.

25. **A** This and all subsequent paragraphs are about Roosevelt and his legislative action when he took office in 1933. Of the four answers, the only one that mentions Roosevelt is (A), and this answer effectively sets up the information that is to follow.

26. **C** This sentence describes Roosevelt's action to send *government workers to inspect each bank*. The reports from these inspectors would allow government officials to determine *which banks would be safe and sustainable to reopen*. There is a cause-and-effect relationship established between these ideas, which (A) and (B) disrupt. Choice (D) provides the appropriate relationship, but this word cannot be used idiomatically with the non-underlined word, *determining*, that follows. Only (C) remains—it establishes the correct relationship and can be used in the context.

27. **B** Read the question carefully. It asks for the choice that *provides the most specific information on the areas that Roosevelt hoped to stimulate*. Choices (A), (C), and (D) may each be true, but none fulfills the question's demand for *specific information*. Only (B) does so in listing two specific sectors of the economy.

28. **C**   This sentence refers to an action that would control *demand*. The best combination of words that refers to this action is *level off*, as in (C). Choice (A), *level with*, means "to be honest with." Choices (B) and (D) do not create idiomatically logical phrases.

29. **C**   Read the question carefully. It asks for a detail that *emphasizes the importance of the TVA in Roosevelt's larger economic project*, a project, as the passage indicates, of stimulating the economy and reducing unemployment. Choices (A) and (D) do not fulfill any part of this purpose, and (B) gives a detail about the TVA but does not connect it to Roosevelt's larger project. Therefore, (C) most effectively fulfills the goal outlined in the question.

30. **B**   All four answers express essentially the same idea, so the most effective answer will be the most concise. In this case, that answer is (B), which expresses in a single word what the other answers express in more.

31. **A**   The underlined pronoun refers back to *Roosevelt's "New Deal,"* which is singular, thus eliminating (C), which is plural, and (D), which is not a pronoun. The underlined pronoun should be the contraction *it is*, as in (A). The possessive pronoun given in (B) would create a sentence fragment, in addition to the fact that the *it* is not in possession of anything.

32. **A**   This sentence refers to the *day-to-day lives* belonging to *people*. Therefore, the best answer is (A), which gives the possessive form *people's*. Choice (C) is not possessive. With (B) and (D), remember that everything that comes before the apostrophe must be a word—*peoples* (when used in this way) is not a word.

33. **C**   This paragraph describes a debate about the legacy of Roosevelt's legislative activity, citing arguments from those on either side of the issue. Only (C) remains neutral in this debate with the words *In either case*.

34. **D**   All four choices express a similar idea, that of an actress who excels in some way. Choice (A) is informal and potentially sarcastic, so it can be eliminated. Choices (B) and (C) are unnecessarily elevated, as they are written in a tone that is not in keeping with that of the rest of the passage. Choice (D) is the most direct and keeps with the tone of the passage, in that it is sufficiently formal but not overblown in its use of language.

35. **B**   This sentence states that *the Japanese film industry had divided loyalties at the time,* and it cites a *debt to American cinema* and *tensions with the United States and others,* which led to war. There is no contrast established in the sentence, eliminating (A) and (C). Nor was it the Japanese film industry's loyalties that *enabled* the tensions between nations that led to war, eliminating (D). Only (B) works effectively in this contrast by establishing the correct relationship between the ideas in the sentence.

36. **D**   This paragraph mentions the Japanese film industry's divided loyalties and tensions between nations, and the underlined portion explains how these tensions played out in the particular

film. The underlined portion should be kept because this information is not given anywhere else in the passage, thus eliminating (A) and (B). The information in the underlined portion refers to something that *would become Axis propaganda* and is more general than specific, eliminating (C). Choice (D) is the correct answer in that it correctly states that the underlined portion should be kept because it clarifies the idea about divided loyalties that comes before it and connects to the sentence that follows it.

37. **D** This part of the sentence describes the film *Late Spring* in the present tense, as evidenced by the verbs *plays* and *is*. The underlined verb should therefore be in the present tense as well, eliminating (A), (B), and (C), leaving only (D) as the correct answer.

38. **A** This paragraph as a whole celebrates Hara's performance in *Late Spring*. The last sentence of the paragraph contributes to that celebration, so it should be introduced with a word that indicates a continuation, as only (A) does. Choice (B) can be eliminated because this sentence contains a detail, not a summation. Choice (C) can be eliminated because there is nothing in this sentence that contrasts with previous information. Choice (D) can be eliminated because it suggests a concurrent event, when in fact this sentence gives an additional detail about an event already being described.

39. **B** All four answers express essentially the same idea, so the most effective answer will be the most concise. In this case, that answer is (B), which expresses in a two words what the other answers express in more.

40. **C** This sentence refers to *very few sets*, suggesting that the terms in this list must each represent one of those sets. Choice (A) suggests that one of those sets is an *office kitchen*, which does not make sense. Choices (B) and (D) create similar errors in suggesting *living* and *kitchen living*, respectively, as possible sets. Only (C) creates a logical list by separating as possible sets an *office*, a *kitchen*, and a *living room*.

41. **D** The word *council* is used only as a noun and typically refers to a group of people brought together to deliberate a significant issue. The word *counsel* can be used as either a noun or a verb, and the word refers to either giving advice (in the verb form) or the advice itself (in the noun form). In this sentence, the word refers to the advice of *her friends and family*, so *counsel* must be used, eliminating (A) and (B). Then, the character is receiving the advice *of* this group, making (D) the better of the remaining answers.

42. **D** The first part of the sentence characterizes the plot and conflicts as *simple*, while the second part suggests that the plots are also very *profound*. As a result, the conjunction that links the ideas must indicate a contrast, eliminating (A), (B), and (C) and leaving only (D).

43. **A** The underlined pronoun refers back to the noun *viewers*, meaning that the pronoun must be plural. Of the available choices, only (A), *their*, provides such a pronoun. Though *your* can be plural, the viewers would not be referred to as "you."

44. **B** Note the first word of the proposed sentence: *Others*. This word must link with some first group. That group is indicated in sentence 3 by the word *Some*. Therefore, the most effective placement of the proposed sentence would be between sentences 3 and 4, or after sentence 3, as (B) states.

Section 3: Math (No Calculator)

1. **B** Come up with the expression in bite-sized pieces. Notice that all of the choices use the variable y, which represents the number of hours for (A) and (B) but the number of essays for (C) and (D). The number of essays is given but the number of hours is not. Therefore, the variable has to represent the unknown value, the number of hours. Eliminate (C) and (D). The editor is paid $25 per hour. The total amount that the editor is paid for his or her time can be found by multiplying 25 by the number of hours. The remaining choices use y to represent the number of hours, so the product is $25y$. Eliminate the remaining choice that doesn't include $25y$, which is (A). Only one choice remains. To see why (B) is correct, note that the $50 bonus must be added to the editor's earnings for time spent. Also, the bonus is for *all three* essays rather than *each* essay, so it should only be added once. The answer is (B).

2. **B** Use bite-sized pieces and eliminate answer choices after each step. Start by combining $-mn^2 + 2mn^2$ to get mn^2, and use this to eliminate (C) and (D). Now combine the $2n^2$ terms, which cancel and should not appear in the correct answer. Use this to eliminate (A). The answer is (B).

3. **B** The question is made more complicated by fractions, so get rid of the fractions. Multiply both sides of the first equation by 12 to get $x - y = 156$. Multiply both sides of the second equation by 6 to get $2x - y = 120$. Subtract the first equation from the second equation.

$$
\begin{aligned}
2x - y &= 120 \\
-\underline{(x - y \;=\; 156)} & \\
x &= -36
\end{aligned}
$$

Eliminate any choice that doesn't include $x = -36$. Eliminate (A), (C), and (D). Only one choice remains. To see why $y = -192$, plug $x = -36$ into the non-fraction version of the first equation to get $-36 - y = 156$, and solve for y. The answer is (B).

4. **D** The problem discusses how many shoes Kelly must sell in a month. Eliminate (C) because 300 days does not fit the problem. Since x is the number of days she works each month, plug in $x = 0$ to see how many shoes she starts with at the beginning of the month. The value for S would be 300 at day 0. Therefore, (D) is the answer.

5. **C** Since there are actual numbers in the answer choices, plug in the answers, starting with one of the middle two choices. Start with (B), which is 35. The question asks for the number of all-day passes sold, so assume that there were 35 all-day passes sold. Since there were a total of 70

passes sold, there must have been a total of 70 – 35 = 35 half-day passes sold. The park sells all-day passes for $80 and half-day passes for $40. Since there were 35 of each sold, the park took in a total of $80 × 35 = $2,800 for all-day passes and $40 × 35 = $1,400 for half-day passes. Therefore, the park took in a total of $2,800 + $1,400 = $4,200. However, the question states that the park took in $4,600, so eliminate (B). Since the total should be greater, the park needs to sell more of the $80 tickets. Therefore, the number of all-day passes sold has to increase. Eliminate (A) as well. Only (C) and (D) remain. Since 60 is easier to work with than 45, try (D). If 60 all-day passes are sold, then 70 – 60 = 10 half-day passes are sold. The park takes in $60 × 80 = $4,800 from all-day passes. Since this is already too high, eliminate (D). Only one choice remains. The answer is (C).

6. **D** To find the solutions to a quadratic equation, either factor or use the quadratic formula. When the coefficient on the x^2 term is not 1, factoring is more difficult than usual but not impossible. Since 5 is prime, one factor will have $5x$ and the other will have x, so write $(5x \quad)(x \quad) = 0$. Now find two factors of 6 that fit the equation. Since the sign on 6 is negative, one factor is negative and one is positive. To fit the equation, one of the factors must be multiplied by 5 and added to the other to get 7. The only pairs of factors of 6 are 1 and 6 and 2 and 3. Since $5 \times 2 + (-3) = 7$, the equation can be factored as $(5x - 3)(x + 2) = 0$. Set each factor to 0 to get $5x - 3 = 0$ and $x + 2 = 0$. Solve each factor to get $x = \frac{3}{5}$ and $x = -2$. Another way to find the values for x of a quadratic in the form $ax^2 + bx + c$ is to use the quadratic formula, $x = \frac{-b \pm \sqrt{b^2 - 4ac}}{2a}$. In this case, $a = 5$, $b = 7$, and $c = -6$. Either way of solving yields the solutions $\frac{3}{5}$ and -2. Since the question specifies that $a < b$, $a = -2$ and $b = \frac{3}{5}$. The question asks for $b - a$, which is $\frac{3}{5} - (-2) = \frac{3}{5} + 2 = \frac{3}{5} + \frac{10}{5} = \frac{13}{5}$. The answer is (D).

7. **A** Look at the denominators of the fractions to find easy numbers to plug in. Try $t = 11$. Now look at the numerator to see that $t + u = 12$, so u would then equal 1. Plug these values into the answers to see which is true. Only (A) works, so it must be the answer.

8. **C** Opposite sides of a parallelogram are parallel, and parallel lines have the same slope. Use the slope formula: $\frac{y_1 - y_2}{x_1 - x_2}$. Segment AB has a slope of $\frac{18 - 0}{0 - (-6)} = \frac{18}{6} = 3$. Segment DC is

parallel to AB and must have the same slope, so $3 = \dfrac{0-(-12)}{j-0}$. Then $3 = \dfrac{12}{j}$, so $3j = 12$, and

$j = 4$. The answer is (C).

9.　**B**　Since the problem involves algebra and asks for the least possible value of y, plug in the answers

starting with the smallest number. Try (D). If $y = 4$, then $x = \dfrac{4(4-3)}{2} = \dfrac{4(1)}{2} = \dfrac{4}{2} = 2$, so a

polygon with 4 sides only has 2 diagonals. This is not at least 7, so eliminate (D) and try (C). If

$y = 5$, then $x = \dfrac{5(5-3)}{2} = \dfrac{5(2)}{2} = \dfrac{10}{2} = 5$. This is not at least 7, so eliminate (C) and try (B). If

$y = 6$, then $x = \dfrac{6(6-3)}{2} = \dfrac{6(3)}{2} = \dfrac{18}{2} = 9$. This is greater than 7, so choose (B).

10.　**A**　The question asks for the value of the car y years from now. Determine the value of the car each

year. The car is driven 10,000 miles each year. Set up a proportion to determine the decrease

in the value each year. Since the car's value decreases $500 for every 1,000 miles driven, set

up a proportion: $\dfrac{\$500}{1{,}000 \text{ miles}} = \dfrac{x}{10{,}000 \text{ miles}}$. Cross-multiply to get $1{,}000x = 5{,}000{,}000$.

Divide both sides by 1,000 to get $x = 5{,}000$. Therefore, the car's value decreases by $5,000

each year. Plug in a value for y, such as $y = 2$, and calculate the value of the car. After 2 years,

the car's value decreases by $10,000, so the value then would be $13,000. Go through each

answer, plug in $y = 2$, and eliminate each choice that is not equal to $13,000. Choice (A) is

$23,000 − $5,000(2) = $23,000 − $10,000 = $13,000. Keep (A). Choice (B) is $23,000 −

$500(2) = $23,000 − $1,000 = $22,000. Eliminate (B). Choice (C) is $23,000 − $0.02(2) =

$23,000 − $0.04 = $22,999.96. Eliminate (C). Choice (D) is $23,000 − $0.0002(2) = $23,000

− $0.0004 = $22,999.9996. Eliminate (D). The answer is (A).

11.　**D**　The problem states that the system of equations has no solution, which means that the lines

are parallel and the slopes are equal. The slope of a line in standard form $Ax + By = C$ is given

by $-\dfrac{A}{B}$, so the slope of the first line is $-\dfrac{7}{-c} = \dfrac{7}{c}$. The slope of the second line is $-\dfrac{5}{2}$. Set the slopes equal to each other to solve for c: $\dfrac{7}{c} = -\dfrac{5}{2}$. Now cross-multiply to get $-5c = 14$, and divide both sides by -5 to find that $c = -\dfrac{14}{5}$. Alternatively, convert each line into the form $y = mx + b$ to find the slopes and set them equal. In either case, the answer is (D).

12. **B** Start by multiplying both the numerator and denominator of the given expression by the complex conjugate of the denominator: $\dfrac{4 - 7i}{6 + 3i} \times \dfrac{6 - 3i}{6 - 3i}$. Use FOIL to get $\dfrac{24 - 12i - 42i + 21i^2}{36 - 18i + 18i - 9i^2}$. Combine like terms to get $\dfrac{24 - 54i + 21i^2}{36 - 9i^2}$. Plug in $i^2 = -1$, since the problem says that $i = \sqrt{-1}$. This gives $\dfrac{24 - 54i + 21(-1)}{36 - 9(-1)} = \dfrac{24 - 54i - 21}{36 + 9} = \dfrac{3 - 54i}{45}$. To make this look like the answer choices, turn the expression into two fractions and reduce: $\dfrac{3}{45} - \dfrac{54i}{45} = \dfrac{1}{15} - \dfrac{6i}{5}$, which is (B).

13. **C** If a polynomial is divisible by x, each term in the simplified form of the polynomial must have x as a factor. Write $g(x)$ in simplified form. If $g(x) = 2(x^2 + 14x + 7) - 7(x + c)$, distribute to get $g(x) = 2x^2 + 28x + 14 - 7x - 7c$. Combine like terms to get $g(x) = 2x^2 + 21x + 14 - 7c$. The two terms without x as a factor are 14 and $-7c$. In order for the polynomial to be divisible by x, $14 - 7c$ must equal 0, so that only the terms with x as a factor remain. If $14 - 7c = 0$, add $7c$ to both sides to get $14 = 7c$. Divide both sides by 7 to get $c = 2$. The answer is (C).

14. **C** Plugging in would normally be a good idea for a question like this, but this is the no-calculator section. Exponent questions are always easier to handle when the bases are the same, so rewrite 27 as 3^3. Use the rules of exponents to work out the expression as $\dfrac{27^r}{3^s} = \dfrac{(3^3)^r}{3^s} = \dfrac{3^{3r}}{3^s}$. Now that the terms have the same base, remember the MADSPM rule that division means subtraction of the exponents, so $\dfrac{3^{3r}}{3^s} = 3^{3r - s}$. The problem states that $3r - s = 10$, so $3^{3r - s} = 3^{10}$ and (C) is the answer.

15. **A** This question contains variables in the question and in the answer choices, so plug in. Use $n = 10$ so the calculations are straightforward. Then, $\dfrac{4n + 9}{n - 5} = \dfrac{4(10) + 9}{10 - 5} = \dfrac{40 + 9}{5} = \dfrac{49}{5}$. This is the target value, so plug 10 in for n in the choices to find the one that matches the

target. Start with (A): $4 + \dfrac{29}{n-5} = 4 + \dfrac{29}{10-5} = 4 + \dfrac{29}{5} = \dfrac{20}{5} + \dfrac{29}{5} = \dfrac{49}{5}$. This matches the

target, so keep (A) but remember to check all four choices when plugging in. Move to (B):

$4 + \dfrac{9}{n-5} = 4 + \dfrac{9}{10-5} = 4 + \dfrac{9}{5} = \dfrac{20}{5} + \dfrac{9}{5} = \dfrac{29}{5}$. This doesn't match the target, so eliminate

(B). Try (C): $4 - \dfrac{9}{5} = \dfrac{20}{5} - \dfrac{9}{5} = \dfrac{11}{5}$. This doesn't match the target, so eliminate (C). Try (D):

$-\dfrac{4+9}{5} = -\dfrac{13}{5}$, which will be a negative number and won't match the target, so eliminate (D).

Choice (A) is the answer.

16. **800**   To solve for x, isolate the variable. First, add 3 to both sides to get $40 = \dfrac{x}{20}$. Then, multiply both sides by 20 to get $x = 40 \times 20 = 800$. The answer is 800.

17. $\dfrac{8}{10}, \dfrac{4}{5}$, or **0.8**

In any triangle with angles of 90°, x°, and y°, $\cos x = \sin y$. Therefore, if $\cos p = 0.8$, then

$\sin q = 0.8$ as well. Alternatively, remember from SOHCAHTOA that the cosine of an angle

is the ratio of the adjacent side to the hypotenuse. The value 0.8 can also be written as $\dfrac{8}{10}$.

Plug in 8 as the base of the triangle (adjacent to p°) and 10 as the hypotenuse. Sine is opposite

over hypotenuse. To find the sine of q°, find the opposite side, which is 8, and the hypotenuse,

which is 10. The sine of q° is therefore $\dfrac{8}{10}$, which can also be written as $\dfrac{4}{5}$ or 0.8. Any of these

are acceptable answers.

18.   **25**   Plug in a value for a that will be easy to use without a calculator. If $a = 2$, then

$\dfrac{9(5a)^2}{(3a)^2} = \dfrac{9(5 \times 2)^2}{(3 \times 2)^2} = \dfrac{9(10)^2}{(6)^2} = \dfrac{9(100)}{36}$. Reduce this fraction now, rather than multiplying it

out, since 36 is divisible by 9. The fraction becomes $\dfrac{100}{4}$, which is 25. The answer is 25.

19.   **20**   Vertical angles are congruent, so $\angle HLI = \angle JLK$. Also, $\angle IHL = \angle KJL$ because $\overline{HI} \parallel \overline{JK}$. Like-

wise, $\angle HIL = \angle JKL$. These triangles are similar, and similar triangles have proportional side

lengths, so set up a proportion, which will help find $\overline{HJ}$: $\dfrac{3}{9} = \dfrac{5}{JL}$. Cross-multiply to find that

$45 = 3(\overline{JL})$, and divide both sides by 3 to find that $\overline{JL} = 15$. The question asks for the length of

$\overline{HJ}$, which is 5 (from $\overline{HL}$) plus 15 (from $\overline{JL}$) for a total length of 20, which is the answer.

20. **225** Start by plugging $z = 5\sqrt{3}$ into the second equation to get $3(5\sqrt{3}) = \sqrt{3y}$. Distribute the 3 on the left side to get $15\sqrt{3} = \sqrt{3y}$. Square both sides to get rid of the square root signs: $225 \times 3 = 3y$. Divide both sides by 3 to get $225 = y$.

Section 4: Math (Calculator)

1. **D** Translate the information in the question into an expression in bite-sized pieces. The monthly fee is $20.00 and the data usage fee is $2.50 per gigabyte. Start with the fee for data usage. The usage is $2.50 per gigabyte used, so to get the fee in a month in which David used g gigabytes, multiply g by 2.50 to get 2.50g. Eliminate any answer choice that doesn't include 2.50g: (A), (B), and (C). Thus, only (D) remains. To determine why (D) is correct, note that the word *and* translates to +, so add 20 to 2.50g to get 20 + 2.50g. The answer is (D).

2. **B** The question asks for the greatest change between consecutive years. Go through each year and determine the change in each. From 2000 to 2001, there is a decrease of $50,000 – $40,000 = $10,000. From 2001 to 2002, there is an increase of $55,000 – $40,000 = $15,000. From 2002 to 2003, there is an increase of $60,000 – $55,000 = $5,000. From 2003 to 2004, there is an increase of $75,000 – $60,000 = $15,000. From 2004 to 2005, there is a decrease of $75,000 – $65,000 = $10,000. From 2005 to 2006, there is no change. From 2006 to 2007, there is an increase of $95,000 – $65,000 = $30,000. The greatest is $30,000, which is (B). Alternatively, ballpark. Look at the graph and notice that the change from 2006 to 2007 appears to be the steepest, so this difference would have to be the answer. The answer is (B).

3. **A** There are variables in the answers, so plug in. Currently Jim can do 14 pull-ups in a minute. He believes that he can increase this amount by 7 each year. Therefore, he believes that in 1 year he can do 14 + 7 = 21 pull-ups, and in 2 years he can do 21 + 7 = 28 pull-ups. Now plug $y = 2$ into each of the choices and eliminate any that isn't equal to 28. Choice (A) is 7(2) + 14 = 28, so keep (A). Choice (B) is 7(2) + 30 = 44, so eliminate (B). Choice (C) is 14(2) + 7 = 35, so eliminate (C). Choice (D) is 14 – 7(2) = 0, so eliminate (D). The answer is (A).

4. **D** The question gives an equation and a value for one of the variables in the equation. Plug in the given value to solve for the value of the other variable. If $v = 67$, the equation becomes $67 = 17 + 2.5t$. Subtract 17 from both sides to get $50 = 2.5t$. Divide both sides by 2.5 to get $t = 20$, so the answer is (D).

5. **A** The question asks for the equation of a function that could possibly define h. Each of the equations in the choices is in factored form. If a factor of the equation of a function is in the form $(x – r)$, r is one of the roots, or one of the x-intercepts. Since the roots of this function are –4, 2, and 4, the roots are $(x – (–4))$ or $(x + 4)$, $(x – 2)$, and $(x – 4)$. The only equation with all of these factors is (A), so the answer is (A).

6. **C** Translate the first statement into an equation. The phrase *three times a number n* translates to $3n$. The phrase *is added to* translates to +. The word *is* translates to =. Therefore, the sentence translates to $3n + 9 = 3$. Solve this for n: subtract 9 from both sides to get $3n = -6$, then divide both sides by 3 to get $n = -2$. This is (A). However, the question does not ask for the value of n, so (A) is a trap answer. The question asks for *the result when 4 times n is added to 14*. The phrase *4 times n* translates to $4n$. The phrase *is added to 14* translates to + 14. Therefore, *4 times n is added to 14* translates to $4n + 14$. Since $n = -2$, $4n + 14 = 4(-2) + 14 = -8 + 14 = 6$. The answer is (C).

7. **B** The question asks for how many 16-ounce cups can be filled from a 64-gallon urn. First, convert the 64 gallons into ounces. Use a proportion: $\dfrac{1 \text{ gallon}}{128 \text{ ounces}} = \dfrac{64 \text{ gallons}}{x \text{ ounces}}$. Cross-multiply to get $x = (128)(64) = 8{,}192$. Now determine the number of 16-ounce cups that can be filled from an 8,192-ounce urn. Use another proportion: $\dfrac{1 \text{ cup}}{16 \text{ ounces}} = \dfrac{y \text{ cups}}{8{,}192 \text{ ounces}}$. Cross-multiply to get $16y = 8{,}192$. Divide both sides by 16 to get $y = 512$. The answer is (B).

8. **C** To determine the slope of a line, use the slope formula, $slope = \dfrac{y_2 \quad y_1}{x_2 \quad x_1}$. Let $\left(1, -\dfrac{1}{3}\right)$ be (x_1, y_1) and $\left(5, \dfrac{8}{3}\right)$ be (x_2, y_2). The slope is $\dfrac{\dfrac{8}{3} - \left(-\dfrac{1}{3}\right)}{5 - 1} = \dfrac{\dfrac{8}{3} + \dfrac{1}{3}}{4} = \dfrac{\dfrac{9}{3}}{4} = \dfrac{3}{4}$. The answer is (C).

9. **A** The question asks for the average number of fish per tank. The average is $\dfrac{total}{number\ of\ things}$. The *things* in this case are the tanks. Since the title of the graph says that there are 18, the average is $\dfrac{total}{18}$. The *total* is the number of fish. To determine this, use the histogram. There are 2 tanks with 2 fish each, so these 2 tanks have a total of $2 \times 2 = 4$ fish. There are 4 tanks with 3 fish, so these 4 tanks have a total of $4 \times 3 = 12$ fish. There are no tanks with 4 fish, so ignore that column. There are 3 tanks with 5 fish, so these 3 tanks have a total of $3 \times 5 = 15$ fish. There are 5 tanks with 6 fish, so these 5 tanks have a total of $5 \times 6 = 30$ fish. There is 1 tank with 7 fish, so this 1 tank has a total of $1 \times 7 = 7$ fish. There are 3 tanks with 8 fish, so these 3 tanks have a total of $3 \times 8 = 24$ fish. Therefore, all the tanks have a total of $4 + 12 + 15 + 30 + 7 + 24 = 92$ fish, and the average number of fish per tank is $\dfrac{92}{18} = 5.\bar{1}$. The question asks for the *closest* choice, which is (A).

10. **A** The question asks for the design flaw in the survey. The survey was conducted to determine whether people in City C are more likely to work 9-to-5 office jobs than other jobs. The survey was conducted exclusively during the time in which people would be working at 9-to-5 office jobs.

Therefore, people at this type of job would be less likely to answer the call. Choice (A) matches the prediction, so keep (A). Choice (B) is population size. Population size is not necessarily a design flaw, since the population size is not given. Eliminate (B). Choice (C) is sample size. If the sample size were significantly less than the population size, this fact could lead to unreliable results. However, since population size is not known, sample size cannot be determined to be a design flaw. Eliminate (C). Choice (D) refers to the fact that the telephone was used. Since the problem does not mention telephone use by people with different types of jobs, there's no reason to believe that using a telephone to conduct the survey would make the results less reliable. Eliminate (D). The correct answer is (A).

11. **D** The question asks which graph could represent $y = p(x)$ and says that function p has exactly four roots. A *root* of a function is an x-value for which the y-value is 0. The y-value is 0 for all points on the x-axis, so p has to have exactly four x-intercepts (points where the graph intersects the x-axis). Go through each choice and determine the number of x-intercepts. Choices (A) and (C) have three x-intercepts, so eliminate these. Choice (B) has five intercepts. Since the question states that p has *exactly* four roots rather than *at least* four, eliminate (B) as well. Only (D) has exactly four x-intercepts, so the answer is (D).

12. **A** The question states that 85% of the customers ordered the brunch special. Since the question asks for which choice could be the number of customers, plug in the answers by taking 85% of each choice. Eliminate any choice that doesn't result in a whole number of customers. Start with (A): 85% of 40 is $(0.85)(40) = 34$. Since this is a whole number, this could be the number of customers, so the answer is (A).

13. **A** The question includes variables and uses the phrase *in terms of*, so plug in. Since an equation is given with d isolated, plug in for the other variables, t, v, and h, and calculate d. Let $t = 2$, $v = 10$, and $h = 20$. In this case, $d = -8t^2 + vt + h = -8(2)^2 + (10)(2) + 20 = 8$. The question asks for the value of v, so the target answer is 10. Go through the choices and eliminate any answer that is not 10. Choice (A) is $v = \dfrac{8 - 20}{2} + 8(2) = 10$, so keep (A). Choice (B) is $v = \dfrac{8 + 20}{2} - 8(2) = -2$, so eliminate (B). Choice (C) is $v = \dfrac{8 - 20 + 8}{2} = -2$, so eliminate (C). Choice (D) is $v = 8 + 20 - 8(2) = 12$, so eliminate (D). Only (A) matches, so the answer is (A).

14. **D** The question asks for what could be the median of 22 scores. The median of an even number of numbers is the average of the middle two when the numbers are listed in order. In this case, it is the average of the 11th and 12th score. Find the location of the 11th and 12th scores on the histogram. There is 1 score from 50 to 60. There are 4 scores from 60 to 70, so there are 5 scores from 50 to 70. There are 2 scores from 70 to 80, so there are 7 scores from 50 to 80. There are 11 scores from 80 to 90, so there are 18 scores from 50 to 90. Since the 11th and 12th scores were passed at the 80 to 90 interval, they must be in this interval. Therefore, the median must be within this interval, as well. The only choice within this interval is 84, so the answer is (D).

15. **C** The question asks for a percent, which is $\dfrac{part}{whole} \times 100$. The *part* is the total number of those surveyed who use public transit, which is 51, and the *whole* is the total number of those surveyed, which is 130. Therefore, the percent is $\dfrac{51}{130} \times 100 \approx 39$. The answer is (C).

16. **C** The proportion of people who fit the requirements in the survey can be expected to be the same proportion of people who will fit the requirements in the general population. First, find the number of commuters surveyed who used public transit and had an average daily commute of at least 1 hour. Find the column for *Commutes by Public Transit* and the row for *At least 1 hour*. At the intersection is 29, so this is the number of those surveyed who used public transit and had an average daily commute of at least 1 hour. Since the total number of those surveyed is 130 and the total population of the population is 13,000,000, set up the proportion $\dfrac{29}{130} = \dfrac{x}{13,000,000}$. Cross-multiply to get $130x = 377,000,000$. Divide both sides by 130 to get $x = 2,900,000$. The answer is (C).

17. **B** The question asks how many times more likely it is for a commuter whose average daily commute is less than 1 hour not to take public transit than it is for a commuter whose average daily commute is at least 1 hour not to take public transit. The term *more likely* refers to probability, so determine the probability of each. Go to the table and find the number of commuters who commute less than 1 hour and do NOT commute using public transit. Find the *Does Not Commute by Public Transit* column and the *Less than 1 hour* row. At the intersection is 46, so this is the number of commuters who commute less than 1 hour and do NOT commute using public transit. Now look in the same row under the *Total* column to find that the total number of commuters who commute less than 1 hour is 68. Therefore, the probability is $\dfrac{46}{68}$. Now do the same for the probability that someone who commutes at least one hour does not take public transit. Find the row for those who commute *At least 1 hour* and the columns for *Does Not Commute Using Public Transit* and *Total*. In this row, the number under *Does Not Commute by Public Transit* is 33 and the number under *Total* is 62, so the probability is $\dfrac{33}{62}$. The question asks *how many times more likely* is the first probability than the second. Set up the equation $\dfrac{46}{68} = \dfrac{33}{62}x$. Divide both sides by $\dfrac{33}{62}$ to get $x \approx 1.27$. The answer is (B).

18. **C** The question asks for the best conclusion from the study. The study takes a random sample of subjects without sleep disorders and gives half of them beverage *C*. The subjects who consume beverage *C* sleep less than the subjects who don't consume it. This would seem to indicate that beverage *C* caused people without sleep disorders to sleep less. Go through each of the choices. Choice (A) is incorrect because the study doesn't compare different caffeinated beverages. It only compares consuming beverage *C* to not consuming it. Choice (B) is incorrect, because the study does not indicate *substantial* loss is sleep. Furthermore, the sample only includes people without sleep disorders, so any conclusion must be restricted to this population. Choice (C) is similar to the prediction, so keep this choice. Choice (D), like (B), does not restrict the conclusion to people without sleep disorders. The answer is (C).

19. **C** The question involves algebra, asks for a value, and includes numbers in the answers, so plug in the answers. First, eliminate any answers that don't make sense: since *n* is 40% larger than the sum of the other three numbers, *n* will have to be greater than half of 1,764. Eliminate (A) and (B). Try one of the remaining answers, such as (D). If *n* = 1,260, then the remaining three numbers would add up to 1,764 − 1,260 = 504. Since 1,260 is not 40% more than 504, eliminate (D) and choose (C). If desired, check (C): if *n* = 1,029, then the other three numbers add up to 735. Since 735 + 40% (735) = 735 + 294 = 1,029, (C) is the correct answer.

20. **D** The question asks how much more the 11.5 m³ object weighed than was predicted by the line of best fit. This question can be solved by determining the actual weight of the object and the weight predicted by the line of best fit. However, finding the actual amounts is not necessary. Instead, simply find the difference between the two. Volume is represented by the horizontal axis, so find 11.5 on the horizontal axis. Trace straight up to the data point. From that point, trace the line downward, counting the number of intervals to the line of best fit. There are four intervals. Go to the vertical axis to determine the number of kilograms per interval. The labels are 5,000 kilograms apart, and there are 5 intervals between each label. Therefore, each interval is $\frac{5,000}{5} = 1,000$, so 4 intervals are 4,000 kg. The answer is (D).

21. **C** The question asks the percent increase in total sales. Since the number of laptops and the number of tablets are different, don't just add the two percent increases. Thus, (D) is a trap answer. A percent change is always equal to the expression $\frac{difference}{original} \times 100$. The *original* is the total number of units sold last week, which is 90 + 210 = 300. To get the difference, get the increase in laptops and the increase in tablets separately and then add. There is a fifty percent increase in laptop sales,

so the increase is $\dfrac{50}{100} \times 90 = 45$. There is a thirty percent increase in tablet sales, so the increase is $\dfrac{30}{100} \times 210 = 63$. Therefore, the total *difference* is $45 + 63 = 108$, and the percent increase is $\dfrac{108}{300} \times 100 = 36\%$. The answer is (C).

22.   **B**   According to the question, $\cos(x°) = \sin(y°)$. This can only be the case if the two angles are complementary, meaning the measures of the two angles have a sum of 90°. The question asks for the value of c, and there are numbers in the answer choices, so plug in the answers. Start with (B). If $c = 15.5$, then $x = 3(15.5) - 23 = 23.5$ and $y = 66.5$, so $x + y = 23.5 + 66.5 = 90$. Thus, the two angles are complementary, and the answer is (B).

23.   **A**   The question asks for the maximum value for $-3 \le x \le 6$. This is the domain sketched in the graph, so only worry about the points on the sketch. The value of the function is equal to each y-value. Although the values of the function appear to be increasing toward ∞, they do not actually go to ∞ within the points sketched, so eliminate (D). Since the question asks for the maximum value of the function, which is the maximum y-value, find the highest point on the graph. This appears on the far left. Draw a horizontal line to the y-axis to see that this line crosses the y-axis at 4. Therefore, the y-value at this point, or the maximum value of the function, is 4. The answer is (A).

24.   **B**   The question says that the width is 8 feet more than 4 times the length. Take this statement and translate it into an equation. Translate *the width* to w. Translate *is* to =. Translate *8 feet more than* to ____ + 8, leaving room on the left for what follows. Translate *4 times the length* to $4l$. Therefore, the statement translates to $w = 4l + 8$. The question also says that the area is 5,472. The area of a rectangle can be found using the formula $A = lw$. Substitute $A = 5,472$ and $w = 4l + 8$ to get $5,472 = l(4l + 8)$. Distribute the l on the left side to get $5,472 = 4l^2 + 8l$. Since this is a quadratic equation, get one side equal to 0 by subtracting 5,472 from both sides to get $0 = 4l^2 + 8l - 5,472$. This is a difficult quadratic to factor, so use the quadratic formula, $l = \dfrac{-b \pm \sqrt{b^2 - 4ac}}{2a}$, where $a = 4$, $b = 8$, and $c = -5,472$. Substitute these values to get $l = \dfrac{-8 \pm \sqrt{8^2 - 4(4)(-5,472)}}{2(4)}$. Use a calculator to get that $8^2 - 4(4)(-5,472) = 87,616$ and that

$l = \dfrac{-8 \pm \sqrt{87{,}616}}{2(4)}$. Take the square root of 87,616 to get $l = \dfrac{-8 \pm 296}{2(4)} = \dfrac{-8 \pm 296}{8}$. Since

length can only be positive, don't take the negative into account and $l = \dfrac{-8 \pm 296}{8}$ becomes

$l = \dfrac{-8 + 296}{8} = \dfrac{288}{8} = 36$. If $l = 36$, then $w = 4l + 8 = 4(36) + 8 = 152$. To find the perimeter, use

$P = 2l + 2w = 2(36) + 2(152) = 376$. The answer is (B).

25.　**D**　The line intersects the origin as well as the points $(c, 3)$ and $(27, c)$. Questions about lines in the

xy-plane often involve slope, so determine the slope of this line. Any two points can be used to find

the equation of a line (including the slope). Note that since the line intersects the origin, it inter-

sects point $(0, 0)$ as well as the other two points. Use points $(0, 0)$ and $(c, 3)$ to calculate the slope:

$slope = \dfrac{y_2 - y_1}{x_2 - x_1} = \dfrac{3 - 0}{c - 0} = \dfrac{3}{c}$. The slope can also be determined using points $(0, 0)$ and $(27, c)$:

$\dfrac{c - 0}{27 - 0} = \dfrac{c}{27}$. Since these two slopes must be equal, $\dfrac{3}{c} = \dfrac{c}{27}$. Cross-multiply to get $c^2 = 81$. Take

the square root of both sides to get $c = \pm 9$. Since only 9 is a choice, the answer is (D).

26.　**B**　Since $\overline{FG}$ is a chord that includes the center, it is a diameter. Therefore, arc $\overparen{FXG}$ is a semicircle.
Since the length of the semicircular arc is 14π, the circumference of the circle is $14\pi \times 2 = 28\pi$. The
formula for circumference is $C = 2\pi r$, so $28\pi = 2\pi r$. Divide both sides by 2π to get $r = 14$. The question asks for the length of the segment $\overline{XO}$. Since $\overline{XO}$ is a radius, the length is 14. The answer is (B).

27.　**B**　Since the question says *must be*, plug in multiple values of p and q. Make sure that all values of p
and q satisfy the inequality $-|p| < q < |p|$. Let $p = 4$ and $q = 2$. Go through each statement and
eliminate any statement that is false. Statement (I) is $4 > 0$, which is true, so keep statement (I).
Statement (II) is $|4| > -2$, which is true, so keep statement (II). Statement (III) is $4 > |2|$, which is
true, so keep statement (III). Try other values that might change the results. Since the question
involves absolute values, try negative numbers. Let $p = -4$ and $q = -2$. In this case, statement (I)
is $-4 > 0$, which is false, so cross out (I). Eliminate (A) and (D), since they include statement (I).
Since both remaining choices include statement (II), statement (II) must be true, and no more
testing of statement (II) is necessary. Test statement (III) using the same values of $p = -4$ and
$q = -2$: $-4 > |-2|$. This is false, so cross out statement (III), and eliminate (C). The answer is (B).

28.　**B**　The question asks for a reasonable estimate for the number of blue jelly beans in the entire container.
The number of blue jelly beans is given for each of ten regions. Determine the total number of regions

in the container. The container has a base of 10 feet by 10 feet, so the area of the base of the entire container is $A = s^2 = (10)^2 = 100$. Each region has a base of 1 foot by 1 foot, so the area of the base of each region is $A = s^2 = (1)^2 = 1$. To get the number of regions, divide the area of the base of the container by the area of the base of each region to get $\frac{100}{1} = 100$. One way to get an estimate of the number of blue jelly beans in the entire container would be to find the average number of blue jelly beans in the counted regions and multiply that number by 100. The question asks for an approximation, though, and the answer choices are spread apart, so ballpark. All of the numbers in the table are around 25. Therefore, 25 is a reasonable estimate for the average number of blue jelly beans, and the total number of jelly beans should be about $25 \times 100 = 2,500$. The answer is (B).

29. **C** The question states that there are four times as many vanilla ice creams sold as vanilla frozen yogurts. Let x be the number of vanilla frozen yogurts sold; therefore, $4x$ is the number of vanilla ice creams sold. The question also says that there are six times as many chocolate ice creams sold as chocolate frozen yogurts, so let y be the number of chocolate frozen yogurts sold and $6y$ be the number of chocolate ice creams sold. Since there are a total of 32 frozen yogurts sold, $x + y = 32$. Since there are a total of 152 ice creams sold, $4x + 6y = 152$. Since there are two equations with two variables, it is possible to solve for the variables. Stack and add the two equations, trying to eliminate the chocolates to solve for the vanillas. Multiply both sides of the first equation by -6 to get $-6x - 6y = -192$, then stack and add the equations like this:

$$
\begin{array}{rl}
4x + 6y = & 152 \\
\underline{-6x - 6y =} & \underline{-192} \\
-2x \quad\;\; = & -40
\end{array}
$$

Divide both sides by -2 to get $x = 20$. The question asks for the probability that a randomly selected ice cream sold is vanilla, which will be calculated by dividing the number of vanilla ice creams sold ($4x$) by the total number of ice creams sold (152). Since $x = 20$, the number of vanilla ice creams sold is $4x = 4(20) = 80$. The probability that one ice cream is vanilla is $\frac{80}{152} \approx 0.526$. The answer is (C).

30. **D** To graph an inequality, start by graphing the equation. If the inequality sign is $\geq$, draw the equation as a solid line and shade above. If the inequality sign is $\leq$, draw the equation as a solid line and shade below. If the sign is $>$ or $<$, use the same rule as $\geq$ or $\leq$, respectively, but use a dashed line instead of a solid line. Use the inequalities given. Start with $y \geq x$. Since the inequality sign

is ≥ rather than >, the graph is the one with the solid line. Since the inequality sign is ≥, shade the solution above the line. Therefore, since only Sectors W and X are above the solid line, eliminate any choice that includes Y and Z. Eliminate (A) and (B). Now look at the inequality $3y < 2x - 3$. Divide both sides by 3 to get $y < \frac{2}{3}x - 1$. Since the inequality sign is <, the solution is below the dashed line. Since Sector W is above the dashed line, eliminate (C). The answer is (D).

31. **5 or 6** Martina spends between $20 and $25, inclusive, and she buys one hamburger at a cost of $5. This would leave her at least $20 – $5 = $15 and at most $25 – $5 = $20 for hot dogs. In the first case, $15 total divided by $3 per hot dog would get her 5 hot dogs, so 5 is one possible value for h. If she spent up to $20 on hot dogs, she could get $20 divided by $3 per hot dog for 6.67 hot dogs. She can only buy whole hot dogs, so 6 is another possible value of h. Therefore, the two possible correct answers are 5 and 6.

32. **19.4** The question asks for the average, so get the total and divide by the number of things. To get the total, add the number of states for each nation. The total is 6 + 9 + 26 + 16 + 29 + 13 + 31 + 4 + 36 + 2 + 10 + 17 + 50 + 23 = 272. Divide 272 by the 14 nations to get $\frac{272}{14} \approx 19.4285714$. Rounded to the nearest tenth, the answer is 19.4.

33. **10** The question gives the equation of a function and a point on the graph of the function. Plug the point into the equation. Substitute $x = -2$ and $y = g(x) = 6$ to get $6 = 2(-2)^2 + k(-2) + 18$. Simplify the right side to get $6 = 26 - 2k$. Subtract 26 from both sides to get $-20 = -2k$. Divide both sides by -2 to get $10 = k$. The answer is 10.

34. **11** The question asks how many rooms will be assigned three students. Consider the possibility that all rooms have three students. How many left over students would there be? If 26 rooms are assigned three students, then there are 26 × 3 = 78 students. However, the question says that there are 108 students, so there are 108 – 78 = 30 left over. These left over students have to be assigned to 5 student rooms. Since each room already has three students, to make five student rooms, pair the remaining students and add each pair to one of the three student rooms. Since there are 30 left over students, they make 15 pairs, so 15 rooms of three students become five-student rooms. Since there are a total of 26 rooms, there are 26 – 15 = 11 three-person rooms. The answer is 11.

35. $\frac{7}{12}$ The question asks for what fraction Town A's 1970 population was of Town A's 2000 population. To determine the population in 1970, find 1970 on the horizontal axis, trace straight up to the curve, then straight across to the vertical axis. It hits the vertical axis on the only line between 30 and 40, so the population in 1970 was 35,000. (Note that the vertical axis label indicates that the population is in thousands.) To determine the population in 2000, find 2000 on the horizontal

axis, trace straight up to the curve, then straight across to the vertical axis. It hits the vertical axis at 60, so the population in 2000 was 60,000. Therefore, the fraction is $\dfrac{35,000}{60,000} = \dfrac{35}{60} = \dfrac{7}{12}$. The answer is $\dfrac{7}{12}$.

36. **4** The question states that the volume of the cylinder is 64π cubic centimeters. The formula for volume of a cylinder is $V = \pi r^2 h$. Plug in $V = 64\pi$ and $h = 16$, as indicated by the figure, to get $64\pi = \pi r^2(16)$. Divide both sides by 16π to get $4 = r^2$. Take the square root of both sides to get $2 = r$. Note, however, that the question asks for the *diameter* and not the radius. Since the diameter is twice the radius, $d = 2r = 2(2) = 4$. The answer is 4.

37. **321** This question asks for angular position, which is in equation 1 and represented by θ. Write down known variables and solve. When the carousel changes direction, the angular velocity is 0. Use the first equation, $\omega^2 = \omega_0^2 + 2\alpha\theta$. Plug in $\omega = 0$, $\omega_0 = 90$, and $\alpha = -12.6$ to get $0 = 90^2 + 2(-12.6)\theta$. Simplify the right side to get $0 = 8,100 - 25.2\theta$. Add 25.2θ to both sides to get $25.2\theta = 8,100$. Divide both sides to get $\theta = 321.4286$. Rounded to the nearest degree, the answer is 321.

38. **7** The question asks for time. Write down known variables, then choose the equation that gives only time as the unknown. This is equation 2. When the carousel changes direction, the angular velocity is 0. Use the second equation, $\omega = \omega_0 + \alpha t$. Plug in $\omega = 0$, $\omega_0 = 90$, and $\alpha = -12.6$ to get $0 = 90 + (-12.6)t$. Simplify the right side to get $0 = 90 - 12.6t$. Add $12.6t$ to both sides to get $12.6t = 90$. Divide both sides by 12.6 to get $t = 7.1429$. Rounded to the nearest second, the answer is 7.

Chapter 4
Practice Test 2

Reading Test

65 MINUTES, 52 QUESTIONS

Turn to Section 1 of your answer sheet to answer the questions in this section.

DIRECTIONS

Each passage or pair of passages below is followed by a number of questions. After reading each passage or pair, choose the best answer to each question based on what is stated or implied in the passage or passages and in any accompanying graphics (such as a table or graph).

Questions 1–10 are based on the following passage.

This passage is excerpted from Gloria Steinem, *My Life on the Road*. © 2015 by Random House. The narrator, a writer, recalls her childhood in the United States of America.

There were only a few months each year when my father seemed content with a house-dwelling life. Every summer, we stayed in the small house he had
Line built across the road from a lake in rural Michigan,
5 where he ran a dance pavilion on a pier over the water. Though there was no ocean within hundreds of miles, he had named it Ocean Beach Pier, and given it the grandiose slogan "Dancing Over the Water and Under the Stars."
10 On weeknights, people came from nearby farms and summer cottages to dance to a jukebox. My father dreamed up such attractions as a living chess game, inspired by his own love of chess, with costumed teenagers moving across the squares of the dance floor.
15 On weekends, he booked the big dance bands of the 1930s and 1940s into this remote spot. People might come from as far away as Toledo or Detroit to dance to this live music on warm moonlit nights. Of course, paying the likes of Guy Lombardo or Duke Ellington
20 or the Andrews Sisters meant that one rainy weekend could wipe out a whole summer's profits, so there was always a sense of gambling. I think my father loved that, too.

But as soon as Labor Day had ended this precarious
25 livelihood, my father moved his office into his car. In the first warm weeks of autumn, we drove to nearby

country auctions, where he searched for antiques amid the household goods and farm tools. After my mother, with her better eye for antiques and her reference
30 books, appraised them for sale, we got into the car again to sell them to roadside antique dealers anywhere within a day's journey. I say "we" because from the age of four or so, I came into my own as the wrapper and unwrapper of china and other small items that
35 we cushioned in newspaper and carried in cardboard boxes over country roads. Each of us had a role in the family economic unit, including my sister, nine years older than I, who in the summer sold popcorn from a professional stand my father bought her.
40 But once the first frost turned the lake to crystal and the air above it to steam, my father began collecting road maps from gas stations, testing the trailer hitch on our car, and talking about such faraway pleasures as thin sugary pralines from Georgia, all-
45 you-can-drink orange juice from roadside stands in Florida, or slabs of salmon fresh from a California smokehouse.

Then one day, as if struck by a sudden whim rather than a lifelong wanderlust, he announced that it was
50 time to put the family dog and other essentials into the house trailer that was always parked in our yard, and begin our long trek to Florida or California.

Sometimes this leave-taking happened so quickly that we packed more frying pans than plates, or left a
55 kitchen full of dirty dishes and half-eaten food to greet us like Pompeii on our return. My father's decision

CONTINUE ➜

always seemed to come as a surprise, even though his fear of the siren song of home was so great that he refused to put heating or hot water into our small
60 house. If the air of early autumn grew too chilly for us to bathe in the lake, we heated water on a potbellied stove and took turns bathing in a big washtub next to the fireplace. Since this required the chopping of wood, an insult to my father's sybaritic soul, he had invented
65 a wood-burning system all his own: he stuck one end of a long log into the fire and let the other protrude into the living room, then kicked it into the fireplace until the whole thing turned to ash. Even a pile of cut firewood in the yard must have seemed to him a
70 dangerous invitation to stay in one place.

　　After he turned his face to the wind, my father did not like to hesitate. Only once do I remember him turning back, and even then my mother had to argue strenuously that the iron might be burning its way
75 through the ironing board. He would buy us a new radio, new shoes, almost anything rather than retrace the road already traveled.

1

Over the course of the passage, the main focus shifts from

A) a description of the narrator's father to a portrayal of a significant place the family often visited.

B) a depiction of the family's settled life to a description of the family's life on the road.

C) an allegorical display of domesticity to an example of its rejection by the narrator's father.

D) an anecdote about the poverty of the narrator's childhood to a speculation concerning the causes of that poverty.

2

The main purpose of the second paragraph (lines 10–23) ("On weeknights . . . too") is to

A) analyze the source of the father's compulsive desire to travel.

B) introduce the figures who play a role in the narrator's remembrances.

C) illustrate the father's delusions of grandeur that harmed the family's financial well-being.

D) describe the father's unique approach to living life that is expanded upon later in the passage.

3

The word "precarious" is used in line 24 to

A) emphasize the danger inherent to dancing over the water.

B) caution against burning firewood in an unapproved manner.

C) underscore the joy that this dancehall brought to so many.

D) highlight the uncertainty regarding the summer profits.

4

The narrator indicates that she participated in the family business

A) in a way that matched her age and abilities.

B) much less than her older siblings.

C) despite not being paid for her work.

D) on a volunteer basis until her teenage years.

CONTINUE ➤

5

With which of the following statements about her father would the narrator most likely agree?

A) He objected to train travel as a mode of transportation.

B) He had no consideration for his family's wishes.

C) He feared the expense of installing a heater into the family home.

D) He seemed mostly discontent with a settled, domestic life.

6

Which choice provides the best evidence for the answer to the previous question?

A) Lines 1–2 ("There were . . . life")

B) Lines 22–23 ("I think . . . too")

C) Lines 36–39 ("Each of . . . her")

D) Lines 59–60 ("he refused . . . house")

7

As used in line 48, "struck" most nearly means

A) battered.

B) boycotted.

C) inspired.

D) disturbed.

8

It can reasonably be inferred from the passage that the main reason that the narrator's father started the cross-country trip is because

A) he was struck by a sudden desire to escape the monotony of the house.

B) his desire to travel stemmed from a basic personality trait.

C) the family had already depleted the resources at one site.

D) he was surprised by the sudden change in the weather.

9

Which choice provides the best evidence for the answer to the previous question?

A) Lines 25–28 ("In the . . . tools")

B) Lines 40–47 ("But once . . . smokehouse")

C) Lines 48–52 ("Then one . . . California")

D) Lines 53–56 ("Sometimes this . . . return")

10

Which statement best characterizes the mother's role in the family?

A) She resented the father's impulsive nature.

B) She shared the father's wanderlust equally.

C) She sometimes played a more practical role than the father did.

D) She rescued the family's possessions from the flames.

CONTINUE →

Questions 11–21 are based on the following passage and supplementary material.

This passage is adapted from "Stanford researchers uncover patterns in how scientists lie about their data," by Bjorn Carey, originally published in November 2015 by Stanford University.

Even the best poker players have "tells" that give away when they're bluffing with a weak hand. Scientists who commit fraud have similar, but even more subtle,
Line tells, and a pair of Stanford researchers have cracked
5 the writing patterns of scientists who attempt to pass along falsified data. The work, published in the *Journal of Language and Social Psychology*, could eventually help scientists identify falsified research before it is published.
10 There is a fair amount of research dedicated to understanding the ways liars lie. Studies have shown that liars generally tend to express more negative emotion terms and use fewer first-person pronouns. Fraudulent financial reports typically display higher
15 levels of linguistic obfuscation—phrasing that is meant to distract from or conceal the fake data—than accurate reports.

To see if similar patterns exist in scientific academia, Jeff Hancock, a professor of communication
20 at Stanford, and graduate student David Markowitz searched the archives of PubMed, a database of life sciences journals, from 1973 to 2013 for retracted papers. They identified 253, primarily from biomedical journals, that were retracted for documented fraud and
25 compared the writing in these to unretracted papers from the same journals and publication years, and covering the same topics.

They then rated the level of fraud of each paper using a customized "obfuscation index," which
30 rated the degree to which the authors attempted to mask their false results. This was achieved through a summary score of causal terms, abstract language, jargon, positive emotion terms and a standardized ease of reading score.
35 "We believe the underlying idea behind obfuscation is to muddle the truth," said Markowitz, the lead author on the paper. "Scientists faking data know that they are committing a misconduct and do not want to get caught. Therefore, one strategy to evade this may be
40 to obscure parts of the paper. We suggest that language can be one of many variables to differentiate between fraudulent and genuine science."

The results showed that fraudulent retracted papers scored significantly higher on the obfuscation index
45 than papers retracted for other reasons. For example, fraudulent papers contained approximately 1.5 percent more jargon than unretracted papers. "Fraudulent papers had about 60 more jargon-like words per paper compared to unretracted papers," Markowitz said.
50 "This is a non-trivial amount."

The researchers say that scientists might commit data fraud for a variety of reasons. Previous research points to a "publish or perish" mentality that may motivate researchers to manipulate their findings or
55 fake studies altogether. But the change the researchers found in the writing, however, is directly related to the author's goals of covering up lies through the manipulation of language. For instance, a fraudulent author may use fewer positive emotion terms to curb
60 praise for the data, for fear of triggering inquiry.

In the future, a computerized system based on this work might be able to flag a submitted paper so that editors could give it a more critical review before publication, depending on the journal's threshold
65 for obfuscated language. But the authors warn that this approach isn't currently feasible given the false-positive rate. "Science fraud is of increasing concern in academia, and automatic tools for identifying fraud might be useful," Hancock said. "But much more
70 research is needed before considering this kind of approach. Obviously, there is a very high error rate that would need to be improved, but also science is based on trust, and introducing a 'fraud detection' tool into the publication process might undermine that trust."

CONTINUE →

Frequencies of Language Categories in Publications, Reviewed by Markowitz and Hancock

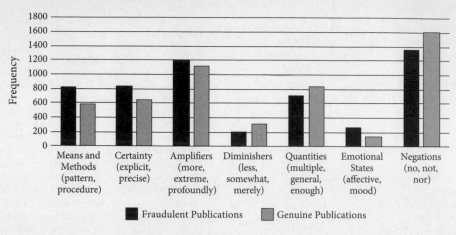

Data sourced from "Linguistic Traces of a Scientific Fraud: The Case of Diederik Stapel," © David M. Markowitz and Jeffrey T. Hancock, August 25, 2014.
http://journals.plos.org/plosone/article/figure?id=10.1371/journal.pone.0105937.t001

11

The primary purpose of this passage is to

A) defend scientists who have incorporated fraudulent data into their reports in order to succeed in a competitive field.

B) contrast various methodologies for spotting false information in different industries and research fields.

C) describe an experiment designed to find the differences between fraudulent and genuine scientific data and caution against a possible solution.

D) reveal the secrets of those who successfully convince others of the veracity of false information.

12

The first paragraph serves mainly to

A) introduce a concept at the foundation of the research discussed in the passage.

B) propose additional applications for the results of the study in the passage.

C) introduce the development of general methods of fraud detection.

D) present an idea about scientific development that will be questioned later in the passage.

13

As used in line 10, "fair" most nearly means

A) ample.

B) lawful.

C) equal.

D) favorable.

CONTINUE ➜

14

As used in line 40, "obscure" most nearly means

A) hide.

B) blind.

C) distort.

D) characterize.

15

The passage indicates that scientific papers with fraudulent data can potentially be spotted by looking for

A) references to research studies that did not happen.

B) writing that uses deliberately distracting and confusing words and phrases.

C) results that differ from those of other studies by more than 1.5 percent.

D) authors who have published more than 60 papers in academic journals.

16

Which choice provides the best evidence for the answer to the previous question?

A) Lines 31–34 ("This was . . . score")

B) Lines 43–45 ("The results . . . reasons")

C) Lines 58–60 ("For instance . . . inquiry")

D) Lines 61–65 ("In the future . . . language")

17

Which hypothetical situation would Hancock most likely agree could be a consequence of action without further research into science fraud?

A) A scientist runs his paper through a computer program to check for confusing language before publication.

B) A scientist includes fraudulent data in a paper that does not affect the conclusion of the experiment.

C) A scientist publishes a genuine paper in a journal that has been known to publish fraudulent papers.

D) A scientist is less likely to submit a paper to a journal that uses automatic tools to detect fraud.

18

Which choice provides the best evidence for the answer to the previous question?

A) Lines 39–40 ("Therefore, one . . . paper")

B) Lines 52–55 ("Previous research . . . altogether")

C) Lines 65–67 ("But the . . . rate")

D) Lines 71–74 ("Obviously, there . . . trust")

19

According to the graph, the greatest difference between the language used in fraudulent and genuine research occurred in which category?

A) Means and Methods

B) Amplifiers

C) Quantities

D) Emotional States

CONTINUE

20

Which of the following statements is supported by the graph?

A) Scientists who published fraudulent data were more likely to use quantities-related language in their papers than were scientists who published genuine data.

B) Scientists who published fraudulent data used means and methods-related language nearly as often as they used certainty-related language.

C) Scientists who used more negation-related language were more likely to have published fraudulent data than scientists who used less negations-related language.

D) Scientists who used more amplifiers and diminishers were more likely to publish genuine data than scientists who used fewer amplifiers and diminishers.

Based on information in the graph and passage, which statement from the passage best supports the claim that jargon would be classified as "means and methods?"

A) Lines 2–6 ("Scientists who . . . data")

B) Lines 11–13 ("Studies have . . . pronouns")

C) Lines 47–49 ("Fraudulent papers . . . said")

D) Lines 69–71 ("But much . . . approach")

CONTINUE

Questions 22–31 are based on the following passage and supplementary material.

This passage is adapted from "The Story of YInMn Blue," originally published by Mas Subramanian, Joseph Tang, and Oregon State University.

YInMn Blue, or "MasBlue" as it is commonly referred to at Oregon State University ("OSU"), is a serendipitous discovery of a bright blue pigment
Line by scientists led by Mas Subramanian at OSU while
5 researching materials for electronics applications. The pigment contains the elements Yttrium, Indium, Manganese, and Oxygen.

In 2009, graduate student Andrew Smith was exploring the electronic properties of manganese oxide
10 by heating it to approximately 1,200°C (~2,000°F). Instead of a new, high-efficiency electronic material, what emerged from the furnace was a brilliant blue compound—a blue that Subramanian knew immediately was a research breakthrough. "If I hadn't
15 come from an industry research background—DuPont has a division that developed pigments and obviously they are used in paint and many other things—I would not have known this was highly unusual, a discovery with strong commercial potential," he says.
20 Blue pigments dating back to ancient times have been notoriously unstable—many fade easily and contain toxic materials. The fact that this pigment was synthesized at such high temperatures signaled to Subramanian that this new compound was extremely
25 stable, a property long sought in a blue pigment, he says. . . .

The chemical formula of YInMn Blue is $YIn_{1-x}Mn_xO_3$. These compositions adopt a crystal structure in which the chromophore responsible for
30 the intense blue color (Mn^{3+}) resides in the trigonal bipyramidal site. The intensity of the color can be systematically tuned by adjusting the In:Mn ratio. . . .

By measuring the spectral properties of this series, it was found that $YIn_{1-x}Mn_xO_3$ exhibits high absorbance
35 in the UV region and high reflectivity in the near-infrared region when compared to currently-used Cobalt Blue pigments. . . .

In May 2012, the Subramanian team received a patent with the U.S. Patent Office for the new pigment
40 (US82822728). Shepherd Color Co. subsequently began rigorous testing of the pigment. They concluded that the increased UV absorbance and stability in outdoor weathering and heat buildup tests

demonstrate that YInMn blue is superior to Cobalt
45 Blue ($CoAl_2O_4$). In addition, the high solar reflectance (compared to similarly colored pigments) indicates that this 'cool pigment' can find use in a variety of exterior applications by reducing surface temperatures, cooling costs, and energy consumption. As a result of
50 this testing, Shepherd Color Co. has licensed the patent for commercialization efforts.

Recently, several local artists (including OSU art students) have used this pigment in their own professional endeavors, utilizing it in watercolors and
55 drypoint.

The excitement of discovering a brilliant blue, heat reflecting, thermally stable, and UV absorbing pigment did not stop them from exploring beyond the blues. Since then, Subramanian and his team have expanded
60 their research and have made a range of new pigments to include almost every color, from bright oranges to shades of purple, turquoise and green.

They continue to search for a new stable, heat reflecting, and brilliant red, the most elusive color to
65 synthesize.

CONTINUE ➡

Reflectance vs. Wavelength

Figure 1

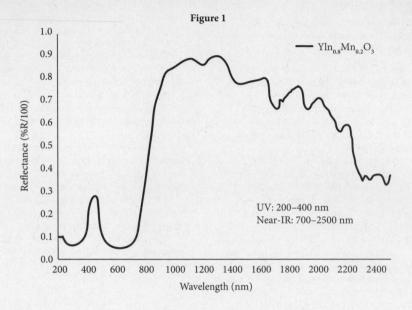

UV: 200–400 nm
Near-IR: 700–2500 nm

Figure 2

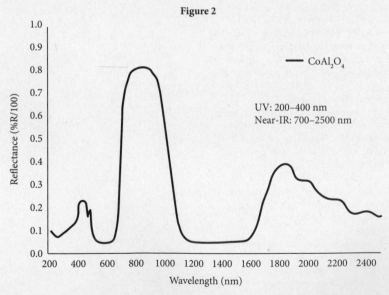

UV: 200–400 nm
Near-IR: 700–2500 nm

Images provided courtesy of Oregon State University.

CONTINUE →

22

One main idea of the passage is that

A) chemically-engineered substances can be both beneficial and dangerous.

B) unexpected findings can have significant implications.

C) pigments can be described most effectively in terms of chemical composition.

D) increased UV absorbance is directly related to pigment stability.

23

Which choice best describes the overall structure of the passage?

A) A description of a discovery, a scientific explanation, and the practical applications of the discovery

B) A comparison of the properties of a synthetic compound and the presentation of a natural compound alternative

C) A historical account of several accidental discoveries and an unbiased critique of the resulting products

D) A listing of chemical compounds, a description of how those compounds work together, and a comparison of the benefits of each compound

24

As used in line 5, "applications" most nearly means

A) requests.

B) forms.

C) uses.

D) industries.

25

Which choice provides the best evidence for the claim that Smith did not intend for his experiment to produce the results that it did?

A) Lines 6–7 ("The pigment . . . Oxygen")

B) Lines 11–14 ("Instead of . . . breakthrough")

C) Lines 49-51 ("As a . . . efforts")

D) Lines 63–65 ("They continue . . . synthesize")

26

As used in line 21, "unstable" most nearly means

A) impermanent.

B) threatening.

C) careless.

D) antiquated.

27

According to the passage, researchers have identified which of the following factors as most indicative of stable pigments?

A) Toxic materials

B) Oxygenated indium

C) Extreme temperatures

D) High pressure

CONTINUE ➡

28

Based on the passage, which choice best describes the relationship between the new YInMn Blue pigment and the Cobalt Blue pigment currently used?

A) Cobalt Blue is superior for exterior conditions, while YInMn Blue is preferred for interior conditions.

B) YInMn Blue was specifically engineered to provide a color that can be chemically-adjusted for intensity, while Cobalt Blue was not.

C) YInMn Blue pigment is as hard to synthesize as purple pigment is, while Cobalt Blue is simpler.

D) Cobalt Blue has a lower UV absorbency and infrared reflectivity than does YInMn Blue.

29

Which choice provides the best evidence for the answer to the previous question?

A) Lines 20–22 ("Blue pigments . . . materials")

B) Lines 34–37 ("$YIn_{1-x}Mn_xO_3$ exhibits . . . pigments.")

C) Lines 41–45 ("They concluded . . . $(CoAl_2O_4)$")

D) Lines 56–58 ("The excitement . . . blues")

30

According to Figure 2, at which of the following wavelengths does $CoAl_2O_4$ have a reflectance of 0.4%?

A) 2400 nm

B) 1800 nm

C) 1200 nm

D) 600 nm

31

Based on information in the passage and the graph, which of the following ranges of wavelengths most clearly illustrates the thermal advantages of YInMn Blue over Cobalt Blue?

A) 200–400

B) 400–600

C) 800–1000

D) 1200–1400

CONTINUE

Questions 32–41 are based on the following passages.

Passage 1 is adapted from President Grover Cleveland's *1895 Annual Message to the Congress of the United States*. Passage 2 is adapted from William Jennings Bryan's speech at the 1896 Democratic National Convention. The Coinage Act of 1873 ended the United States' federal policy of accepting both gold- and silver-backed currency, establishing a gold monetary standard. This decision was a primary point of contention in the 1896 presidential race.

Passage 1

While I have endeavored to make a plain statement of the disordered condition of our currency and the present dangers menacing our prosperity and to
Line suggest a way which leads to a safer financial system, I
5 have constantly had in mind the fact that many of my countrymen, whose sincerity I do not doubt, insist that the cure for the ills now threatening us may be found in the single and simple remedy of the free coinage of silver. They contend that our mints shall be at once
10 thrown open to the free, unlimited, and independent coinage of both gold and silver dollars of full legal-tender quality, regardless of the action of any other government and in full view of the fact that the ratio between the metals which they suggest calls for 100
15 cents' worth of gold in the gold dollar at the present standard and only 50 cents in intrinsic worth of silver in the silver dollar.

Were there infinitely stronger reasons than can be adduced for hoping that such action would secure for
20 us a bimetallic currency moving on lines of parity, an experiment so novel and hazardous as that proposed might well stagger those who believe that stability is an imperative condition of sound money.

No government, no human contrivance or act of
25 legislation, has ever been able to hold the two metals together in free coinage at a ratio appreciably different from that which is established in the markets of the world.

Those who believe that our independent free
30 coinage of silver at an artificial ratio with gold of 16 to 1 would restore the parity between the metals, and consequently between the coins, oppose an unsupported and improbable theory to the general belief and practice of other nations; and to the
35 teaching of the wisest statesmen and economists of the world, both in the past and present, and, what is far more conclusive, they run counter to our own actual experiences.

Twice in our earlier history our lawmakers,
40 in attempting to establish a bimetallic currency, undertook free coinage upon a ratio which accidentally varied from the actual relative values of the two metals not more than 3 per cent. In both cases, notwithstanding greater difficulties and cost
45 of transportation than now exist, the coins whose intrinsic worth was undervalued in the ratio gradually and surely disappeared from our circulation and went to other countries where their real value was better recognized.

50 Acts of Congress were impotent to create equality where natural causes decreed even a slight inequality.

Passage 2

If they tell us that the gold standard is the standard of civilization, we reply to them that this, the most enlightened of all nations of the earth, has never
55 declared for a gold standard, and both the parties this year are declaring against it. If the gold standard is the standard of civilization, why, my friends, should we not have it? So if they come to meet us on that, we can present the history of our nation. More than that, we
60 can tell them this, that they will search the pages of history in vain to find a single instance in which the common people of any land ever declared themselves in favor of a gold standard. They can find where the holders of fixed investments have.

65 Mr. Carlisle said in 1878 that this was a struggle between the idle holders of idle capital and the struggling masses who produce the wealth and pay the taxes of the country; and my friends, it is simply a question that we shall decide upon which side the
70 Democratic Party shall fight. Upon the side of the idle holders of idle capital, or upon the side of the struggling masses? That is the question that the party must answer first; and then it must be answered by each individual hereafter. The sympathies of the
75 Democratic Party, as described by the platform, are on the side of the struggling masses, who have ever been the foundation of the Democratic Party.

There are two ideas of government. There are those who believe that if you just legislate to make the
80 well-to-do prosperous, that their prosperity will leak through on those below. The Democratic idea has been

CONTINUE ▶

that if you legislate to make the masses prosperous their prosperity will find its way up and through every class that rests upon it.

85   You come to us and tell us that the great cities are in favor of the gold standard. I tell you that the great cities rest upon these broad and fertile prairies. Burn down your cities and leave our farms, and your cities will spring up again as if by magic. But destroy our farms
90   and the grass will grow in the streets of every city in the country.

32

As used in line 3, "present" most nearly means

A) prompt.

B) current.

C) instant.

D) gifted.

33

What does Passage 1 suggest about the proponents of implementing a bimetallic system of currency?

A) They doubt the use of gold to back a currency in any situation.

B) They have an honest belief in the potential of their proposed solution.

C) They would rather Congress become impotent than submit to bimetallic currency.

D) They resent the great cities that are pushing the gold standard on the people of the prairies.

34

Which choice provides the best evidence for the answer to the previous question?

A) Lines 4–9 ("I have . . . silver")

B) Lines 9–13 ("They contend . . . government")

C) Lines 29–34 ("Those who . . . nations")

D) Lines 37–38 ("they run . . . experiences")

35

In the final sentence of Passage 1, the main purpose of Cleveland's reference to "Acts of Congress" is to

A) emphasize a disparity between government forces and market forces.

B) summarize Congress's argument for implementing the gold standard.

C) propose a natural alternative to the complex problem facing the nation.

D) assert that only the passage of a law could solve a seemingly intractable debate.

36

As used in line 66, "idle" most nearly means

A) abandoned.

B) ambitious.

C) inactive.

D) cheap.

37

Based on Passage 2, Bryan would be most likely to agree with which claim about the controversy over the gold standard?

A) It would only be settled if gold were the preferred standard of civilization.

B) It has consistently lacked support from large segments of society.

C) It motivated further investigation of the silver standard worldwide.

D) It could have been avoided if Congress had not listened to the prosperous.

CONTINUE

38

Which choice provides the best evidence for the answer to the previous question?

A) Lines 56–58 ("If the . . . it")

B) Lines 59–63 ("More than . . . standard")

C) Lines 74–77 ("The sympathies . . . Party")

D) Lines 78–81 ("There are . . . below")

39

Both passages discuss the issue of the gold standard in relationship to

A) Congress.

B) the Democratic Party.

C) economists.

D) other nations.

40

In the context of each passage as a whole, the historical references in line 39 of Passage 1 and line 65 of Passage 2 primarily function to help each speaker

A) establish that a debate has been ongoing.

B) cite established precedent to support a position.

C) challenge the gold standard status quo.

D) question whether progress has been made.

41

Which choice identifies a central tension between the two passages?

A) Cleveland advocates for new legislation to enact the gold standard, but Bryan questions the necessity of such a move without elite support.

B) Cleveland questions the validity of a proposed solution, but Bryan argues that the alternative is an even more unreasonable path forward.

C) Cleveland demands gold standard proponents reconsider their position, and Bryan defends the specifics of that position.

D) Cleveland presents studies in support of the gold standard, and Bryan asserts that the sources of the evidence are biased.

CONTINUE ➡

Questions 42–52 are based on the following passage.

This passage is adapted from "Zombie ant fungi 'know' brains of their hosts," originally published on August 22, 2014 by Chuck Gill, Penn State College of Agricultural Sciences.

Line
A parasitic fungus that reproduces by manipulating the behavior of ants emits a cocktail of behavior-controlling chemicals when encountering the brain
5 of its natural target host, but not when infecting other ant species, a new study shows. The findings, which suggest that the fungus "knows" its preferred host, provide new insights into the molecular mechanisms underlying this phenomenon, according to researchers.
10 "Fungi are well known for their ability to secrete chemicals that affect their environment," noted lead author Charissa de Bekker, a Marie Curie Fellow in Penn State's College of Agricultural Sciences, and Ludwig Maximilian of the University of Munich. "So we wanted to know what chemicals are employed to
15 control so precisely the behavior of ants."
The research focused on a species from the genus *Ophiocordyceps* — known as "zombie ant fungi" — which control their ant hosts by inducing a biting behavior. Although these fungi infect many insects,
20 the species that infect ants have evolved a mechanism that induces hosts to die attached by their mandibles to plant material, providing a platform from which the fungus can grow and shoot spores to infect other ants. To study this mechanism, the researchers combined
25 field research with a citizen-scientist in South Carolina, infection experiments under laboratory conditions, and analysis using metabolomics, which is the study of the chemical processes associated with the molecular products of metabolism. The scientists used a newly
30 discovered fungal species from North America—initially called *Ophiocordyceps unilateralis sensu lato* while it awaits a new name—that normally controls an ant species in the genus *Camponotus*. To test whether a species of fungus that has evolved to control the
35 behavior of one ant species can infect and control others, they infected nontarget hosts from the same ant genus and another genus (*Formica*).
They found that this obligate killer can infect and kill nontarget ants, but it cannot manipulate their
40 behavior. "The brain of the target species was the key to understanding manipulation," de Bekker said. The researchers next removed ant brains, keeping the organs alive in special media. The fungus then

was grown in the presence of brains from different
45 ant species to determine what chemicals it produced for each brain. "This was 'brain-in-a-jar' science at its best," said co-author David Hughes, assistant professor of entomology and biology, Penn State. "It was necessary to reduce the complexity associated
50 with the whole, living ant, and just ask what chemicals the fungus produces when it encounters the ant brain. "You don't get to see a lot of behavior with fungi," he said. "You have to infer what they are doing by examining how they grow, where they grow and most
55 important, what chemicals they secrete."
"We could see in the data that the fungus behaved differently in the presence of the ant brain it had co-evolved with," said de Bekker, whose Penn State co-authors also included Andrew Patterson, assistant
60 professor of molecular toxicology, and Phil Smith, director of the Metabolomics Core Facility. The researchers found thousands of unique chemicals, most of them completely unknown. This, according to Hughes, is not surprising, since little previous work has
65 mined these fungi for the chemicals they produce. But what did stand out were two known neuromodulators, guanobutyric acid (GBA) and sphingosine. These both have been reported to be involved in neurological disorders and were enriched when the fungus was
70 grown in the presence of brains of its target species. "There is no single compound that is produced that results in the exquisite control of ant behavior we observe," de Bekker said. "Rather, it is a mixture of different chemicals that we assume act in synergy. "But
75 whatever the precise blend and tempo of chemical secretion," she said, "it is impressive that these fungi seem to 'know' when they are beside the brain of their regular host and behave accordingly."
Noted Hughes, "This is one of the most complex
80 examples of parasites controlling animal behavior because it is a microbe controlling an animal—the one without the brain controls the one with the brain. By employing metabolomics and controlled laboratory infections, we can now begin to understand how the
85 fungi pull off this impressive trick." The research also is notable, the scientists contend, because it is the first extensive study of zombie ants in North America.

CONTINUE

42

The primary purpose of the passage is to

A) correct a misconception about the interactions between fungi and host organisms.

B) present the findings of a study that is one of the first of its kind.

C) detail a research study that discovered a new genus of ant.

D) explain the difference between a symbiotic relationship and a parasitic relationship.

43

According to the passage, which statement best explains why the fungi have evolved to control the behavior of the ants?

A) When the infected ant bites a non-infected ant, the fungus is able to spread and grow.

B) When an infected ant dies while biting a plant, the fungus can reproduce more easily.

C) When the infected ant dies on the ground, its corpse is an ideal breeding ground for the fungus.

D) There is no evolutionary benefit for the fungus to control the ant's behavior.

44

In line 37, the mention of the *Formica* genus primarily serves to

A) introduce another ant genus newly-discovered to be controlled by the fungus.

B) provide the scientific name of the ant genus most affected by the fungus.

C) present a new finding about a specific genus of fungus.

D) name a genus of ant that scientists tested to extend their research on the fungus.

45

The use of phrases such as "exquisite control" (line 72), "most complex examples" (lines 79–80), and "impressive trick" (line 85) in the passage communicate a tone that is

A) amused.

B) informative.

C) critical.

D) admiring.

46

Which choice describes a scenario in which the zombie ant fungi would NOT successfully reproduce?

A) Fungus spores infect both *Camponotus* and *Formica* ants.

B) An infected *Camponotus* ant attaches to a twig and dies.

C) A spore-releasing stalk grows from the head of a dead, infected *Camponotus* ant.

D) An infected *Formica* ant dies on a plant-free patch of soil.

47

As used in line 43, "media" most nearly means

A) communications.

B) material.

C) channels.

D) periodicals.

CONTINUE

48

Based on the passage, which part of the research process was the most effective for obtaining an unprecedented amount of information?

A) The researchers grew the fungus in the presence of isolated ant brains.

B) The researchers infected ants not normally targeted by the fungus.

C) The researchers removed the brains from the ants.

D) The researchers observed how the fungus behaved while in the ant brains.

49

Which choice provides the best evidence for the answer to the previous question?

A) Lines 29–33 ("The scientists . . . *Camponotus*")

B) Lines 43–46 ("The fungus . . . brain")

C) Lines 61–63 ("The researchers . . . unknown")

D) Lines 65–67 ("But what . . . sphingosine")

50

Based on the passage, a unique outcome of the chemicals produced by the fungus is

A) a reaction from the host organism that could only be reproduced in the lab.

B) a contagious infection that could not be controlled in the lab.

C) a parasitic relationship notably different from those usually found in nature.

D) a result that can be applied to neurological disorders in human patients.

51

Which choice provides the best evidence for the answer to the previous question?

A) Lines 16–19 ("The research . . . behavior")

B) Lines 38–40 ("They found . . . behavior")

C) Lines 56–58 ("We could . . . de Bekker")

D) Lines 79–82 ("This is . . . brain")

52

Based on the passage, in studying the zombie ants, the research team made the most extensive use of which type of evidence?

A) Observation of the interplay between the ant and the fungus in the natural world

B) Predictions based on research obtained from experiments with a different genus of ant

C) Chemical analysis of the brains of fungi

D) Data obtained from laboratory experiments designed to isolate particular factors

STOP
**If you finish before time is called, you may check your work on this section only.
Do not turn to any other section in the test.**

No Test Material On This Page

Writing and Language Test

35 MINUTES, 44 QUESTIONS

Turn to Section 2 of your answer sheet to answer the questions in this section.

DIRECTIONS

Each passage below is accompanied by a number of questions. For some questions, you will consider how the passage might be revised to improve the expression of ideas. For other questions, you will consider how the passage might be edited to correct errors in sentence structure, usage, or punctuation. A passage or a question may be accompanied by one or more graphics (such as a table or graph) that you will consider as you make revising and editing decisions.

Some questions will direct you to an underlined portion of a passage. Other questions will direct you to a location in a passage or ask you to think about the passage as a whole.

After reading each passage, choose the answer to each question that most effectively improves the quality of writing in the passage or that makes the passage conform to the conventions of standard written English. Many questions include a "NO CHANGE" option. Choose that option if you think the best choice is to leave the relevant portion of the passage as it is.

Questions 1–11 are based on the following passage and supplementary material.

Fast Fashion Slows Down

    In most US cities, the presence of blue recycling bins alongside the ubiquitous black trash bins is no longer **1** an innovation. Most people are used to separating recyclable materials from their landfill-bound trash, even in public waste bins. In many cities composting is even becoming a standard third component of waste separation, but one area that is just **2** kicking off is textile recycling.

1

A) NO CHANGE

B) a deviation.

C) a novelty.

D) a miracle.

2

Which choice best maintains the style and tone of the passage?

A) NO CHANGE

B) fixing to start

C) getting in gear

D) gaining traction

CONTINUE ➡

A few cities have begun to collect textiles as part of their curbside recycling programs, along with the more customary cardboard and glass, but such programs generally require specially-designed multi-compartment recycling **3** trucks—(which most cities don't have). Many areas that don't have curbside textile recycling instead have designated drop-off bins where residents can recycle unwanted clothing and other household textiles, such as sheets and towels.

Textile recycling is in its infancy, but it has the potential to make a big impact. The average American discards 70 pounds of **4** clothing each year, only 15% of which is recycled. Of the most commonly recycled materials, only **5** rubber and leather are recycled at a higher rate than is clothing. Not only can cities save on trash pick-up and disposal costs by encouraging their

3

A) NO CHANGE
B) trucks which
C) trucks—which
D) trucks (which

4

The writer wants to include information from the graph that is consistent with the description of textiles in the passage. Which choice most effectively accomplishes this goal?

A) NO CHANGE
B) paper each year, only 45%
C) rubber and leather each year, only 15%
D) wood each year, only 9%

5

The writer wants to support the paragraph's main idea with accurate, relevant information from the graph. Which choice most effectively accomplishes this goal?

A) NO CHANGE
B) plastic and wood are recycled at a lower
C) yard trimmings are recycled at a higher
D) glass is recycled at a higher

CONTINUE

residents to recycle unwanted textiles, ▮6▮ and re-using clothing can also save resources by reducing the amount of new clothing that needs to be manufactured.

▮7▮ For example, producing enough virgin cotton for one pair of jeans requires 1,800 gallons of water; buying a pair of jeans second-hand saves that water.

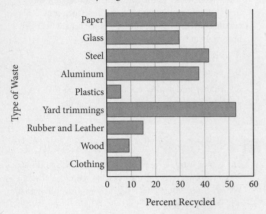

Estimated Recycling Rates in the United States

So-called "fast fashion" chains that produce trendy, low-cost (and, according to critics, low-quality) clothing, are often singled out as one of the primary causes of the increase in clothing waste in the U.S. in recent decades. But at least one such chain, the Swedish retailer H&M, is also trying to ▮8▮ rain in, clothing waste by offering 15% off coupons to consumers who bring unwanted clothing, of any brand, to their stores for recycling. Since the program began in 2013, H&M has collected over 44,000 tons of clothing to recycle. The company's goal is to eventually collect 25,000 tons of clothing for recycling each year.

▮6▮

A) NO CHANGE

B) yet

C) but

D) for

▮7▮

A) NO CHANGE

B) Surprisingly,

C) However,

D) Moreover,

▮8▮

A) NO CHANGE

B) rain in

C) rein in,

D) rein in

CONTINUE ➤

9 Hopefully other retailers will institute similar programs. The first step is reuse: any items still in useable condition are sold second-hand. Non-useable items are shredded for use as insulation, **10** they are repurposed as cleaning rags, or recycled to make fabric for new clothing.

The technology for recycling textile fibers into new fabrics **11** are currently limited, however. The ultimate goal of H&M and other environmentally-conscious retailers is to establish a "closed loop" manufacturing system, in which 100% of the fibers they use to create their clothing can be recycled into new clothing. This may seem like a lofty goal, but it is worth pursuing.

9

Which choice provides the most effective transition from the previous paragraph?

A) NO CHANGE

B) Recycling that quantity of clothing is done in several steps.

C) Low-quality fast fashion should make that goal easily attainable.

D) Offering a bigger discount might help H&M meet its goal.

10

A) NO CHANGE

B) repurposed as cleaning cloths,

C) cleaning cloths are repurposed,

D) alternatively they are repurposed as cleaning cloths,

11

A) NO CHANGE

B) is

C) were

D) have been

CONTINUE

Questions 12–22 are based on the following passage.

Celebrating Death

At dusk on the night of November 1, Lake Pátzcuaro in the southern Mexican state of Michoacán begins to glow as residents float across the lake in candlelit boats. The people are going to the island of Janitzio for an all-night vigil at the cemeteries where [12] its loved ones are buried. This vigil is the culmination of the Day of the Dead celebrations that begin with the construction of [13] *ofrendas. Ofrendas* are altars that honor the dead. The festivities begin in early October, when towns host markets [14] dedicated to the bright skeleton decorations and colorful flowers used to adorn the altars.

[1] The origins of the Mexican Day of the Dead tradition date back nearly 3,000 years to pre-Columbian times, when dead ancestors were celebrated in rituals that lasted for an entire month in the late summer of the Aztec calendar. [2] After Europeans brought Catholicism to North America, the Aztec rituals were combined with the Christian tradition of All Souls Day and moved to November 1–2. [3] During these two days, the spirits of the dead are believed to come back to the land of the living to visit their families. [4] The Aztec tradition was that the dead would be offended by mourning, [15] but it's sad when family members die. [5] The *ofrendas* that help to

12

A) NO CHANGE
B) it's
C) they're
D) their

13

Which choice most effectively combines the sentences at the underlined portion?

A) *ofrendas*, in Spanish; those are
B) *ofrendas*; the Spanish word *ofrendas* means
C) *ofrendas*,
D) *ofrendas*; moreover, *ofrendas* are

14

A) NO CHANGE
B) dedicated, to the bright skeleton decorations,
C) dedicated to the bright, skeleton, decorations,
D) dedicated to the bright skeleton decorations—

15

Which choice most effectively completes the explanation of the Aztec tradition?

A) NO CHANGE
B) so they are remembered in a spirit of celebration rather than sadness.
C) though it can be difficult to tell whether an invisible spirit is offended.
D) and the Aztec didn't want to disrespect the wishes of the dead.

CONTINUE ➡

celebrate the dead often have items similar to **16** those found on church altars, such as candles and pictures. **17**

Many Day of the Dead altars are built in private homes, but they can also be found in cemeteries, at churches, in government buildings, and in public squares. Some public altars are meant to call attention to a specific cause. Others are built by local artists, **18** of which many are best known for their elaborate *ofrendas*.

For many families, preparing an *ofrenda* is similar to preparing for a visit from living relatives. The bright colors and fragrance of marigolds are said to lead spirits back to their families. Altars are loaded with food and drink **19** (which smell delicious) and sometimes include pillows and blankets (which provide a resting spot for the spirits). Some families put personal items that belonged to the deceased on the altars, and altars dedicated to children

16

A) NO CHANGE
B) church altars,
C) churches and altars,
D) the structures of church altars,

17

To make this paragraph most logical, sentence 3 should be placed
A) where it is now.
B) before sentence 1.
C) before sentence 2.
D) before sentence 5.

18

A) NO CHANGE
B) many
C) many of whom
D) many of them

19

Which choice provides information that is most consistent in style and content with the information about why pillows and blankets are included on the altars?
A) NO CHANGE
B) (including *pan de muerto*)
C) (which are often homemade)
D) (which provide sustenance for the travelling spirits)

CONTINUE ➤

often include toys. [20] It's more work to provide food for living relatives than for dead ones.

Many of the same items that decorate altars are also part of the cemetery vigils on Janitzio. Graves are covered with candles and [21] marigolds, and families bring ample picnics to sustain both themselves and the spirits of the departed through the night. Living family members spend the night eating, drinking, singing, and telling stories. Rather than focusing on the finality of death, [22] the people's merriment celebrates life.

20

Which choice most effectively concludes the paragraph?

A) NO CHANGE

B) Regardless of what specifically is included on an altar, the dead are always welcomed home, just as they were when they were alive.

C) The toys for children can be new or old.

D) Some altars include religious items such as crucifixes and images of saints.

21

A) NO CHANGE

B) marigolds just as altars are,

C) marigolds like those that also decorate altars,

D) marigolds that attract spirits with their bright colors,

22

A) NO CHANGE

B) life is celebrated by the people through their merriment.

C) the merriment of the people celebrates life.

D) the people celebrate life through their merriment.

CONTINUE ▶

Questions 23–33 are based on the following passage and supplementary material.

Bank Tellers: Machine v. Human

When automated teller machines (ATMs) were first installed in the 1970s, there were widespread predictions that the machines would replace human bank tellers. Such predictions did not immediately come true, however. **23** In fact, throughout the 1990s, as the number of ATMs increased most quickly, the number of human bank tellers also increased.

[1] While many simple bank transactions now happen at ATMs, people still rely on human tellers to cash **24** checks, transfer money between accounts; provide specific bill denominations, and dispense information about bank products and services. [2] Some of these duties, particularly the marketing aspect of advising customers about bank services, have changed with the advent of ATMs. [3] They also limit the amount of cash a customer can get in a single day, place restrictions on how soon funds from deposits are available, and generally don't offer much choice in currency denominations. [4] Before the rise of banking machines, tellers were primarily responsible for handling cash, but machines have proven to be faster and **25** more rock solid with cash than people are.

23
A) NO CHANGE
B) As a result,
C) For example,
D) Therefore,

24
A) NO CHANGE
B) checks; transfer money between accounts;
C) checks; transfer money between accounts,
D) checks, transfer money between accounts,

25
Which choice best fits with the tone of the rest of the passage?
A) NO CHANGE
B) more impeccable
C) more reliable
D) safer

CONTINUE

26 [5] On the other hand, ATMs are far more vulnerable to theft. **27**

26

At this point, the writer is considering adding the following graph.

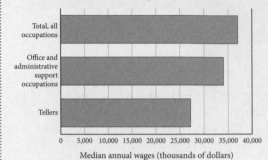

Annual Wage Comparison:
Tellers versus Other Occupations
Median annual wages, May 2016

Median annual wages (thousands of dollars)

Note: All Occupations includes all occupations in the U.S. Economy.
Source: U.S. Bureau of Labor Statistics, Occupational Employment Statistics

Should the writer make this addition here?

A) Yes, because it provides evidence that supports the idea that the number of bank tellers is rising.

B) Yes, because it effectively contradicts the idea that ATMs are faster at counting money than people are.

C) No, because it does not make a comparison between wages for tellers and those for loan officers.

D) No, because it gives information that distracts from the paragraph's focus on the duties performed by tellers.

27

To make this paragraph most logical, sentence 3 should be placed

A) where it is now.

B) after sentence 1.

C) after sentence 4.

D) after sentence 5.

CONTINUE ▶

With the rise of tech-savvy customers who are increasingly [28] custom to using their smartphones in all aspects of life, mobile banking apps are the latest mechanized challenge to the need for human bank tellers. Apps are also beginning to improve upon some banking functions that had largely been taken over by ATMs. Mobile apps [29] are used consistently by only about 50% of smartphone owners. Apps also usually offer less waiting time before funds from a check deposit are available for use, but they cannot handle cash. That doesn't mean there's a need for human tellers, [30] though. Without a teller, customers can still go to a traditional ATM to deposit or withdraw cash.

28

A) NO CHANGE
B) accustomed for
C) accustomed to
D) custom at

29

Which choice provides the best supporting example for the main idea of the paragraph?

A) NO CHANGE
B) can quickly and easily perform the more complex balance inquiries and transfers that not all ATMs are capable of.
C) are not always designed well, though user ratings through an app store can help consumers decide which one is best.
D) are also highly susceptible to theft or fraud, particularly when they are used over public Wi-Fi networks.

30

Which choice most effectively combines the sentences at the underlined portion?

A) though: customers
B) though, because it's true that customers
C) though, without them customers
D) though; it's the case that customers

CONTINUE

Physical banks have begun to respond to the rising popularity of mobile banking by replacing their old-fashioned teller windows [31] with an automated kiosk that combine all the functions of both mobile banking apps and ATMs.

Such kiosks are not replacing ATMs, nor are they replacing humans altogether. What they are doing is changing, again, the job description of human bank employees. Todd Barnhart, head of branch distribution for PNC bank, stresses the continued need for humans in bank branches. Employees are now trained to answer questions about how to use mobile apps, [32] as well as trained to handle deposits and provide loan advice. "We're not building branches with teller lines but with places where customers and employees can have meaningful conversations," he said. So while the old-fashioned notion of a bank teller may be on the way [33] out, machines are not yet close to replacing human bank employees altogether.

31
A) NO CHANGE
B) to an automated kiosk
C) each for automated kiosks
D) with automated kiosks

32
A) NO CHANGE
B) as well as handle
C) also to answer questions about
D) and in addition to handle

33
A) NO CHANGE
B) out; machines
C) out. Machines
D) out, nevertheless machines

CONTINUE ➤

Questions 34–44 are based on the following passage.

Bacteria in Space

Ever since antibiotics began to be widely used in the 1940s, scientists have been engaged in an arms race against bacteria. Bacteria continue to evolve and develop resistance to antibiotics; 34 as a result, scientists must continually develop newer, stronger antibiotics to overcome the resistant bacteria. Since scientists generally want to 35 count the number of bacteria mutations, it may seem strange that they would intentionally make bacteria more aggressive, but researchers from Arizona State University (ASU) are doing just that by sending some strains of bacteria to the International Space Station to be studied.

NASA scientists first began studying bacteria and other pathogens in space because they wanted to keep astronauts healthy. Extended trips to space 36 that last a long time have long been understood to weaken astronauts' immune systems, so studies were designed to determine whether pathogens, including bacteria, are similarly affected by microgravity. Scientists were surprised

34
A) NO CHANGE
B) however,
C) nevertheless,
D) for example,

35
Which choice most effectively establishes scientists' goal, related to information presented earlier in the paragraph?
A) NO CHANGE
B) facilitate
C) stay ahead of
D) shoot at

36
A) NO CHANGE
B) that are extensive
C) continuing for many weeks
D) DELETE the underlined portion.

CONTINUE

to find that pathogens of any kind 37 mutated more rapidly and became more virulent in space. A team led by Cheryl Nickerson of the Biodesign Institute at ASU 38 speculated that microgravity would cause a fluid shear stress reduction (the friction between cells and the fluids they interact with). Fluid shear stress affects gene expression in pathogens, and reducing it allows mutations to occur more quickly. The ASU scientists believe that microgravity mimics the reduced fluid shear stress conditions that bacteria encounter inside the human body 39 .

Although pathogen studies in space were initially intended just to help protect astronauts' health during flight, the implications of these 40 subjects now have a much broader application. Scientists are looking more closely at the specific mechanics of various pathogens'

37

A) NO CHANGE
B) had mutated more rapidly and had become
C) mutates more rapidly and becomes
D) mutate more rapidly and becomes

38

A) NO CHANGE
B) thought that fluid shear stress would be reduced by microgravity
C) speculated that microgravity reduces fluid shear stress
D) believed that microgravity lessens the shear stress caused by fluid

39

At this point, the writer is considering adding the following.

so that studying something like *Salmonella* in space allows, in effect, a glimpse into how that pathogen behaves in the human digestive tract

Should the writer make this addition here?

A) Yes, because it makes clear that researchers cannot actually see inside the human digestive tract.
B) Yes, because it further explains the benefits of conducting bacteria studies in space.
C) No, because it repeats information stated earlier in the paragraph.
D) No, because it is not relevant to the discussion of what fluid shear stress is.

40

Which choice provides the most precise description of the proceeding depicted in the first part of the sentence?

A) NO CHANGE
B) examinations
C) experiments
D) tests

CONTINUE

mutations so that they **41** could have developed treatments, especially vaccines, that attack those changes. Nickerson and her team are working on developing a vaccine for *Salmonella*. The virus is one of the leading **42** causes of food-borne illness, in the United States and one of the leading causes of infant mortality worldwide, so an effective vaccine has the potential to have a major impact on public health.

43 *Salmonella* is already playing an important role in vaccine research, though in an unexpected way. A promising new vaccine technology, recombinant attenuated *Salmonella* vaccine (RASV), uses a genetically modified form of *Salmonella* as a delivery vehicle. RASVs quickly and efficiently deliver **44** antigens, substances, that stimulate the production of antibodies to multiple body systems with just a single dose, and can be taken orally, eliminating the need for more expensive vaccine shots. Such a vaccine already exists for *Streptococcus pneumonia*, the bacterium responsible for pneumonia and meningitis among other things. Next up on the researchers' list: an RASV to guard against *Salmonella* itself.

41

A) NO CHANGE
B) can develop
C) were developing
D) developed

42

A) NO CHANGE
B) causes of food-borne illness in the United States
C) causes, of food-borne illness in the United States
D) causes of food-borne illness, in the United States,

43

Which choice provides the most effective transition between ideas in the paragraph?

A) NO CHANGE
B) Such a vaccine hasn't yet been developed for *Salmonella*, however.
C) Researchers would also like to be able to develop better vaccines against a number of other particularly nasty bacteria.
D) This potential positive impact is part of the reason the *Salmonella* studies have expanded beyond the International Space Station.

44

A) NO CHANGE
B) antigens, substances that stimulate the production of antibodies, to multiple body systems
C) antigens, substances that stimulate the production of antibodies to multiple body systems,
D) antigens substances that stimulate the production of antibodies to multiple body systems

STOP
If you finish before time is called, you may check your work on this section only.
Do not turn to any other section in the test.

Math Test – No Calculator

25 MINUTES, 20 QUESTIONS

Turn to Section 3 of your answer sheet to answer the questions in this section.

DIRECTIONS

For questions 1–15, solve each problem, choose the best answer from the choices provided, and fill in the corresponding circle on your answer sheet. **For questions 16–20,** solve the problem and enter your answer in the grid on the answer sheet. Please refer to the directions before question 16 on how to enter your answers in the grid. You may use any available space in your test booklet for scratch work.

NOTES

1. The use of a calculator **is not permitted**.
2. All variables and expressions used represent real numbers unless otherwise indicated.
3. Figures provided in this test are drawn to scale unless otherwise indicated.
4. All figures lie in a plane unless otherwise indicated.
5. Unless otherwise indicated, the domain of a given function f is the set of all real numbers x for which $f(x)$ is a real number.

REFERENCE

$A = \pi r^2$
$C = 2\pi r$

$A = \ell w$

$A = \frac{1}{2} bh$

$c^2 = a^2 + b^2$

Special Right Triangles

$V = \ell wh$

$V = \pi r^2 h$

$V = \frac{4}{3}\pi r^3$

$V = \frac{1}{3}\pi r^2 h$

$V = \frac{1}{3}\ell wh$

The number of degrees of arc in a circle is 360.
The number of radians of arc in a circle is 2π.
The sum of the measures in degrees of the angles of a triangle is 180.

CONTINUE ➡

1

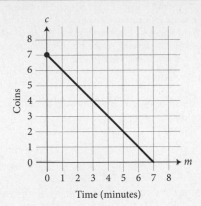

Time (minutes)

In a certain game, players start with a certain number of coins and then spend their coins. The graph above shows the number of coins, c, possessed by Erica at m minutes. Which of the following equations correctly relates c and m ?

A) $c = -\dfrac{1}{7}m$

B) $c = -m$

C) $c = -m + 7$

D) $c = -7m + 7$

2

$$\frac{2A + B + 2C}{5} = D$$

Based on the number of pages of algebra homework, A, biology homework, B, and chemistry homework, C, she is assigned, Katerina uses the above formula to determine the amount of time, D, in hours, she spends per page of homework assigned by her teachers. Which of the following correctly gives B in terms of A, C, and D ?

A) $B = \dfrac{2A + 2C - D}{5}$

B) $B = \dfrac{D - 2A - 2C}{5}$

C) $B = 2A + 2C - 5D$

D) $B = 5D - 2A - 2C$

3

$$a + a - 9 = 4a + a + a + a - 3 - 1$$

In the equation above, what is the value of a ?

A) -1

B) $\dfrac{9}{4}$

C) $\dfrac{13}{5}$

D) 5

CONTINUE

4

$$3y < 7$$
$$x < 3y + 4$$

Which of the following consists of the x-coordinates of all the points that satisfy the system of inequalities above?

A) $x < \dfrac{7}{3}$

B) $x < 3$

C) $x < \dfrac{19}{3}$

D) $x < 11$

5

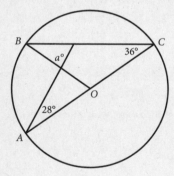

In the figure above, O is the center of the circle. What is the value of a ?

A) 100

B) 80

C) 72

D) 64

6

A traffic island is shaped like an isosceles triangle. The equal sides each have a length of s meters, and the third side is 4 meters shorter than the equal sides. Which of the following represents the perimeter, in meters, of the traffic island in terms of s ?

A) $2s - 4$

B) $\dfrac{s^2 - 4s}{2}$

C) $3s - 4$

D) $\dfrac{s - 4}{2}$

7

Point A has coordinates $(-11, 1)$, point B has coordinates $(-11, 7)$, and $\overline{AB}$ is the diameter of a circle. What is the equation of that circle?

A) $(x - 11)^2 + (y + 4)^2 = 9$

B) $(x + 11)^2 + (y - 1)^2 = 36$

C) $(x - 11)^2 + (y - 7)^2 = 36$

D) $(x + 11)^2 + (y - 4)^2 = 9$

8

$$a - 6 = \sqrt{8a - 7} - 4$$

What is the solution set of the equation above?

A) $\{0\}$

B) $\{1\}$

C) $\{11\}$

D) $\{1, 11\}$

CONTINUE

9

$$h(a) = a^2 + a - 20$$
$$k(a) = a^3 - 16a$$

Which of the following is equal to $\dfrac{h(a)}{k(a)}$, for $a > 4$?

A) $\dfrac{a+5}{a(a+4)}$

B) $\dfrac{a+5}{a(a-4)}$

C) $\dfrac{a+5}{a+4}$

D) $a+5$

10

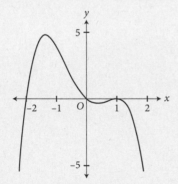

Which of the following could be the equation of the graph above?

A) $y = -x(x-1)(x+2)$

B) $y = -x(x+1)(x-2)$

C) $y = -x(x-1)^2(x+2)$

D) $y = -x(x+1)^2(x-2)$

11

If $\dfrac{x}{3y} = 3$, what is the value of $\dfrac{y}{x}$?

A) $\dfrac{1}{9}$

B) $\dfrac{1}{3}$

C) 3

D) 9

12

Taylor's garden produced 296 tomatoes, and he is preserving all the tomatoes in jars that hold either 3 or 5 tomatoes each. Taylor has a total of 80 jars. If he uses all the jars and preserves all the tomatoes, exactly how many of the jars hold 3 tomatoes?

A) 50

B) 52

C) 54

D) 56

13

$$f(x) = 2 - [g(x)]^2$$
$$g(x) = 3x - 3$$

The functions f and g are defined above. Which of the following is the value of $f(0)$?

A) -7

B) -3

C) 2

D) 11

CONTINUE ➡

14

The population of Bulgaria was approximately 9 million people in 1989. Bulgaria's population decreased to 7.4 million people in 2011. If the decrease in population was linear, which of the following linear functions P best models the population of Bulgaria, in millions of people x years after the year 1989?

A) $P(x) = -\dfrac{74}{220}x + 9$

B) $P(x) = -\dfrac{16}{220}x + 9$

C) $P(x) = \dfrac{16}{220}x + 9$

D) $P(x) = \dfrac{74}{220}x + 9$

15

$$y = x^2 + 2x + k$$
$$y = 2x$$

If the system of equations above has exactly one real solution, which of the following is the value of k ?

A) -4

B) 0

C) 2

D) 4

CONTINUE

3   3

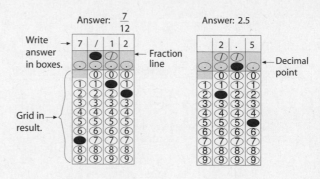

DIRECTIONS

For questions 16–20, solve the problem and enter your answer in the grid, as described below, on the answer sheet.

1. Although not required, it is suggested that you write your answer in the boxes at the top of the columns to help you fill in the circles accurately. You will receive credit only if the circles are filled in correctly.

2. Mark no more than one circle in any column.

3. No question has a negative answer.

4. Some problems may have more than one correct answer. In such cases, grid only one answer.

5. **Mixed numbers** such as $3\frac{1}{2}$ must be gridded as 3.5 or 7/2. (If is entered into the grid, it will be interpreted as $\frac{31}{2}$, not as $3\frac{1}{2}$.)

6. **Decimal Answers:** If you obtain a decimal answer with more digits than the grid can accommodate, it may be either rounded or truncated, but it must fill the entire grid.

Acceptable ways to grid $\frac{2}{3}$ are:

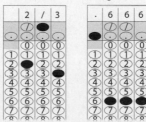

Answer: 201 – either position is correct

NOTE: You may start your answers in any column, space permitting. Columns you don't need to use should be left blank.

CONTINUE ➡

16

When $a^2 + 2a + 4$ is subtracted from $3a^2 - 4a + 27$, the result can be written in the form $xa^2 + ya + z$, where x, y, and z are constants. What is the value of $y + z$?

17

$$n^2 - n - 30 = 0$$

What is the positive solution to the equation above?

18

A student is modeling the number of assignments she has completed in a semester. She models the number of completed assignments by writing an equation in the form $y = mx + b$, where y is the number of assignments she has completed and x is the number of weeks since the start of the month. If at the start of the month she has completed 12 assignments and she completes 3 assignments per week, what is the value of m?

CONTINUE

19

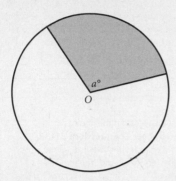

Note: Figure not drawn to scale.

In the figure above, O is the center of the circle and $a = 110$. If the area of the circle is 72, what is the area of the shaded region?

20

$$9x + 2y = 17.75$$
$$x + 2y = 3.75$$

If (x, y) is the solution to the system of equations above, what is the value of x?

STOP
If you finish before time is called, you may check your work on this section only.
Do not turn to any other section in the test.

Math Test – Calculator

55 MINUTES, 38 QUESTIONS

Turn to Section 4 of your answer sheet to answer the questions in this section.

DIRECTIONS

For questions 1–30, solve each problem, choose the best answer from the choices provided, and fill in the corresponding circle on your answer sheet. **For questions 31–38**, solve the problem and enter your answer in the grid on the answer sheet. Please refer to the directions before question 31 on how to enter your answers in the grid. You may use any available space in your test booklet for scratch work.

NOTES

1. The use of a calculator **is permitted**.
2. All variables and expressions used represent real numbers unless otherwise indicated.
3. Figures provided in this test are drawn to scale unless otherwise indicated.
4. All figures lie in a plane unless otherwise indicated.
5. Unless otherwise indicated, the domain of a given function f is the set of all real numbers x for which $f(x)$ is a real number.

REFERENCE

$A = \pi r^2$
$C = 2\pi r$

$A = \ell w$

$A = \frac{1}{2}bh$

$c^2 = a^2 + b^2$

Special Right Triangles

$V = \ell wh$

$V = \pi r^2 h$

$V = \frac{4}{3}\pi r^3$

$V = \frac{1}{3}\pi r^2 h$

$V = \frac{1}{3}\ell wh$

The number of degrees of arc in a circle is 360.
The number of radians of arc in a circle is 2π.
The sum of the measures in degrees of the angles of a triangle is 180.

CONTINUE ▶

1

The figure below shows the total number of tenants living in an apartment building between January 1st of 2005 and January 1st of 2010.

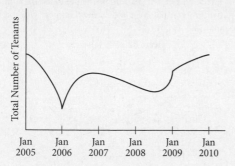

During which of the following years of operation does the number of tenants in the building increase the fastest?

A) 2005

B) 2006

C) 2007

D) 2009

2

A doctor randomly selects 500 residents of an island and finds that 4 of these residents have a specific gene mutation. Based on these results, approximately how many of the island's 15,000 residents likely have this mutation?

A)   75

B)   90

C)   105

D)   120

3

Chris buys one box of cookies for n dollars. At this rate, how much does he pay, in dollars, for 4 boxes of cookies?

A) $\dfrac{n}{4}$

B) $\dfrac{4}{n}$

C) $4n$

D) $n + 4$

4

In the figure above, lines l_1 and l_2 are parallel and $a = 110$. What is the value of b ?

A)   40

B)   70

C)   80

D)   140

CONTINUE

5

A newspaper sells both paper and digital subscriptions. The newspaper reports that 1,800 total subscriptions were sold last month and the total revenue from those subscription sales was $20,760. The digital subscriptions, d, cost $8 a month, and the paper subscriptions, p, cost $20 a month. Which of the following systems of equations could be used to solve for the number of each type of subscription that was sold by the newspaper last month?

A) $d + p = 1,800$
   $20d + 8p = 20,760$

B) $d + p = 1,800$
   $8d + 20p = 20,760$

C) $d + p = 20,760$
   $8d + 20p = 1,800$

D) $d + p = 1,800$
   $8d (20p) = 20,760$

6

A study tracked the maximum heart rate for runners competing in a marathon. The data and line of best fit are shown in the scatterplot below. Based on the line of best fit, what would be the predicted maximum heart rate of a 60-year-old runner competing in the marathon?

Heart Rates of Runners

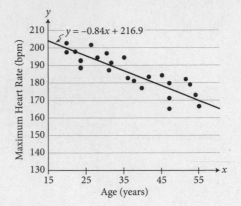

A) 166.5

B) 170.7

C) 183.4

D) 216.9

7

$$\frac{3}{c - 2} = c - 2$$

Which of the following values of $c - 2$ satisfies the equation above?

A) 5

B) 3

C) $\sqrt{3}$

D) $\sqrt{3} - 2$

CONTINUE

8

Which of the following equations, when graphed in the xy-plane, results in a line with a y-intercept of -1 ?

A) $y = x - \dfrac{1}{2}$

B) $y = \dfrac{1}{2}x - 1$

C) $y = -x$

D) $y = 2x + 1$

9

Sarah works at an art school and is purchasing canvases for \$6 each and bottles of paint for \$4 each. She budgets a total of \$1,700 for canvases and paint. She goes over-budget, but purchases more than 360 items. Which of the following systems of inequalities represents all the possible values for the number of canvases, a, and the number of paint bottles, b, that she buys?

A) $6a + 4b < 1,700$
   $a + b > 360$

B) $6a + 4b < 1,700$
   $a + b < 360$

C) $6a + 4b > 1,700$
   $a + b < 360$

D) $6a + 4b > 1,700$
   $a + b > 360$

Questions 10–12 refer to the following information.

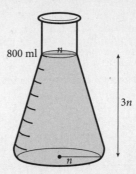

A beaker that can be filled to a maximum volume of 800 milliliters is shown above. For safety reasons, it cannot be filled above the 800-milliliter line. The radius of the base is equal to the diameter of the top, and the volume in cubic inches of the beaker is given by the equation $V = \dfrac{21\pi n^3}{12}$.

10

How many beakers of this size, filled to the 800-milliliter line, would be needed to hold 4 liters of a solution? (1 liter = 1000 mL)

A) 2

B) 4

C) 5

D) 8

CONTINUE

11

Given that the volume of 800 milliliters of liquid is approximately 13.2 cubic inches, which of the following is closest to the radius of the base of the beaker?

A) 1.34 inches

B) 2.28 inches

C) 4.23 inches

D) 8.04 inches

12

The beaker is filled with a solution to the 800-milliliter line and then left outside in the sun where the solution evaporates at a constant rate. The graph of the height of the solution remaining in the beaker over time would have which of the following shapes?

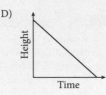

13

The amount of work done to move an object is equal to the product of the mass of the object, in kilograms; the distance the object moves, in meters; and the gravitational constant of 9.8 meters per second squared. What is the power rating of a machine that can move a 100-kilogram object 3.6 meters in 18 seconds? (Power is work per unit time.)

A) 196

B) 54

C) 19.6

D) 5.4

14

If $y = \dfrac{1}{x^3}$, which of the following gives x in terms of y?

A) $y^{\frac{1}{3}}$

B) $y^{-\frac{1}{3}}$

C) $-y^3$

D) y^3

CONTINUE

15

The function $f(x) = \dfrac{5}{x^2 - 5x + 4}$ is graphed in the xy-plane. Which of the following values of x is NOT in the domain of $f(x)$?

A) −1

B) 0

C) 1

D) 5

16

Number of Eggs Laid by Chickens

Number of Eggs	8	7	6	5	4	2
Frequency	1	3	8	5	2	5

A farmer has 24 chickens. At the end of a week he counts the total number of eggs each chicken laid that week. The table above shows the distribution of the number of eggs laid by the chickens. Which of the following statements about the mean, median, and mode of the number of eggs laid is true?

A) The mean is greater than both the mode and the median.

B) The mean is less than both the mode and the median.

C) The mean is greater than the mode but less than the median.

D) The mean is equal to both the mode and the median.

17

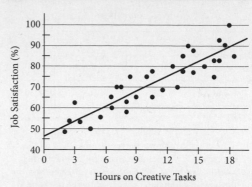

A Human Resources department seeking to increase employee retention commissioned a study to determine the relationship between job tasks and employee satisfaction. The scatterplot above shows the relationship for employees in a particular field between the number of work hours spent on creative tasks per week and their overall job satisfaction. The line of best fit is shown on the figure.

An employee that works in the same field but was not part of the study indicates that he spends 12 hours a week on creative tasks. Which of the following is the best approximation of his predicted job satisfaction based on the line of best fit?

A) 68%

B) 75%

C) 80%

D) 84%

CONTINUE ➡

18

Effectiveness of Ad Campaign

	Favorable	Not Favorable	Total
New Ad	120	130	250
Previous Ad	85	165	250
Total	205	295	500

The table above shows the results of a study on the effectiveness of a new ad campaign. In a randomly selected sample of 500 participants, 250 were shown the new ad campaign for a car while the rest were shown the previous ad campaign. The participants then reported whether their opinion of the car was favorable or not. What proportion of participants who watched the new ad campaign had a favorable opinion?

A) $\dfrac{12}{25}$

B) $\dfrac{41}{100}$

C) $\dfrac{6}{25}$

D) $\dfrac{24}{41}$

Questions 19 and 20 refer to the following information.

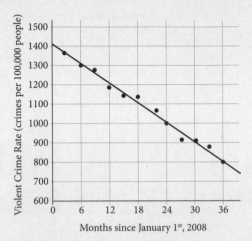

Months since January 1st, 2008

On January 1st, 2008, a city implemented a new program to combat crime. The graph above shows the violent crime rate in the city, measured in violent crimes per 100,000 residents, from January 1st, 2008, to the end of 2010. The line of best fit has the equation $y = 1{,}412 - 16.8x$, where y is the violent crime rate and x is the number of months since the implementation of the program.

19

Which of the following is closest to the percent decrease in the violent crime rate in the city from January 1st, 2010, to January 1st, 2011?

A)   8%

B)   20%

C)   80%

D)   140%

CONTINUE

20

What does the coefficient 16.8 represent in the line of best fit equation?

A) The number of months since the crime reduction program was implemented

B) The average crime rate per month since January 2008

C) The average monthly reduction in the violent crime rate during the first three years that the crime reduction program was in place

D) The violent crime rate in January 2008

▲

21

Samuel's annual salary is $49,500. If he completes an MBA program with a tuition of $73,320, his annual salary will be $64,500. If n represents the number of years that Samuel works at his job after completing his MBA, which of the following inequalities demonstrates the value of n for which his total additional income exceeds the cost of the tuition?

A) $n > \dfrac{73,320}{(64,500 - 49,500)}$

B) $n < \dfrac{73,320}{(64,500 - 49,500)}$

C) $n > \dfrac{(73,320 - 49,500)}{64,500}$

D) $n < \dfrac{(73,320 - 49,500)}{64,500}$

22

Polynomial function g is graphed in the xy-plane. This function has zeroes at -4 and 2, and its range is the set of all real numbers such that $g(x) \geq -3$. Which of the following graphs represents function g?

A)

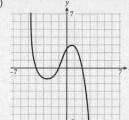

B)
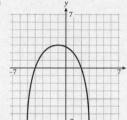

C)
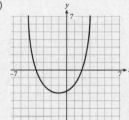

D)
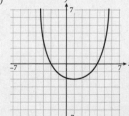

CONTINUE

23

To determine support for a proposition on the state ballot, residents were called on the phone. Of those residents called, 20% did not answer the phone. Approximately 35% of the residents who did answer were contacted on a landline and the other 65% were contacted on a cell phone. Approximately 55% of the respondents contacted on a landline and 30% of the respondents contacted on a cell phone supported the proposition. Which of the following conclusions is best supported by the poll results?

A) The proposition will pass if voter turnout is high on Election Day.

B) Voters over 35 years old were more likely to support the proposition than voters between 18 and 35 were.

C) Participants that were reached on their cell phones were less likely to support the bill than participants that were reached on a landline.

D) If only voters that own a landline vote on Election Day, the proposition will pass.

24

The weight w, in grams, of a newborn panda can be approximated with the equation $w = 109(1.12)^n$, where n represents the number of days since birth. Which of the following equations models the weight, in grams, of a newborn panda x weeks after the panda is born?

A) $w = 109(2.21)^{\frac{x}{7}}$

B) $w = 109(1.12)^{\frac{x}{7}}$

C) $w = 109(1.84)^x$

D) $w = 109(1.12)^{7x}$

25

An activist group wants to determine how frequently the average resident of a county uses the library. The group plans to ask everybody that enters one of the library branches on a Saturday to estimate how many times per year they visit a library. Based on these responses, the group will estimate the number of library visits that the average resident makes each year. Which of the following statements is true?

A) The proposed survey has a small sample size and therefore the results will likely be an unreliable estimate of the average library use of the county's residents.

B) The proposed survey will likely produce a reliable estimate of the average library use of the county's residents only if the group conducts it on both a Saturday and a weekday.

C) The proposed survey will likely produce a reliable estimate of the average library use of the county's residents if the group conducts the survey at the busiest library in the county.

D) Due to a flawed sampling method, the proposed survey will likely produce a biased estimate of the average library use of the county's residents regardless of the sample size and the days of the week on which the survey is conducted.

CONTINUE ➡

26

The point (c, d) lies on a line with a slope of 2 in the xy-plane. The point $(3, 2d)$ lies on a different line with a slope of -3. If the two lines have the same y-intercept and $\dfrac{c}{d} = \dfrac{3}{2}$, what is the value of d?

A) $-\dfrac{9}{4}$

B) $-\dfrac{2}{3}$

C) $\dfrac{3}{2}$

D) $\dfrac{9}{2}$

28

A pool has 750 gallons of water in it when a hose begins adding water at a constant rate. The pool contains 60% more water after the hose has run for 5 hours. Which of the following expressions gives the number of gallons of water in the pool after the hose has run for a total of t hours?

A) $750 + 90t$

B) $750 + 5t$

C) $750(1.6)^{\frac{t}{5}}$

D) $750(1.6)^{5t}$

27

Unemployment Rate in Country X

Year	2010	2013
Unemployment Rate	11.5%	13%

The table above shows the unemployment rate for Country X in 2010 and 2013. If the unemployment rate and year have a linear relationship, which of the following expressions best approximates the unemployment rate of the country n years after 2010?

A) $1.5n + 11.5$

B) $0.5(n - 2{,}010) + 11.5$

C) $0.5n + 11.5$

D) $-1.5n + 11.5$

CONTINUE

29

A table of values for function $f(x)$ and the graph of function $h(x)$ are shown below. If the vertex of $h(x)$ is (a, b), what is $f(h(a))$?

x	–3	–2	–1	0	1	2	3
$f(x)$	11	8	5	2	–1	–4	–7

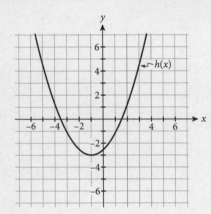

A) –1

B) 2

C) 5

D) 11

30

Researchers allowed 15 participants in a study to get a full night's sleep, while another 15 were awoken after only 3 hours of sleep. The researchers then gave the participants a series of mental tasks and calculated each participant's average completion time. The results are shown below.

Completion time (sec)
Normal Sleep

Completion time (sec)
Reduced Sleep

If the participants with normal sleep make up Group A and the participants with 3 hours of sleep make up Group B, which of the following statements regarding the standard deviations and ranges of the groups is true?

A) The range of Group B is larger than the range of Group A.

B) The standard deviation of Group B is smaller than the standard deviation of Group A.

C) The standard deviation of Group B is equal to the standard deviation of Group A.

D) The range of Group B is equal to the range of Group A.

CONTINUE ➤

DIRECTIONS

For questions 31–38, solve the problem and enter your answer in the grid, as described below, on the answer sheet.

1. Although not required, it is suggested that you write your answer in the boxes at the top of the columns to help you fill in the circles accurately. You will receive credit only if the circles are filled In correctly.

2. Mark no more than one circle in any column.

3. No question has a negative answer.

4. Some problems may have more than one correct answer. In such cases, grid only one answer.

5. **Mixed numbers** such as $3\frac{1}{2}$ must be gridded as 3.5 or 7/2. (If $\boxed{3\ 1\ /\ 2}$ is entered into the grid, it will be interpreted as $\frac{31}{2}$, not as $3\frac{1}{2}$.)

6. **Decimal Answers:** If you obtain a decimal answer with more digits than the grid can accommodate, it may be either rounded or truncated, but it must fill the entire grid.

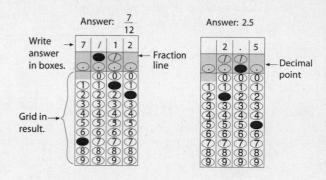

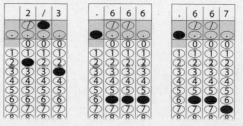

Acceptable ways to grid $\frac{2}{3}$ are:

Answer: 201 – either position Is correct

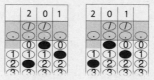

NOTE: You may start your answers in any column, space permitting. Columns you don't need to use should be left blank.

CONTINUE

31

$$nx - 8y = 18$$
$$7x - 4y = 9$$

The equations above both represent line l in the xy-plane. If n is a constant, what is the value of n?

32

One liter of a solution contains one milligram of Solute A and three milligrams of Solute B. How many milligrams of Solute B are there in 22 liters of the solution?

33

$$\frac{1}{3}c + x = 0$$

The equation above is true when $x = -3$. What is the value of c?

34

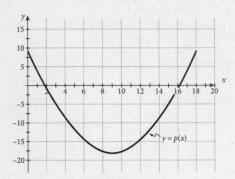

The function p is defined by the equation

$p(x) = \frac{1}{3}(x - 9)^2 - 18$. A portion of the graph of p

is shown above. Function q (not shown) is defined

by the equation $q(x) = 15 - 5x$. If $p(x)$ intersects the

graph of $q(x)$ at the point (r, s) where $r > 0$, what

is the value of r?

CONTINUE

35

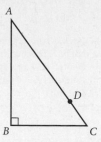

In the figure above, if cos (∠*DBA*) = 0.3, what is the value of cos (∠*DBA*) + sin (∠*DBC*) ?

36

October 28 and 29, 1929 are known as Black Monday and Black Tuesday, respectively. During two days of trading the Dow Jones Industrial Average lost 68.9 points. If there were 5 hours of trading during each of the two days, on average how many points per <u>minute</u>, to the nearest hundredth, did the Dow Jones Industrial Average lose during those two days?

CONTINUE

Questions 37 and 38 refer to the following information.

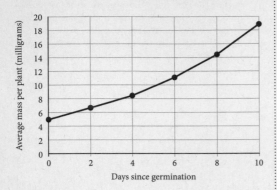

Days since germination

Days since germination	0	2	4	6	8	10
Average mass per plant (milligrams)	5.0	6.6	8.4	11.1	14.4	18.8

Once a seed has germinated and the first leaves begin producing carbohydrates through photosynthesis, a plant grows rapidly until it begins flowering or its growth is restricted by a lack of nutrients or light. An agriculture class grew *Zea mays* L. (sweet corn) in its greenhouse and measured the mass of each plant every other day. The average mass per plant was determined and presented in the graph and table above.

37

$$H(d) = 5.0r^{\frac{d}{2}}$$

The students in the class modeled the average mass per plant using the above function H, where H is average mass in grams d days after germination, and r is a constant. The students found their model matched the data collected within 0.1 grams. To the nearest tenth, what is the value of r?

38

According to the table, what is the positive difference on average, in grams, between a group of 4 plants that germinated 4 days ago and a group of 3 plants that are germinated 8 days ago?

▲

STOP

If you finish before time is called, you may check your work on this section only.
Do not turn to any other section in the test.

No Test Material On This Page

Experimental:
Writing and Language Skills

20 MINUTES, 18 QUESTIONS

Turn to Section 5 of your answer sheet to answer the questions in this section.

The passage below is accompanied by a number of questions. For some questions, you will consider how the passage might be revised to improve the expression of ideas. For other questions, you will consider how the passage might be edited to correct errors in sentence structure, usage, or punctuation. A passage or a question may be accompanied by one or more graphics (such as a table or graph) that you will consider as you make revising and editing decisions.

Some questions will direct you to an underlined portion of the passage. Other questions will direct you to a location in the passage or ask you to think about the passage as a whole.

After reading the passage, choose the answer to each question that most effectively improves the quality of writing in the passage or that makes the passage conform to the conventions of standard written English. Many questions include a "NO CHANGE" option. Choose that option if you think the best choice is to leave the relevant portion of the passage as it is.

Questions 1–18 are based on the following passage.

Metric Mayhem

[1] In the fall of 1999, the metric system caused the $125 million Mars Climate Orbiter to crash on Mars . [2] Somehow, neither group realized the units were different, and the result was that the trajectory of the probe was miscalculated and it crashed. [3] This, at least, is the argument of **2** <u>people</u> who are against adopting the metric system in the U.S. [4] The problem was that two different groups that worked on the project used different systems of measurement. [5] One group used pounds of force per second, a U.S. Customary measurement, and the other group **3** <u>uses</u> newtons, the equivalent metric measurement of force. **4**

1

At this point, the writer is considering adding the following.

> instead of going into orbit around the planet to collect and transmit data

Should the writer make this addition here?

A) Yes, because it gives details that clarify that the crash was unexpected.

B) Yes, because it establishes an important shift in focus in the paragraph's discussion of the Mars Climate Orbiter.

C) No, because it contains information that is not directly related to the main focus of the paragraph.

D) No, because it repeats information given later in the paragraph.

2

A) NO CHANGE

B) them

C) they

D) those ones

3

A) NO CHANGE

B) had used

C) used

D) will have used

4

To make this paragraph most logical, sentence 2 should be placed

A) where it is now.

B) after sentence 3.

C) after sentence 4.

D) after sentence 5.

CONTINUE

The history of the metric system in the Western world began soon after the replacement of Roman numerals with the base-ten Arabic numbering [5] system. The replacement of Roman numerals with Arabic numerals happened in the 15th century. The earliest known treatise promoting the [6] idea, of a decimal, or base-ten system of measurement was printed in 1586. The foundations of the metric system as we know it today were developed over the next two [7] centuries, as commerce, across great distances, became more common. A universal system makes trade vastly simpler because weights and prices can be easily understood, [8] so cheating is difficult.

Which choice most effectively combines the sentences at the underlined portion?

A) system; this replacement

B) system, which

C) system—the adoption of Arabic numerals

D) system, an occurrence that largely

A) NO CHANGE

B) idea of a decimal, or base-ten,

C) idea, of a decimal or base-ten,

D) idea of a decimal—or base-ten,

A) NO CHANGE

B) centuries as commerce, across great distances

C) centuries as commerce, across great distances,

D) centuries as commerce across great distances

Which choice most effectively completes the explanation of how the metric system was important for trade over long distances?

A) NO CHANGE

B) since different currencies make long-distance trade hard enough.

C) regardless of whether buyers and sellers are from the same place.

D) whether the goods are spices, wine, or textiles.

CONTINUE

France was the first country to officially adopt the metric system in the late 18th century, and **9** they organized several international conferences to establish what the universal standards would be. Much of Europe **10** got on board with the metric system quickly on the heels of France, with the exception of Britain. **11** Since the American colonies were part of the British Empire, they used the British Imperial System of measurement. When the United States was established, the Constitution specified that Congress had the power to "fix the Standard of Weights and Measures," and Thomas Jefferson and Ben Franklin were both among the proponents of **12** sacrificing the British system in favor of the metric system.

9
A) NO CHANGE
B) they were organizing
C) it organized
D) it had organized

10
Which choice best maintains the style and tone of the passage?
A) NO CHANGE
B) singled out
C) adopted
D) pinned down

11
A) NO CHANGE
B) Although
C) Therefore,
D) Nevertheless,

12
A) NO CHANGE
B) ducking
C) evading
D) abandoning

In the late 18th century, [13] for example, politics and distance turned out to be insurmountable roadblocks to adopting the metric system in the U.S. Although France had been an American ally during the Revolutionary [14] War. It quickly turned hostile towards the U.S. as diplomatic relations between the U.S. and Britain warmed after the war. There was also concern in the U.S. about the cost of sending a delegation to France [15] for learn about the metric system and worry that political upheaval within France might mean the quick demise of the new system. In the end, the British system was retained, though we now know it as the U.S. Customary System.

[16] There have been multiple attempts over the years to establish the metric system in the U.S. In fact, the metric system was made legal (though not mandatory) by Congress in 1866, and our standards for yards and pounds are defined as fractions of meters and kilograms,

13

A) NO CHANGE
B) moreover,
C) thus,
D) however,

14

A) NO CHANGE
B) War, it
C) War; it
D) War: it

15

A) NO CHANGE
B) to
C) by
D) of

16

Which choice provides the best introduction to this paragraph?

A) NO CHANGE
B) The metric system continued in France, despite Napoleonic rule.
C) Congress deals with a lot of issues that might not seem like they have a big impact on everyday life.
D) Political upheaval also happens in the United States.

CONTINUE ➤

respectively. When Congress passed the Metric Conversion Act in 1975, [17] metric enthusiasts who admired that system were optimistic that the U.S. was finally going to make the switch. But the bill was later amended to make metric conversion voluntary, [18] which is why our speed limit signs are in miles per hour instead of kilometers per hour, and at least in part why the Mars Climate Orbiter crashed.

17

A) NO CHANGE

B) those in enthusiastic favor of the metric system

C) metric enthusiasts

D) enthusiastic metric system admirers

18

Which choice most effectively concludes the essay?

A) NO CHANGE

B) but even though it isn't official, many school children learn about the metric system from an early age.

C) so some businesses have opted to go metric, while most government agencies haven't fully made the switch.

D) which means no one is motivated to make the change even though it wouldn't be that hard.

STOP
**If you finish before time is called, you may check your work on this section only.
Do not turn to any other section in the test.**

SAT Essay

DIRECTIONS

The essay gives you an opportunity to show how effectively you can read and comprehend a passage and write an essay analyzing the passage. In your essay you should demonstrate that you have read the passage carefully, present a clear and logical analysis, and use language precisely.

Your essay must be written on the lines provided in your answer sheet booklet; except for the planning page of the answer booklet, you will receive no other paper on which to write. You will have enough space if you write on every line, avoid wide margins, and keep your handwriting to a reasonable size. Remember that people who are not familiar with your handwriting will read what you write. Try to write or print so that what you are writing is legible to those readers.

You have <u>50 minutes</u> to read the passage and write an essay in response to the prompt provided inside this booklet.

REMINDER

— Do not write your essay in this booklet. Only what you write on the lined pages of your answer booklet will be evaluated.

— An off-topic essay will not be evaluated.

CONTINUE →

As you read the passage below, consider how Stiffler and Dubrow use

- evidence, such as facts or examples, to support claims.
- reasoning to develop ideas and to connect claims and evidence.
- stylistic or persuasive elements, such as word choice or appeals to emotion, to add power to the ideas expressed.

Excerpted from Lisa Stiffler and Aaron Dubrow, "Benefits and Risks of the 'Internet of Things.'" © 2015 by National Science Foundation. Originally posted online on October 23, 2015.

1   Technology publications call 2015 "the year of the car hack."

2   This summer at DEF CON—one of the world's largest computer-hacker conferences—attendees tested the vulnerability of car computer systems at the first "Car Hacking Village." Members of Congress recently introduced the SPY Car Act, aimed at strengthening security in modern cars.

3   In other words, the rest of the world is catching up to the University of Washington's (UW) Security and Privacy Research Lab. Four years ago, with support from the National Science Foundation (NSF), the lab in the UW's Department of Computer Science & Engineering co-led an effort that first exposed weaknesses in car computer systems and demonstrated that hackers could remotely control a vehicle's brakes, door locks and other functions.

4   "We like to look in the places that no one else is looking yet," said computer science and engineering associate professor Yoshi Kohno, who founded the security lab. "You open that area up, and once people start to show up, you move on to the next thing."

5   That trailblazing strategy has put the lab, which Kohno runs jointly with assistant professor Franziska Roesner, at the forefront of computer security and privacy. The UW engineers are international leaders in addressing problems others haven't considered and helping guide the direction of the entire field. Their findings have driven security improvements in cars, medical devices, electronic voting machines and online browsing.

6   The lab's work is increasingly influential as computers are installed in countless everyday devices, making users' lives better and easier, but also putting them at risk for identity theft and even physical harm. This year alone, more than 530 security breaches have compromised more than 140 million records kept by credit card and insurance companies, hospitals, government agencies and others.

7   To combat these and other cyber threats, Kohno and Roesner investigate ways that people can co-opt a computerized product or use online information, warping it into something never intended. Take the car example: The UW researchers, in partnership with alumni Alexei Czeskis and Karl Koscher and computer scientists from the University of California

CONTINUE

at San Diego, were curious about the security of modern vehicles and their computerized systems. So the teams at each university bought cars and plugged their computers into the vehicles' computers to see if they could decode, and ultimately hijack, the cars' software. They did it by listening as the computer systems talked to each other.

8   "If I go to a foreign country and try to learn the language, one of the best ways to do this is to eavesdrop," Kohno said. Then, he said, you "try to repeat things, and see if you get the same reaction."

9   Once the engineers figured out how to talk to the cars' computers and manipulate their functions while plugged in, they moved to the next phase: controlling the cars remotely...

10 "We were surprised by how easy some things were" when it came to commandeering the vehicles, Roesner said. But up to that point, the carmakers hadn't thought to install systems that would make it difficult.

11 That's no longer the case. The car hacking experiments caught the attention of the National Highway Traffic Safety Administration, and the Society of Automotive Engineers created a cybersecurity taskforce. The federal car safety legislation can likewise be traced to the work by the UW lab. While the car hacking work garnered the most public attention, the lab has identified other important security weaknesses....

12 With Kohno's and Roesner's help, many of the UW Computer Science & Engineering students will graduate with a better understanding of risks posed by hackers. Professors there teach an undergraduate course in security and privacy that fills up almost instantly and has a waiting list of a dozen or more.

13 The course essentially turns traditional software development on its head by taking a finished product that works one way and asking how it could be twisted, potentially for nefarious purposes. "It's kind of a surprising mind switch," Roesner said. But, she added, it's important for students to grasp if the industry is going to get a handle on security threats.

14 "In order to build secure systems," she said, "you have to understand how to break them."

Write an essay in which you explain how Stiffler and Dubrow build an argument to advocate for the importance of research that includes hacking into systems. In your essay, analyze how Stiffler and Dubrow use one or more of the features listed in the box above (or features of your own choice) to strengthen the logic and persuasiveness of their argument. Be sure that your analysis focuses on the most relevant features of the passage.

Your essay should not explain whether you agree with the authors' claims, but rather explain how Stiffler and Dubrow build an argument to persuade their audience.

END OF TEST

DO NOT RETURN TO A PREVIOUS SECTION.

Completely darken bubbles with a No. 2 pencil. If you make a mistake, be sure to erase mark completely. Erase all stray marks.

1.

YOUR NAME: _____
(Print)   Last   First   M.I.

SIGNATURE: _____   DATE: __/__/__

HOME ADDRESS: _____
(Print)   Number and Street

_____
City   State   Zip Code

PHONE NO.: _____
(Print)

5. YOUR NAME

First 4 letters of last name | | | | FIRST INIT | MID INIT

IMPORTANT: Please fill in these boxes exactly as shown on the back cover of your test book.

2. TEST FORM

3. TEST CODE   **4. REGISTRATION NUMBER**

6. DATE OF BIRTH

Month	Day	Year
JAN		
FEB	0 0	0 0
MAR	1 1	1 1
APR	2 2	2 2
MAY	3 3	3 3
JUN	4	4 4
JUL	5	5 5
AUG	6	6 6
SEP	7	7 7
OCT	8	8 8
NOV	9	9 9
DEC		

7. SEX
- MALE
- FEMALE

Test 2

Start with number 1 for each new section.
If a section has fewer questions than answer spaces, leave the extra answer spaces blank.

Section 1—Reading

1. Ⓐ Ⓑ Ⓒ Ⓓ
2. Ⓐ Ⓑ Ⓒ Ⓓ
3. Ⓐ Ⓑ Ⓒ Ⓓ
4. Ⓐ Ⓑ Ⓒ Ⓓ
5. Ⓐ Ⓑ Ⓒ Ⓓ
6. Ⓐ Ⓑ Ⓒ Ⓓ
7. Ⓐ Ⓑ Ⓒ Ⓓ
8. Ⓐ Ⓑ Ⓒ Ⓓ
9. Ⓐ Ⓑ Ⓒ Ⓓ
10. Ⓐ Ⓑ Ⓒ Ⓓ
11. Ⓐ Ⓑ Ⓒ Ⓓ
12. Ⓐ Ⓑ Ⓒ Ⓓ
13. Ⓐ Ⓑ Ⓒ Ⓓ
14. Ⓐ Ⓑ Ⓒ Ⓓ
15. Ⓐ Ⓑ Ⓒ Ⓓ
16. Ⓐ Ⓑ Ⓒ Ⓓ
17. Ⓐ Ⓑ Ⓒ Ⓓ
18. Ⓐ Ⓑ Ⓒ Ⓓ
19. Ⓐ Ⓑ Ⓒ Ⓓ
20. Ⓐ Ⓑ Ⓒ Ⓓ
21. Ⓐ Ⓑ Ⓒ Ⓓ
22. Ⓐ Ⓑ Ⓒ Ⓓ
23. Ⓐ Ⓑ Ⓒ Ⓓ
24. Ⓐ Ⓑ Ⓒ Ⓓ
25. Ⓐ Ⓑ Ⓒ Ⓓ
26. Ⓐ Ⓑ Ⓒ Ⓓ
27. Ⓐ Ⓑ Ⓒ Ⓓ
28. Ⓐ Ⓑ Ⓒ Ⓓ
29. Ⓐ Ⓑ Ⓒ Ⓓ
30. Ⓐ Ⓑ Ⓒ Ⓓ
31. Ⓐ Ⓑ Ⓒ Ⓓ
32. Ⓐ Ⓑ Ⓒ Ⓓ
33. Ⓐ Ⓑ Ⓒ Ⓓ
34. Ⓐ Ⓑ Ⓒ Ⓓ
35. Ⓐ Ⓑ Ⓒ Ⓓ
36. Ⓐ Ⓑ Ⓒ Ⓓ
37. Ⓐ Ⓑ Ⓒ Ⓓ
38. Ⓐ Ⓑ Ⓒ Ⓓ
39. Ⓐ Ⓑ Ⓒ Ⓓ
40. Ⓐ Ⓑ Ⓒ Ⓓ
41. Ⓐ Ⓑ Ⓒ Ⓓ
42. Ⓐ Ⓑ Ⓒ Ⓓ
43. Ⓐ Ⓑ Ⓒ Ⓓ
44. Ⓐ Ⓑ Ⓒ Ⓓ
45. Ⓐ Ⓑ Ⓒ Ⓓ
46. Ⓐ Ⓑ Ⓒ Ⓓ
47. Ⓐ Ⓑ Ⓒ Ⓓ
48. Ⓐ Ⓑ Ⓒ Ⓓ
49. Ⓐ Ⓑ Ⓒ Ⓓ
50. Ⓐ Ⓑ Ⓒ Ⓓ
51. Ⓐ Ⓑ Ⓒ Ⓓ
52. Ⓐ Ⓑ Ⓒ Ⓓ

Section 2—Writing and Language Skills

1. Ⓐ Ⓑ Ⓒ Ⓓ
2. Ⓐ Ⓑ Ⓒ Ⓓ
3. Ⓐ Ⓑ Ⓒ Ⓓ
4. Ⓐ Ⓑ Ⓒ Ⓓ
5. Ⓐ Ⓑ Ⓒ Ⓓ
6. Ⓐ Ⓑ Ⓒ Ⓓ
7. Ⓐ Ⓑ Ⓒ Ⓓ
8. Ⓐ Ⓑ Ⓒ Ⓓ
9. Ⓐ Ⓑ Ⓒ Ⓓ
10. Ⓐ Ⓑ Ⓒ Ⓓ
11. Ⓐ Ⓑ Ⓒ Ⓓ
12. Ⓐ Ⓑ Ⓒ Ⓓ
13. Ⓐ Ⓑ Ⓒ Ⓓ
14. Ⓐ Ⓑ Ⓒ Ⓓ
15. Ⓐ Ⓑ Ⓒ Ⓓ
16. Ⓐ Ⓑ Ⓒ Ⓓ
17. Ⓐ Ⓑ Ⓒ Ⓓ
18. Ⓐ Ⓑ Ⓒ Ⓓ
19. Ⓐ Ⓑ Ⓒ Ⓓ
20. Ⓐ Ⓑ Ⓒ Ⓓ
21. Ⓐ Ⓑ Ⓒ Ⓓ
22. Ⓐ Ⓑ Ⓒ Ⓓ
23. Ⓐ Ⓑ Ⓒ Ⓓ
24. Ⓐ Ⓑ Ⓒ Ⓓ
25. Ⓐ Ⓑ Ⓒ Ⓓ
26. Ⓐ Ⓑ Ⓒ Ⓓ
27. Ⓐ Ⓑ Ⓒ Ⓓ
28. Ⓐ Ⓑ Ⓒ Ⓓ
29. Ⓐ Ⓑ Ⓒ Ⓓ
30. Ⓐ Ⓑ Ⓒ Ⓓ
31. Ⓐ Ⓑ Ⓒ Ⓓ
32. Ⓐ Ⓑ Ⓒ Ⓓ
33. Ⓐ Ⓑ Ⓒ Ⓓ
34. Ⓐ Ⓑ Ⓒ Ⓓ
35. Ⓐ Ⓑ Ⓒ Ⓓ
36. Ⓐ Ⓑ Ⓒ Ⓓ
37. Ⓐ Ⓑ Ⓒ Ⓓ
38. Ⓐ Ⓑ Ⓒ Ⓓ
39. Ⓐ Ⓑ Ⓒ Ⓓ
40. Ⓐ Ⓑ Ⓒ Ⓓ
41. Ⓐ Ⓑ Ⓒ Ⓓ
42. Ⓐ Ⓑ Ⓒ Ⓓ
43. Ⓐ Ⓑ Ⓒ Ⓓ
44. Ⓐ Ⓑ Ⓒ Ⓓ

Completely darken bubbles with a No. 2 pencil. If you make a mistake, be sure to erase mark completely. Erase all stray marks.

Test ❷ Start with number 1 for each new section.
If a section has fewer questions than answer spaces, leave the extra answer spaces blank.

Section 3—Mathematics: No Calculator

Section 4—Mathematics: Calculator

Section 5—Experimental: Writing and Language Skills

Chapter 5
Practice Test 2:
Answers and
Explanations

PRACTICE TEST 2 ANSWER KEY

Section 1: Reading		Section 2: Writing & Language		Section 3: Math (No Calculator)		Section 4: Math (Calculator)	
1. B	27. C	1. C	23. A	1. C	13. A	1. B	20. C
2. D	28. D	2. D	24. D	2. D	14. B	2. D	21. A
3. D	29. B	3. D	25. C	3. A	15. B	3. C	22. C
4. A	30. B	4. A	26. D	4. D	16. 17	4. A	23. C
5. D	31. D	5. B	27. D	5. B	17. 6	5. B	24. D
6. A	32. B	6. C	28. C	6. C	18. 3	6. A	25. D
7. C	33. B	7. A	29. B	7. D	19. 22	7. C	26. A
8. B	34. A	8. D	30. A	8. C		8. B	27. C
9. C	35. A	9. B	31. D	9. A	20. $\frac{14}{8}$,	9. D	28. A
10. C	36. C	10. B	32. B	10. C	$\frac{7}{4}$,	10. C	29. D
11. C	37. B	11. B	33. A	11. A	or	11. A	30. B
12. A	38. B	12. D	34. A	12. B	1.75	12. A	31. 14
13. A	39. D	13. C	35. C			13. A	32. 66
14. C	40. A	14. A	36. D			14. B	33. 9
15. B	41. B	15. B	37. A			15. C	34. 6
16. B	42. B	16. A	38. C			16. B	35. 0.6
17. D	43. B	17. A	39. B			17. B	36. 0.11
18. D	44. D	18. C	40. C			18. A	37. 1.3
19. A	45. D	19. D	41. B			19. B	38. 9.6
20. B	46. D	20. B	42. B				
21. C	47. B	21. A	43. A				
22. B	48. A	22. D	44. B				
23. A	49. B						
24. C	50. C						
25. B	51. D						
26. A	52. D						

Section 5:
Experimental
(Writing & Language)

1. A	10. C
2. A	11. A
3. C	12. D
4. D	13. D
5. B	14. B
6. B	15. B
7. D	16. A
8. C	17. C
9. C	18. A

For self-scoring assessment tables, please turn to page 213.

PRACTICE TEST 2 EXPLANATIONS

Section 1: Reading

1. **B** This question asks how the main focus of the passage shifts from the beginning to the end. Because this is a general question, it should be done after the specific questions. The passage begins with the narrator's description of her family's *house-dwelling life* in a house built *across the road from a lake*. She continues with a description of the family's business running a *dance pavilion* with live music and dancing throughout the summer. In the third paragraph, the story focus changes when her father *moved his office into his car* and they drove around buying and selling antiques. The narrator describes her father's *lifelong wanderlust* and how he would suddenly decide it was time to go somewhere else. Eliminate any answer choices that are not consistent with this structure. Choice (A) can be eliminated because there is no *portrayal of a significant place the family often visited* in the passage. Choice (B) is consistent with the shift from her description of life in the summer house to life on the road. Choice (C) can be eliminated because the descriptions in the first part of the passage are concrete descriptions of the narrator's childhood rather than an *allegorical display of domesticity*. Choice (D) can be eliminated because the passage is not an examination of the narrator's childhood financial situation. The correct answer is (B).

2. **D** This question asks about the main purpose of the second paragraph. Carefully read the paragraph to determine what the central focus is. Throughout the paragraph, the narrator describes the dance pavilion her father ran during the summer. He *dreamed up such attractions as a living chess game* and *booked the big dance bands of the 1930s and 1940s*. She says that people would come from *as far away as Toledo or Detroit*, but that *paying the likes of Guy Lombardo or Duke Ellington…meant that one rainy weekend could wipe out a whole summer's profits*. This paragraph establishes the idea that the narrator's father is a man with big ideas who doesn't always play it safe. Eliminate any answer choices that aren't consistent with this idea. Choice (A) can be eliminated because there is no discussion of the father's *compulsive desire to travel* in this paragraph. Choice (B) can also be eliminated, because no one important to the *narrator's remembrances* is *introduced* in this paragraph. Choice (C) might initially look good, but the father is actually bringing in the famous acts rather than suffering *delusions of grandeur*, and while his decisions *could wipe out* the *summer's profits*, that's a risk that is being described rather than an actual negative outcome. Eliminate (C). Choice (D) is consistent with the prediction. The correct answer is (D).

3. **D** This question asks what the word *precarious* does in line 24. Use the line reference to find the window, and read carefully. The narrator describes the family's livelihood as *precarious* after saying that her father's business decisions could *wipe out a whole summer's profits*, which always gave them *a sense of gambling*. The word *precarious* describes their livelihood as "risky" or "a

gamble." Eliminate anything that is not consistent with this prediction. Choices (A) and (B) can be eliminated because there is no mention of their family's financial situation in either answer. Choice (C) might be true in the life of the narrator, but the word *precarious* is used here to highlight the riskiness of the financial situation, so eliminate (C). Choice (D) is a clear paraphrase of the prediction. The correct answer is (D).

4.   **A**   This question asks about the narrator's participation in the *family business*. Use chronology to find the window that talks about the family business and read carefully. The narrator says that *from the age of four*, she *came into [her] own as the wrapper and unwrapper of china*. She goes on to say that each of the family members *had a role in the family economic unit*, including her older sister, who *sold popcorn from a professional stand*. The correct answer should be consistent with the idea of the narrator having her own job within the family business from a young age. Choice (A) is consistent with this idea, so keep it. Choice (B) might be initially attractive, but there is no mention in the text of the time either sister spent doing her job. Choices (C) and (D) can be eliminated because there is no mention in the passage of money, getting paid, or volunteering. The correct answer is (A).

5.   **D**   This question asks which statement the narrator's father would most likely agree with. Notice that this is the first question in a paired set, so it can be done in tandem with Q6. Begin with the answers to Q6. The lines for (6A) say that there were only *a few months each year* when her father was *content with a house-dwelling life*. These lines support (5D), so draw a line connecting those two answer choices. The lines for (6B) say that her father loved the risks of the summer business. These lines do not support any of the answer choices for Q5, so eliminate (6B). The lines for (6C) say that everyone *had a role in the family economic unit* and then go on to explain her sister's role. These lines don't support any of the answers for Q5, so eliminate (6C). The lines for (6D) say that he *refused to put heating or hot water* in their house. Those lines might initially seem to support (5C), but read carefully. The father is not concerned about *the expense* of the water heater; he is concerned about the permanence of it. Eliminate (6D). Without support from Q6, (5A), (5B), and (5C) can all be eliminated. The correct answers are (5D) and (6A).

6.   **A**   (See explanation above.)

7.   **C**   This question asks what *struck* most nearly means in line 48. Go back to the text, find the word *struck*, and cross it out. Carefully read the surrounding text to determine another word that would fit based on the context. The narrator describes how her father is preparing to travel by *collecting road maps..., testing the trailer hitch..., and talking about faraway pleasures*. Then she says he announces it's time to go *as if struck by a sudden whim rather than a lifelong wanderlust*. The missing word must mean "suddenly decided" or "just realized." Eliminate anything that isn't consistent with this prediction. Choice (A), *battered*, is a definition of *struck*, but it doesn't mean "suddenly decided." Eliminate (A). Choice (B), *boycotted*, means "abstained from buying," which does not match the prediction. Eliminate (B). Choice (C), *inspired*, is consis-

tent with the prediction, so keep it. Choice (D), *disturbed*, can be eliminated because it does not mean "suddenly decided" or "just realized." The correct answer is (C).

8.   **B**   This question asks why the father started the cross-country trip. Notice that it is the first question in a paired set, so it can be done in tandem with Q9. Begin with the answers to Q9. The lines for (9A) refer to the family's antiquing business, driving to *nearby country auctions* to search for antiques. There is no mention of the *cross-country trip*, so these lines do not support any of the answers for Q8. Eliminate (9A). The lines for (9B) describe the father's specific actions as he prepares for the trip, including *collecting road maps…, testing the trailer hitch…, and talking about faraway pleasures*. These lines provide details about the trip, but they do not give the *reason* the trip started. Eliminate (9B). The lines for (9C) refer to the father's *lifelong wanderlust* when he announces it's time to go. These lines support (8B), so draw a line connecting those two answers. The lines for (9D) describe the speed of the *leave-taking*, but do not offer a reason for it. Eliminate (9D). Without support from Q9, (8A), (8C), and (8D) can all be eliminated. The correct answers are (8B) and (9C).

9.   **C**   (See explanation above.)

10. **C**   This question asks about the mother's role in the family. Carefully read the window where the mother is mentioned. She is first mentioned in line 28 when the narrator discusses the family antiquing business. She says that her mother had a *better eye for antiques and reference books* and was the one who *appraised them for sale*. Then, in the last paragraph (lines 71–77), the narrator again mentions her mother as the one who remembered the iron was still on and *might be burning its way through the ironing board*. The correct answer should have something to do with the mother being reasonable and practical in the family. Choice (A) can be eliminated because there is no evidence that she *resented* her husband's *impulsive nature*. Choice (B) can also be eliminated because she goes along with her husband, but there is no evidence in the text that she *shared the…wanderlust equally*. Choice (C) is consistent with the prediction, so keep it. Choice (D) can be eliminated because, although she was worried about the iron, it did not actually set the house on fire. The correct answer is (C).

11. **C**   This question asks about the primary purpose of the passage. Because it is a general question, it should be done after the specific questions have been completed. The passage begins by introducing the idea that liars and bluffers have *tells* that indicate when they aren't being truthful. The passage then expands this idea into a discussion about a pair of Stanford researchers who identified patterns that show up in reports with falsified data and could potentially be used to spot fraudulent papers. The passage ends with a warning that systems designed to detect fraudulent papers by simply counting words could have negative repercussions. The correct answer should be consistent with this prediction. Eliminate (A) because this passage is not *defend*[ing] anyone. Choice (B) can also be eliminated because the passage is focused on scientific publications, not *different industries and research fields*. Choice (C) is consistent with the

prediction, so keep it. Eliminate (D) because the passage is about research into detecting fraud, not *reveal[ing] secrets* of those who successfully lie. The correct answer is (C).

12. **A**   This question asks about the function of the first paragraph. Carefully read the paragraph to determine the author's reason for including the given information. The paragraph begins by mentioning how *poker players* have "tells" that give away *when they're bluffing*. The paragraph goes on to say that this idea of *tells* can also happen with *scientists* who *commit fraud* by attempting to *pass along falsified data*. The paragraph ends by saying *a pair of Stanford researchers* have *cracked the writing patterns* of the tells, which could help *identify falsified research* before it is published. The paragraph is there to provide context for research discussed later in the passage. Eliminate any answer choices that are not consistent with that prediction. Choice (A) is consistent with the prediction, as the paragraph introduces the concept of *tells*, which is what the later research is about. Keep (A). Choice (B) can be eliminated because there is no mention in the paragraph of *additional applications* of the research results. Choice (C) can be eliminated: although there is mention of *fraud detection*, the paragraph does not introduce *general methods* of fraud detection. Choice (D) can be eliminated because the idea is not *questioned* later in the passage, but expanded upon. The correct answer is (A).

13. **A**   This question asks what the word *fair* means in line 10. Go back to the text, find the word *fair*, and cross it out. Carefully read the surrounding text to determine another word that would fit in the blank based on the context of the passage. The text says that there is a *fair amount of research* dedicated to understanding how liars lie. The text continues with a mention of the results of some of these studies. The missing word must mean something like "enough" or "plenty." Eliminate any answer choices that aren't consistent with that prediction. Choice (A), *ample*, is consistent with "plenty," so keep it. Choice (B), *lawful*, can be eliminated because there is no mention in the text about the legality of the evidence. Choice (C) can be eliminated because the amount of research is not compared to anything else, so it can't be *equal*. Choice (D) can be eliminated because the text focuses on the amount of research, not the quality of the research or whether the outcomes were positive or negative. The correct answer is (A).

14. **C**   This question asks what the word *obscure* means in line 40. Go back to the text, find the word *obscure*, and cross it out. Carefully read the surrounding text to determine another word that would fit in the blank based on the context of the passage. The passage says that scientists who don't want to get caught *committing a misconduct* may *obscure parts of the paper*. The text also says that these same fraudsters may *muddle the truth*. Therefore, the missing word must mean something like "muddle" or "confuse." Eliminate anything that isn't consistent with this prediction. Choice (A) might initially look good because the scientists would want to *hide* the fact that they are lying. However, *hide* does not mean "muddle" or "confuse," and the scientists aren't actually hiding parts of their papers. Eliminate (A). Choice (B), *blind*, can be eliminated because the scientists are trying to make parts of their papers "confusing," not *blind[ing]*. Choice (C), *distort*, is consistent with "muddle" or "confuse," so keep it. Choice (D), *characterize*, is not consistent with the predictions at all. Eliminate (D). The correct answer is (C).

15.   **B**   This question asks how papers with fraudulent data can be spotted. Notice that this is the first question in a paired set, so it can be done in tandem with Q16. Begin with the answers to Q16 first. The lines for (16A) say that the [rating] was done through *summary score of causal terms, abstract language, jargon, positive emotion terms and…an ease of reading score*. These lines explain how the obfuscation index was determined, but there are no specifics about how to spot the papers that are fraudulent. These lines do not support any of the answers for Q15, so eliminate (16A). The lines for (16B) say that *fraudulent retracted papers scored significantly higher on the obfuscation index*. These lines indicate that a fraudulent paper will have a higher obfuscation index, which would mean more *abstract language and jargon*. These lines could support (15B), so draw a line connecting those two answers. The lines for (16C) say that a *fraudulent author* may use *fewer positive emotion terms*. While this could be a way to spot a fraudulent paper, these lines do not support any of the answer choices for Q15. Eliminate (16C). The lines for (16D) talk about a *computerized system* that might be able to *flag a submitted paper*. These lines don't give any specifics about how to spot the paper, so these lines don't support any of the answers for Q15. Eliminate (16D). Without support from Q16, eliminate (15A), (15C), and (15D). The correct answers are (15B) and (16B).

16.   **B**   (See explanation above.)

17.   **D**   This question asks which hypothetical situation Hancock would most likely agree could be a consequence of action without further research. Notice that this is the first question in a paired set. Although *Hancock* could be a good lead word, the whole passage is about his experiment, so his ideas are not in once place. Do this question in tandem with Q18. Begin with the answer choices for Q18. The lines for (18A) refer to avoiding getting caught publishing fraudulent data by *obscur[ing] parts of the paper*. These lines don't support any of the answers for Q17, so eliminate (18A). The lines for (18B) talk about the *publish or perish* mentality that motivates researchers to publish manipulated or fake findings. These lines do not support any of the answers for Q17, so eliminate (18B). The lines for (18C) warn of the *false-positive rate* of the computerized fraud-detection system. These lines might seem to connect to (17A) because both mention *computer programs*, but there is no connection between the ideas or to the question. Eliminate (18C). The lines for (18D) refer back to the *high error rate*, and also say that *science is based on trust* and if a publication introduces a *fraud detection tool*, it might *undermine that trust*. These lines support (17D), so draw a line connecting those two answers. Without support from Q18, (17A), (17B), and (17C) can all be eliminated. The correct answers are (17D) and (18D).

18.   **D**   (See explanation above.)

19.   **A**   This question asks which category of language had the greatest difference between *language used in fraudulent and genuine research*, according to the graph. The difference between the two in Means and Methods is a little over 200, so keep (A) for now. The difference between them in Amplifiers is less than 100, so eliminate (B). Quantities has a difference of about 125,

so eliminate (C). Emotional States has a difference of about 75, so eliminate (D). The correct answer is (A).

20. **B** This question asks which of the statements is supported by the graph. Go through each of the answer choices and eliminate anything not supported by the graph. Eliminate (A) because *Quantities* is higher in Genuine Publications rather than Fraudulent ones. Keep (B) because the bars for *Means and Methods* and *Certainty* are about the same for Fraudulent publications. Eliminate (C) because the Genuine publications have higher occurrences of *Negations* than the Fraudulent publications. Eliminate (D) because there is no consistency for *Amplifiers* and *Diminishers*. The correct answer is (B).

21. **C** This question asks which statement supports the idea that *jargon* could be classified as *means and methods*, using both the graph and the passage. Carefully read each answer choice and eliminate any that do not address the connection between *jargon* and *means and methods*. Choice (A) can be eliminated because it is only a general statement that scientists who falsify data have certain writing patterns they use. There is no specific connection to *jargon* or the graph. Choice (B) mentions a specific characteristic of the writing of liars in general, but there is no connection to the study discussed in the passage. Eliminate (B). Choice (C) says that the *fraudulent papers* had *60 more jargon-like words per paper*. The graph shows that fraudulent papers contain more *Means and Methods* language than genuine papers, so that could support the idea in question. Keep (C). Choice (D) simply says that *more research is needed*, with no specifics about types of language or types of papers. Eliminate (D). The correct answer is (C).

22. **B** This question asks about a main idea of the passage. Because this is a general question, it should be done after the specific questions have been completed. The passage begins with an introduction of a new, blue pigment, a *serendipitous discovery* made while *researching materials for electronics applications*. The passage then goes on to describe how the pigment was discovered, what makes the pigment particularly notable, and ends with a discussion of further discoveries that have resulted from the discovery of this pigment. Eliminate any answers that are inconsistent with the ideas in the passage. Choice (A) can be eliminated because there is no discussion of how the pigment is *dangerous*. Choice (B) is consistent with the idea of a *serendipitous discovery* of a *superior* new pigment. Choice (C) is consistent with the passage naming the new pigment by its chemical composition, but that is not the *main idea* of the passage, nor is there mention of the chemical composition being the *most effective* way to describe a pigment. Eliminate (C). Choice (D) can be eliminated because it is too narrow: The relationship between *UV absorbance* and *pigment stability* is mentioned in the passage, but it is not the *main idea*. The correct answer is (B).

23. **A** This question asks about the *overall structure of the passage*. Because this is a general question, it should be done after the specific questions have been completed. The passage begins with an introduction of a new pigment, goes on to describe how the pigment was discovered and what makes the pigment particularly notable, and then ends with a discussion of further discoveries

that have resulted from the discovery of this pigment. Eliminate any answer choices that aren't consistent with this prediction. Choice (A) is similar to the prediction, so keep it. Choice (B) can be eliminated because the focus of the passage is the new, synthetic pigment. There is no *natural alternative* presented. Choice (C) can also be eliminated because only one accidental discovery is mentioned, rather than *several accidental discoveries*. Choice (D) can be eliminated because there is no discussion about how compounds *work together* in the passage. The correct answer is (A).

24. **C** This question asks what the word *applications* means in line 5. Go back to the text, find the word *applications*, and cross it out. Carefully read the surrounding text to determine another word that would fit in the blank based on the context of the passage. The text says that a scientist discovered the pigment while *researching materials for electronics applications*. It goes on to say that the researchers were trying to create a *high-efficiency electronic material*. The missing word must mean something like "functions" or "materials." Eliminate (A), *requests*, because it does not mean "functions." Choice (B), *forms*, can also be eliminated because it is not consistent with the prediction. Choice (C), *uses*, is consistent, so keep it. Choice (D), *industries*, might initially look attractive, but the text says that they were trying to develop *material* rather than "businesses." Eliminate (D). The correct answer is (C).

25. **B** This question asks for the best evidence that Smith did not intend for his experiment to produce the results it did. Carefully read each of the lines provided and eliminate any that do not answer the question. Choice (A) can be eliminated because the lines simply describe the pigment, not an experiment or results. Choice (B) answers the question, saying that *instead of… high-efficiency material, what emerged…was a brilliant blue compound*. Keep (B). Choice (C) can be eliminated because the patent process is not related to the discovery process. Choice (D) can also be eliminated because those lines indicate the researchers are continuing to research the accidental discovery, hoping to find additional new pigments. The correct answer is (B).

26. **A** This question asks what the word *unstable* means in line 21. Go back to the text, find the word *unstable*, and cross it out. Carefully read the surrounding text to determine another word that would fit in the blank based on the context of the passage. The text describes blue pigments as *notoriously unstable* and then goes on to say that they *fade easily*. The missing word must mean something like "fades easily" or "doesn't last." Eliminate any answer choices that are inconsistent with this prediction. Choice (A), *impermanent*, means "doesn't last." Keep (A). Choice (B) can be eliminated because the pigments are not *threatening*. Choice (C) can be eliminated because *careless* does not mean the same thing as "doesn't last." Choice (D) might initially look attractive because the passage does mention *ancient times*, but *antiquated* does not mean "doesn't last." Eliminate (D). The correct answer is (A).

27. **C** This question asks which factor has been identified as *most indicative of stable pigments*. In lines 22–25, the author says that the fact that *this pigment was synthesized at such high temperatures*

signaled to researchers that *this new compound was extremely stable*. Therefore, synthesis at high temperatures indicates a stable compound. The correct answer is (C).

28. **D** This question asks about the relationship between the *YInMn Blue pigment and the Cobalt Blue pigment currently used*. The fifth paragraph, lines 33–37, discusses the relationship between the two pigments. The paragraph says that $YIn_{1-x}Mn_xO_3$ exhibits *high absorbance in the UV region and high reflectivity in the near-infrared region when compared to currently-used Cobalt Blue pigments*. Therefore, Cobalt Blue has *lower UV absorbency* and *lower reflectivity in the near-infrared region*. Eliminate any answer choices that aren't consistent with this prediction. Eliminate (A): although the text mentions *outdoor weathering*, YInMn is superior to Cobalt Blue for exterior applications. Choice (B) can be eliminated because, although *YInMn* can be *chemically-adjusted,* it was not *specifically engineered* to be so. Choice (C) can be eliminated because there is no discussion of the comparative difficulty of engineering purple, YInMn, or Cobalt Blue. Choice (D) is consistent with the prediction. The correct answer is (D).

29. **B** This is the best evidence for a specific question, so simply look at the lines used to answer Q28: $YIn_{1-x}Mn_xO_3$ *exhibits high absorbance in the UV region and high reflectivity in the near-infrared region when compared to currently-used Cobalt Blue pigments*. This statement is in lines 34–37. Although (C) mentions *increased UV absorbance*, there is no mention of *infrared reflectivity*, so (C) is not the best evidence to support Q28. The correct answer is (B).

30. **B** This question asks at which wavelength $CoAl_2O_4$ has a reflectance of 0.4%. Go to Figure 2 and find the reflectance of 0.4. Draw a line across the graph and see which wavelengths correspond to that reflectance. There are several places where $CoAl_2O_4$ has a reflectance of 0.4%, but the only one that is an answer choice is 1800 nm. The correct answer is (B).

31. **D** This question asks which range of wavelengths illustrates the thermal advantages of YInMn Blue over Cobalt Blue based on both the graph and the passage. The passage says that *high solar reflectance [of YInMn Blue] indicates that this 'cool pigment' can find use in a variety of exterior applications by reducing surface temperatures, cooling costs, and energy consumption*. Eliminate any answer choices that aren't consistent with this prediction. Choices (A), (B), and (C) all offer wavelength ranges in which the reflectance for YInMn Blue and Cobalt Blue are similar. This would not give YInMn Blue any thermal advantages, so eliminate all three. Choice (D), 1200–1400, gives a range in which the reflectance of YInMn Blue is much higher than Cobalt Blue, which, according to the passage, would give YInMn Blue an advantage. The correct answer is (D).

32. **B** This question asks what the word *present* means in line 3. Go back to the text, find the word *present*, and cross it out. Carefully read the surrounding text to determine another word that would fit in the blank based on the context of the passage. The author says that he is trying to be clear about the *disordered condition of…currency and the present dangers*, while also trying to *suggest a way which leads to a safer financial system*. He is contrasting the current situation with what he hopes will be a better situation in the future. The missing word must mean something

like "at this moment" or "at this time." Eliminate any answers that aren't consistent with that prediction. Choice (A), *prompt*, means that something happens right away, but not necessarily "at this time." Eliminate (A). Eliminate (C) for the same reason. Choice (B), *current*, is consistent with "at this time," so keep (B). Choice (D) can be eliminated because *present* and *gifted* might seem similar, but *gifted* does not mean "at this time." The correct answer is (B).

33. **B** This question asks what Passage 1 suggests about those who support implementing the bimetallic system of currency. Notice that this is the first question in a paired set, so it can be done in tandem with Q34. Read the lines for Q34 first. The lines for (34A) say that *many countrymen...insist that the cure for the ills is the free coinage of silver*. These lines support (33B), so draw a line connecting those two answers. The lines for (34B) say that those who support the bimetallic system think *mints shall be...thrown open to the free, unlimited, and independent coinage of both gold and silver*. These lines don't support any of the answers to Q33, so eliminate (34B). The lines for (34C) say that those who believe *independent coinage...would restore the parity between the metals...oppose an unsupported and improbable theory*. While these lines do describe those who support the bimetallic system, these lines don't support any of the answers for Q33. Eliminate (34C). The lines for (34D) say that the ideas *run counter to our own actual experiences*. These lines give the author's feelings about the system, but not about those who support the system. The lines don't support any of the answers for Q33, so eliminate (34D). Without support from Q34, (33A), (33C), and (33D) can be eliminated. The correct answers are (33B) and (34A).

34. **A** (See explanation above.)

35. **A** This question asks why Cleveland refers to Acts of Congress, which is in line 50. Go back to the text and carefully read the window to determine why he mentions them. The line says that the Acts of Congress were *impotent to create equality where natural causes decreed even a slight inequality*. The correct answer must have something to do with the idea that the Acts of Congress could not create equality when outside forces set up an inequality. Choice (A) is a direct paraphrase of this prediction, so keep it. Choice (B) can be eliminated, because Cleveland mentions the acts to show a contrast, not to *summarize* anything. Choice (C) can be eliminated because the acts would not be a viable *alternative* if they are *impotent to create equality*. Choice (D) can be eliminated for the same reason as (C). The correct answer is (A).

36. **C** This question asks what the word *idle* means in line 66. Go back to the text, find the word *idle*, and cross it out. Carefully read the surrounding text to determine another word that would fit in the blank based on the context of the passage. The text contrasts the *idle holders of idle capital* with the *struggling masses who produce the wealth and pay the taxes*. Therefore, the missing word must mean something like "not working" or "not producing anything." Eliminate any answer choices that aren't consistent with that prediction. Choice (A) can be eliminated, because the holders of the capital have not *abandoned* anything. Choice (B) might initially make sense, because those who hold a great deal of money are likely to be *ambitious*, but *ambitious*

does not mean "not producing anything." Eliminate (B). Choice (C), *inactive*, is consistent with "not working." Keep (C). Choice (D), *cheap*, is not consistent with the prediction, so it can be eliminated. The correct answer is (C).

37. **B** This question asks which claim Bryan would most likely agree with about the gold standard controversy. Notice that this is the first question in a paired set, so it can be done in tandem with Q38. Begin with the answers to Q38 first. The lines for (38A) say that if the gold standard is the standard of civilization, *should we not have it?* Those lines could support (37A), so draw a line connecting those two answers. The lines for (38B) say that a person could *search the pages of history in vain to find a single instance in which the common people…declared themselves in favor of a gold standard*. Those lines support (37B), so draw a line connecting those two answer choices. The lines for (38C) say that *the sympathies of the Democratic Party…are on the side of the struggling masses*. These lines don't mention anything about Bryan's views about the gold standard controversy, and these lines don't support any of the answer choices for Q37. Eliminate (38C). The lines for (38D) say what others believe about legislation to make the *well-to-do prosperous*, but there is no mention of Bryan's thoughts about the gold standard controversy. Eliminate (38D). Go back to the remaining pairs of answer choices and reread the question. The question asks which statement *Bryan would be most likely to agree with*. Choices (37A) and (38A) present an idea that Bryan refutes later in the passage, so eliminate those two answer choices. The correct answers are (37B) and (38B).

38. **B** (See explanation above.)

39. **D** This question asks how both passages discuss the issue of the gold standard. Because this question asks about both passages, it should be done after the questions are done for each individual passage. Use POE to go through the answers one passage at time. Passage 1 mentions *Acts of Congress* in line 50, *economists* in line 35, and *other nations* in line 34. Because Passage 1 does not mention *the Democratic Party*, eliminate (B). Now look for the remaining three answers in Passage 2. Passage 2 does not mention *Congress* or *economists*, so eliminate (A) and (B). Passage 2 mentions *all nations of the earth* in line 54. The correct answer is (D).

40. **A** This question asks how the two historical references mentioned help each speaker. The reference in Passage 1 says that *twice in our earlier history* and the Passage 2 reference says that someone *said in 1878 that this was a struggle*. Both of these references show this debate occurring in the past, which allows both speakers to say something to the effect of, "We've been talking about this for a while now." Eliminate any answer choice that is not consistent with this prediction. Choice (A) is a direct paraphrase of the prediction, so keep it. Choice (B) can be eliminated because there is no *established precedent*, just an idea that's been discussed previously. Choices (C) and (D) can be eliminated because the lines neither *challenge* nor *question* any of the ideas in the debate. The correct answer is (A).

41. **B** This question asks about a *central tension* between the passages. Because this is a general question about both passages, it should be done after all the other questions have been completed.

Use POE to go through the answers one passage at a time. Choice (A) can be eliminated because Cleveland is not advocating for *new legislation to enact the gold standard*. He is against the gold standard and says that *Acts of Congress were impotent to create equality* when the market said otherwise. Choice (B) looks good for Passage 1, because Cleveland is *questioning* the validity of the *free coinage bimetallic* proposal, so keep (B) for now. Choice (C) can be eliminated because Cleveland does not *demand gold standard proponents reconsider their position.* Choice (D) can be eliminated, because Cleveland never *presents studies.* The correct answer is (B).

42. **B** This question asks about the primary purpose of this passage. Because this is a general question, it should be done after the specific questions are complete. The passage begins with introducing the discovery of *a parasitic fungus* that manipulates *the behavior of ants.* The passage goes on to describe the research and the fungus. The primary purpose of the passage is to explain a new discovery. Eliminate any answers that aren't consistent with this prediction. Choice (A) can be eliminated because the passage was not written to *correct* any *misconception.* The first part of (B), *present the findings*, is consistent with the prediction, and the second part of the answer choice is supported by the final sentence of the passage (*The research also is... the first extensive study of zombie ants in North America*). Choice (C) can be eliminated because a new fungus has been discovered, not a new ant. Choice (D) can be eliminated because the passage is not explaining differences between types of relationships. The correct answer is (B).

43. **B** This question asks why fungi have evolved to control the behavior of the ants. Go back to the text and find the window in which the author discusses how the fungi works. In the second paragraph, the author says that the fungus species that infects ants *induces hosts to die attached by their mandibles to plant material.* The author goes on to say that the dead ant attached to the plant provides *a platform from which the fungus can grow and shoot spores to infect other ants.* Find an answer that is consistent with this information. Choice (A) can be eliminated because the fungus spreads through spores, not through bite wounds. Choice (B) is consistent with the information in the text, so keep it. Choice (C) can be eliminated because the text says the fungus wants the ant to die attached to a plant. Choice (D) can be eliminated because it is the opposite of what the text says. The correct answer is (B).

44. **D** This question asks about the role of the *Formica* ant in the passage. Use the lead word to find the window and read carefully to determine why the author mentioned the *Formica* ant. In line 37, the author mentions the *Formica* ant as *another genus* of ant not normally targeted by the fungus. Researchers infected the *Formica* ants as well as ants from the *Camponotus* genus, the genus typically targeted by the fungus. Eliminate any answer choices that aren't consistent with the prediction. Choice (A) can be eliminated because the scientists already know that the *Formica* ants are *nontarget ants.* Choice (B) can be eliminated for the same reason as (A): *Formica* ants aren't *most affected* because they are *nontarget ants.* Choice (C) can be eliminated because it doesn't address the role of the ant in the research. Choice (D) is consistent with the prediction. The correct answer is (D).

45. **D** This question asks what tone the author communicates with the use of phrases such as *exquisite control…, most complex examples…,* and *impressive trick.* Use the lines provided to find the window, and read carefully for context. The phrases come from a quote from one of the researchers talking about how evolved the fungus is. The use of the words *exquisite* and *impressive* gives a positive tone, so eliminate (B) and (C). There is no evidence that the researcher is *amused* by the fungus, but he is impressed. Eliminate (A). The correct answer is (D).

46. **D** This question asks about a scenario in which zombie ant fungi would not successfully reproduce. Carefully read the second paragraph, in which the fungus reproduction is explained. The fungus infects *Camponotus* ants and *induces [them] to die attached by their mandibles to plant material.* The dead ant, attached to the plant, provides *a platform from which the fungus can grow and shoot spores to infect other ants.* Remember, because this is a *NOT* question, cross out the *NOT* and mark each answer choice as "true" or "false." Choice (A) is true. Although the fungus cannot control the *Formica* ant, it can infect and kill it. Keep (A). Choice (B) is true, so keep it. Choice (C) is true, so keep it. Choice (D) is false. A *Formica* ant that doesn't die on a plant will not provide any sort of platform for the fungus to grow from. The correct answer is (D).

47. **B** This question asks what the word *media* means in line 43. Go back to the text, find the word *media*, and cross it out. Carefully read the surrounding text to determine another word that would fit in the blank based on the context of the passage. The text describes the experiment and how the researchers *removed ant brains* and then kept them *alive in special media.* The missing word must mean something like "material" or "substance." Eliminate anything that is not consistent with this prediction. Choice (A), *communications*, might initially seem to be consistent with the word *media,* but it does not mean "substance" or "material." Eliminate (A). Choice (B) is consistent with the prediction, so keep it. Choice (C), *channels,* and (D), *periodicals,* may also be tempting because of the connection with *media,* but neither of those words is consistent with the prediction. The correct answer is (B).

48. **A** This question asks which part of the research was *most effective for obtaining an unprecedented amount of information.* The text says that the *researchers found thousands of unique chemicals, most of them completely unknown.* That is the *unprecedented information,* but remember that the question is asking about the *part of the research* that allowed them to obtain that information. Carefully read the window. The researchers were able to find out this information by growing the fungus *in the presence of brains from different ant species to determine what chemicals it produced for each brain.* Eliminate any answer choice that is not consistent with this prediction. Choice (A) is an exact paraphrase of the prediction, so keep it. Choice (B) was a part of the process, but not the one that allowed them to obtain all the information. Eliminate it. Choice (C), as with (B), was a part of the research, but not the key piece. Eliminate (C). Choice (D) might initially look attractive, but the scientists weren't actually looking at the fungus *in the ant brains.* Eliminate (D). The correct answer is (A).

49. **B** This is the best evidence question for a specific question, so simply look at the lines used to answer Q48. Remember, although (C) might look attractive, the question asks about the *part of the research* that allowed them to *obtain unprecedented information*, not the information itself. The correct answer is (B).

50. **C** This question asks about a unique outcome of the chemicals produced by the fungus. Notice that this is the first question in a paired set, so it can be done in tandem with Q51. Consider the answer for Q51 first. The lines for (51A) introduce the fungus, but don't mention anything about the chemicals the fungus produces. Eliminate (51A). The lines for (51B) say that the killer *can infect and kill nontarget ants* but cannot *manipulate their behavior*. These lines do not support any of the answers for Q50. Eliminate (51B). The lines for (51C) say *the fungus behaved differently in the presence of the ant brain it had co-evolved with*. These lines could look attractive on their own, but they do not support any of the answers for Q50. Eliminate (51C). The lines for (51D) say that the fungus/ant relationship is *one of the most complex examples of parasites controlling animal behavior*. These lines support the idea in (50C) that the complexity of this relationship is different than those *usually found in nature*. Draw a line connecting those two answers. Without support from Q51, (50A), (50B), and (50D) can be eliminated. The correct answers are (50C) and (51D).

51. **D** (See explanation above.)

52. **D** This question asks what type of evidence the team mostly used while studying the zombie ants. Most of their work took place in the lab, so eliminate (A). Choice (B) can also be eliminated because researchers were making observations rather than *predictions*. Choice (C) might initially look attractive, but the researchers were using the brains of *ants* in their research. Choice (D) is consistent with information in the passage. The correct answer is (D).

Section 2: Writing and Language

1. **C** The vocabulary is changing in the answer choices, so this question is testing word choice. Look for a word whose definition is consistent with the other ideas in the passage. The sentence discusses the *presence of blue recycling bins*, and the next sentence says that *most people are used to separating recyclable materials*. The underlined portion is preceded by *no longer*, so the definition should mean "out of the ordinary." An *innovation* is "a new way of doing something." While this is close, it is not the bins themselves that were an innovation, so eliminate (A). A *deviation* is "a departure from the norm." While this is close, the bins were not "going against the system," so eliminate (B). A *novelty* is "something new and unusual." The presence of the bins is now a normal, everyday sight, so keep (C). A *miracle* is "an extraordinary event," so eliminate (D). The correct answer is (C).

2. **D** The vocabulary is changing in the answer choices, so this question is testing word choice. All of the choices have similar meanings, so choose the answer whose tone best matches the passage. Choices (A), (B), and (C) are too informal, so eliminate them. The correct answer is (D).

3. **D**   The punctuation is changing in the answer choices, so the question is testing STOP and GO punctuation. However, notice that the sentence ends with a closed parenthesis. Therefore, the phrase must start with an open parenthesis; eliminate (B) and (C). There is no reason to use a dash to separate an idea already separated by parentheses, so eliminate (A). The correct answer is (D).

4. **A**   Note the question! The question asks for information that is *consistent with the description of textiles. Clothing* is a type of textile, so keep (A). *Paper, rubber*, and *wood* are not textiles, so eliminate (B), (C), and (D). The correct answer is (A).

5. **B**   Note the question! The question asks for information that is supported by the graph. The sentence is comparing the recycling rate of clothing to that of the other items in the graph. First, look up clothing on the graph and find that its rate is about 15%. Then look up each choice to see whether it's true, keeping in mind that the underlined part follows the word *only*. The rate for rubber and leather is about 16%, which is higher than that of clothing, but many other materials are also recycled at higher rates than clothing. Since rubber and leather aren't the only ones with higher rates, eliminate (A). The rate for plastic is 5% and wood is 9%, which is lower than that of clothing, so keep (B). The rate for yard trimmings is 53%, which is higher than that of clothing. Again, it is not the only higher rate, so eliminate (C). The rate for glass is 30%, which is another rate higher than that of clothing, so eliminate (D). It is true that *only* plastics and wood are lower. The correct answer is (B).

6. **C**   The conjunction is changing in the answer choices, so the question is testing consistency of ideas. Determine how the ideas before and after the conjunction relate to each other and select the appropriate transition. The sentence begins with *Not only*, which should be followed by *but also*. The correct answer is (C).

7. **A**   The transitional phrase is changing in the answer choices, so the question is testing consistency of ideas. Determine how the ideas before and after the transitional phrase relate to each other and select the appropriate transition. The previous sentence says that *re-using clothing can also save resources*. The next sentence says that *buying a pair of jeans second-hand saves that water*. The second sentence is similar in idea to the first, so eliminate (B) and (C) because they indicate a change of idea. *Moreover*, indicates a new idea that is similar to the first, but the second sentence is a specific example of the general idea in the first sentence; eliminate (D). The correct answer is (A).

8. **D**   First, commas are changing in the answer choices, so the question is testing the four ways to use a comma. The sentence does not contain a list, and the phrase *clothing waste by offering 15% off coupons to consumers who bring unwanted clothing* is a necessary part of the sentence. Therefore, there is no reason to use a comma; eliminate (A) and (C). Next, the vocabulary is changing, so the question is testing word choice. The meaning of the sentence is that *H&M is trying to* "reduce" *clothing waste. Rain* means "water that falls from clouds," so eliminate (B). *Rein* means to "control." The correct answer is (D).

9.   **B**   Note the question! The question asks for the most effective transition from the previous paragraph. Determine the subject of each paragraph to determine how they should be linked. The previous paragraph discusses H&M's desire to reduce clothing waste and the beginning of its plan to collect and recycle unwanted clothing. The next paragraph discusses the specific steps taken to recycle the clothing. The correct answer will connect these two ideas. Introducing *other retailers* does not connect the ideas, so eliminate (A). Introducing the *several steps* of recycling does connect the ideas, so keep (B). Introducing *low-quality fast fashion* does not connect the ideas, so eliminate (C). Introducing *a bigger discount* does not connect the ideas, so eliminate (D). The correct answer is (B).

10.   **B**   The phrases are changing in the answer choices, so the question is testing consistency and precision. Notice that the sentence contains a list. Therefore, all of the items in the list should be in a consistent format. The first part of the list says that items are *shredded*; the third part of the list says the items are *recycled*. Therefore, the underlined portion must be consistent in this verb phrasing. Choice (B), *repurposed*, is consistent with *shredded* and *recycled*. No other choice starts with the consistent verb phrasing. The correct answer is (B).

11.   **B**   Verbs are changing in the answer choices, so the question is testing consistency of verbs. A verb must be consistent with its subject and with the other verbs in the sentence. The subject of the verb is *the technology*, which is singular. To be consistent, the verb in the answer choices must also be singular. Eliminate (A), (C), and (D) because they are plural. The correct answer is (B).

12.   **D**   Apostrophes are changing in the answer choices, so the question is testing apostrophe usage. In this sentence, the pronoun refers to *people*, who possess the *loved one*. Therefore, the apostrophe is not needed because possessive pronouns do not use apostrophes. Eliminate (B) and (C). Next, pronouns are changing in the choices, so the question is testing consistency of pronouns. A pronoun must be consistent in number with the noun it is replacing. Since *people* is plural, the pronoun must also be plural. Eliminate (A). The correct answer is (D).

13.   **C**   Note the question! The question asks for the choice that combines the sentences, so it's testing precision and concision. Select the choice that keeps the intended meaning of the sentences using the fewest words. Consider (C) first because it's the shortest. The choice ends with *ofrendas*, and then a comma, and then the non-underlined portion is a modifier that describes the *ofrendas*. This creates a sentence that is both precise and concise. The correct answer is (C).

14.   **A**   Commas are changing in the answer choices, so the question is testing the four ways to use a comma. The sentence does not contain a list, so check for unnecessary information. Read the sentence with the phrases between the commas removed to see if the sentence retains the same meaning without it. In this case, all of the phrases are necessary, so there's no need for commas. Eliminate (B) and (C). The long dash cannot be followed by *and*, so eliminate (D). The correct answer is (A).

15. **B**   Note the question! The question asks for the explanation of the Aztec tradition, so it's test-ing consistency of ideas. The first part of the sentence says that *the dead would be offended by mourning*. The correct answer must be consistent with a "tradition" that would not offend the dead. Eliminate (A) because it describes an emotion (*sad*) but not a tradition. Keep (B) be-cause it describes a tradition of *celebration rather than sadness*. Eliminate (C) and (D) because neither describes a tradition. The correct answer is (B).

16. **A**   The phrases are changing in the answer choices, so the question is testing consistency and pre-cision. The sentence uses the phrase *similar to*, so it's comparing two things. The "thing" in the underlined portion must be consistent with the "thing" in the non-underlined portion. The sentence says that *ofrendas ... have items*. Thus, the correct answer must reference the "items" on *church altars*. The pronoun *those* could refer to the *items*, so keep (A). Choices (B) and (C) only mention the *altars* and not the *items* on the altars, so eliminate them both. Eliminate (D) because it mentions the *structures* and not the *items*. The correct answer is (A).

17. **A**   Note the question! The question asks where sentence 3 should be placed, so it's testing con-sistency. Determine the subject matter of the sentence, and find the other sentence that also discusses that information. Sentence 3 says *During these two days*, so it should be placed after a sentence that references two days. Sentence 2 discusses *November 1–2*, so sentence 3 should be placed after sentence 2. The correct answer is (A).

18. **C**   The pronouns are changing in the answer choices, so the question is testing consistency. The pronoun must be consistent with the noun it is referring to. The phrase *are best known for their elaborate ofrendas* refers to the *local artists*, so the pronoun should also refer to the artists. Eliminate (A) because *which* refers to things, and not people. Eliminate (B) because it creates two complete ideas which are separated by a comma; STOP punctuation is needed. Keep (C) because *whom* refers to people. Although *them* can refer to people, (D) also creates two com-plete ideas separated by a comma. Eliminate (D). The correct answer is (C).

19. **D**   Note the question! The question asks for information that is most consistent in style and con-tent with the information about why pillows and blankets are included on the altars, so it's testing consistency of ideas. The sentence includes the phrase *pillows and blankets (which pro-vide a resting spot for the spirits)*, which describes their function or use. *Smells delicious* describes a characteristic but not a function, so eliminate (A). *Pan de muerto* is an example but not a function, so eliminate (B). *Homemade* describes a characteristic but not a function, so elimi-nate (C). *Provide sustenance* describes a function, so keep (D). The correct answer is (D).

20. **B**   Note the question! The question asks for the choice that best concludes the paragraph, so it's testing consistency of ideas. The first sentence of the paragraph says that the celebration of the dead is *similar to preparing for a visit from living relatives*. The remaining sentences discuss the many items placed on the altars. Therefore, a concluding sentence should be consistent with each of those ideas. Claiming that it is *more work* would highlight how the situations are dif-ferent, not similar; since it's not consistent, eliminate (A). Mentioning both what is *included*

on an altar and the similarity to *when they were alive* is consistent, so keep (B). The *toys* is consistent with the items on the altars but does not conclude the paragraph by discussing the similarities for *preparing for a visit from living relatives*; eliminate (C). Eliminate (D) for the same reason as (C). The correct answer is (B).

21.   **A**   The phrases are changing in the answer choices, so the question is testing precision and concision. Select the shortest answer whose meaning is clear. Keep (A) because it does not contain any words after marigolds, so it is probably correct. The first sentence already states that *Many of the same items that decorate altars are also part of the cemetery vigils*, so there's no need to repeat that idea. Eliminate (B) and (C) because they are redundant. The phrase *that attract spirits with their bright colors* does not play a precise role in the sentence, so eliminate (D). The correct answer is (A).

22.   **D**   The phrases are changing in the answer choices, so the question is testing precision. The beginning of the sentence (*focusing on the finality of death*) is a modifying phrase that does not have a subject. Therefore, the subject must be placed immediately after the comma. In (A) and (C), it is the *merriment* that is *focusing on the finality of death*; this is not the correct meaning, so eliminate (A) and (C). In (B), it is *life* that is *focusing on the finality of death*; this is not the correct meaning, so eliminate (B). In (D), it is *the people* who are *focusing on the finality of death*. This is the precise intended meaning. The correct answer is (D).

23.   **A**   The transitional phrase is changing in the answer choices, so the question is testing consistency of ideas. Determine how the ideas before and after the transitional phrase relate to each other and select the appropriate transition. The previous sentence states that the *predictions that the machines would replace human bank tellers...did not immediately come true*. The next sentence states that *the number of human bank tellers also increased*. The second idea supports the first with evidence. *In fact* indicates support, so keep (A). *As a result* indicates an effect of a previous cause, so eliminate (B). *For example* is close, but the second sentence is not a specific example but rather general evidence; eliminate (C). *Therefore* indicates causality, so eliminate (D). The correct answer is (A).

24.   **D**   The punctuation is changing in the answer choices, so the question is testing punctuation. After reading the sentence, it should be clear that the sentence contains a list. The non-underlined portion of the list is separated by a comma: *provide specific bill denominations, and dispense information*. Therefore, all the items in the list must be separated by commas. Eliminate (A), (B), and (C) because they contain semicolons. The correct answer is (D).

25.   **C**   The vocabulary is changing in the answer choices, so the question is testing word choice. The sentence intends to say that *machines* are "more accurate" *with cash than people are*. The meaning of *rock solid* is unclear and the phrase is too informal for the passage, so eliminate (A). *Impeccable* means "without blame or fault," so eliminate (B). *Reliable* means "accurate," so keep (C). *Safer* means "protected" or "more secure," so eliminate (D). The correct answer is (C).

26. **D** Note the question! The question asks whether the graph should be added, so it's testing consistency of ideas. The graph should be added only if the information in the graph is consistent with the information in the passage. The passage compares and contrasts the services provided by human tellers and ATMs. The graph shows the income for different groups of people. The information is not consistent, so the graph should not be added; eliminate (A) and (B). The passage does not contrast *tellers and loan officers*, so eliminate (C). The wage data does *distract from the paragraph's focus*. The correct answer is (D).

27. **D** Note the question! The question asks where sentence 3 should be placed, so it's testing consistency. Determine the subject matter of the sentence, and find the other sentence that also discusses that information. Sentence 3 says that *They also limit the amount of cash...*, which lists another downside of ATMs. Thus, sentence 3 should follow another sentence about the downside of ATMs. Sentence 5 gives a downside when it states *ATMs are far more vulnerable to theft*. The correct answer is (D).

28. **C** The vocabulary is changing in the answer choices, so the question is testing word choice. The sentence intends to say that *tech-savvy customers are increasingly* "familiar with" *their smart phones. Custom* means "personalized," so eliminate (A) and (D). *Accustomed* means "familiar with" or "used to," so keep (B) and (C). The proper idiom is *accustomed to*. The correct answer is (C).

29. **B** Note the question! The question asks for a supporting example for the main idea of the paragraph, so it's testing consistency of ideas. The paragraph as a whole compares and contrasts human tellers, ATMs, and mobile apps. The previous sentence contrasts mobile apps with ATMs by claiming that the apps are better at some tasks, so the underlined portion must be consistent with that idea. The percentage of people using the app is not consistent, so eliminate (A). Comparing the mobile apps to what *ATMs are capable of* is consistent, so keep (B). Stating that mobile apps are *not always designed well* and stating that they are *highly susceptible to theft or fraud* is not consistent with the apps outperforming ATMs, so eliminate (C) and (D). The correct answer is (B).

30. **A** Note the question! The question asks for the most effective combination of the two sentences, so it's testing precision and concision. Select the shortest answer that keeps the intended meaning of the sentence. Choice (A) is the shortest answer. It keeps the intended meaning of the sentence and uses proper punctuation — the colon is HALF-STOP punctuation which can separate two complete ideas. The correct answer is (A).

31. **D** First, nouns are changing in the answer choices, so the question is testing consistency of nouns. A noun must be consistent in number with the other nouns in the sentence. The sentence contains the noun *teller windows*, which is plural. To be consistent, the noun in the answer choice must also be plural. Eliminate (A) and (B) because they contain the singular noun *kiosk*. Next, the adjoining phrase is changing, so the question is testing precision of language. The proper idiom is *replacing...with*, so the banks are *replacing* teller windows *with* kiosks. The correct answer is (D).

32. **B**   First, the transitions are changing in the answer choices, so the question is testing consistency. The sentence states what the employees are *trained* to do: they are *trained to answer questions* and to *handle deposits and provide loan advice*. The phrases *as well as* can join the phrases, so keep (A) and (B). *Also* cannot join the phrases, so eliminate (C). The *comma + and* acts as STOP punctuation. In this case, it would separate a complete idea and an incomplete idea, which is not allowed; eliminate (D). Next, the difference between (A) and (B) is the number of words, so the question is testing concision and precision. Both choices have the same meaning, so select the more concise answer. Eliminate (A). The correct answer is (B).

33. **A**   The punctuation is changing in the answer choices, so the question is testing STOP and GO punctuation. Use the vertical line test, and identify the ideas as complete or incomplete. Draw the vertical line between the words *out* and *machines*. The first phrase is an incomplete idea, and the second phrase is a complete idea. Therefore, GO punctuation is needed. The semicolon and the period are STOP punctuation, so eliminate (B) and (C). The sentence starts with *So while*, so there is no need to add *nevertheless*. Eliminate (D). The correct answer is (A).

34. **A**   The transitional phrase is changing in the answer choices, so the question is testing consistency of ideas. Determine how the ideas before and after the transitional phrase relate to each other and select the appropriate transition. The first sentence states that there is *an arms race against bacteria*. Then it says that *Bacteria...develop resistance to antibiotics* and follows with *scientists must continually develop newer, stronger antibiotics*. The second is an effect of the first. *As a result* indicates an effect, so keep (A). *However* and *nevertheless* indicate opposite ideas, so eliminate (B) and (C). Developing new antibiotics is not an *example* of bacterial resistance, so eliminate (D). The correct answer is (A).

35. **C**   Note the question! The question asks for the scientists' goal, so it's testing consistency of ideas. Earlier in the paragraph it says that *scientists have been engaged in an arms race against bacteria* and that they need to *overcome the resistant bacteria*, so the correct answer must be consistent with "outcompete." *Count the number* is not consistent, so eliminate (A). *Facilitate* means "to help," which is not consistent, so eliminate (B). *Stay ahead of* is consistent, so keep (C). *Shoot at* is too literal of the arms race and is not consistent with "outcompete," so eliminate (D). The correct answer is (C).

36. **D**   The phrases are changing in the answer choices with the option to DELETE, so the question is testing concision and precision. Consider the option to DELETE carefully, as it is often correct. The sentence already says *extended trips*, so there's no reason to repeat that idea. Choices (A), (B), and (C) are each redundant and unnecessary, so eliminate them. The correct answer is (D).

37. **A**   Verbs are changing in the answer choices, so the question is testing consistency of verbs. A verb must be consistent with its subject and with the other verbs in the sentence. The subject of the verb is *pathogens*, which is plural. Therefore, the verbs must also be plural. *Becomes* is singular, so eliminate (C) and (D). Next, check the other verbs in the sentence for consistency.

The non-underlined verb *were surprised* is past tense, so the correct answer should also be in the past tense. *Mutated* and *became* are past tense, so keep (A). *Had mutated* and *had become* are the past perfect tense, but the non-underlined verb does not contain *had*. Eliminate (B) because it's not consistent with the sentence. The correct answer is (A).

38. **C**   The order of the phrases is changing in the answer choices, so the question is testing precision. To create precise meaning, the modifying phrase must be placed immediately next to the thing that it modifies. The modifier in the following parentheses (*the friction between cells and the fluids they interact with*) is describing the *fluid shear stress*. Therefore, the *fluid shear stress* must be placed just before the parentheses. Only one choice places *fluid shear stress* last. The correct answer is (C).

39. **B**   Note the question! The question asks whether the phrase should be added, so it's testing consistency and concision. The phrase should be added only if the information is consistent with the information in the passage and is not redundant. The first part of the sentence states how scientists believe microgravity will affect *bacteria inside the human body*. The new phrase says that studying this allows for *a glimpse into how that pathogen behaves in the human digestive tract*. The idea is consistent and is not redundant, so it should be added. Eliminate (C) and (D). The new phrase shifts from what scientists believe to actually studying it. The correct answer is (B).

40. **C**   Note the question! The question asks for the most precise description of the proceeding depicted in the first part of the sentence, so it's testing precision. The first part of the sentence discusses the *studies*, so the correct answer should match that precisely. *Subject* could mean "ideas" or "participants." Neither matches "studies," so eliminate (A). *Examinations* means "inspections," so eliminate (B). *Experiments* means "studies" or "acts of discovery," so keep (C). *Tests* means "methods to assess," so eliminate (D). The correct answer is (C).

41. **B**   Verbs are changing in the answer choices, so the question is testing consistency of verbs. A verb must be consistent with its subject and with the other verbs in the sentence. The subject of the verb is *they*, which is plural. Since all the answers are plural, check the other verbs. The other verbs in the sentence are *are looking* and *attack*, which are present tense. Choices (A), (C), and (D) are past tense, so eliminate them. The correct answer is (B).

42. **B**   Commas are changing in the answer choices, so the question is testing the four ways to use a comma. The sentence does not contain a list, so check for unnecessary information. Removing any of the phrases between the commas would cause the sentence to not make sense. The information is necessary, so there is no need to use commas. The correct answer is (B).

43. **A**   Note the question! The question asks for the most effective transition, so it's testing consistency of ideas. Determine how the ideas before and after the sentence relate to each other and select the appropriate transition. The previous sentences discuss the need for *developing a vaccine for Salmonella*. The following sentences discuss using *Salmonella as a delivery vehicle* for another

vaccine. The correct transition will shift from needing a vaccine to cure *Salmonella* to using *Salmonella* as a vaccine to cure some other illness. *Salmonella...playing an important role in vaccine research... in an unexpected way* connects the two ideas, so keep (A). Stating that a *vaccine hasn't yet been developed* does not connect to the second part, so eliminate (B). Wanting to *develop better vaccines against... other* illnesses connects to the second part, but doesn't mention *Salmonella*, so eliminate (C). *Studies...beyond the International Space Station* do not connect the ideas, so eliminate (D). The correct answer is (A).

44.　**B**　Commas are changing in the answer choices, so the question is testing the four ways to use a comma. The sentence does not contain a list, so check for unnecessary information. Removing only the word *substances* would change the meaning of the sentence to mean that some *antigens stimulate the production of antibodies*, while others do not; eliminate (A). Removing the phrase *substances that stimulate the production of antibodies* would not change the meaning of the sentence, and is therefore unnecessary; keep (B). Removing the phrase *substances that stimulate the production of antibodies to multiple body systems* would change the meaning of the sentence; the antigens would no longer be delivered to multiple body systems. Eliminate (C). Choice (B) is better than (D) because it separates the unnecessary information from the rest of the sentence with commas. The correct answer is (B).

Section 3: Math (No Calculator)

1.　**C**　The question asks for an equation that represents a graph. To find the best equation, compare features of the graph to the answer choices. The graph for this question has a y-intercept of 7 and a negative slope. Eliminate answer choices that do not match this information. All the choices are already in $y = mx + b$ form, in which m is the slope and b is the y-intercept. Choices (A) and (B) have y-intercepts of 0; eliminate (A) and (B). The difference between (C) and (D) is the slope, so calculate slope using the formula $slope = \dfrac{y_2 - y_1}{x_2 - x_1}$. The graph goes through the points (0, 7) and (7, 0), so $slope = \dfrac{0 - 7}{7 - 0}$, which is $\dfrac{-7}{7}$ or –1. Eliminate (D). The correct answer is (C).

2.　**D**　The question asks for an equation in terms of a specific variable. Although there are variables in the answer choices, plugging in on this question would be difficult, given the lack of calculator use and the four different variables. Instead, solve for B. To begin to isolate B, start by multiplying both sides by 5 to get $2A + B + 2C = 5D$. Next, subtract $2A$ and $2C$ from both sides to get $B = 5D - 2A - 2C$. The correct answer is (D).

3. **A**   The question asks for the value of *a*. Although there are numbers in the answer choices, plugging in the answers would be difficult, given the lack of calculator use and the fractions in (B) and (C). Instead, solve for *a*. To begin to isolate *a*, combine like terms on both sides of the equation to get $2a - 9 = 7a - 4$. Next, subtract $2a$ from both sides to get $-9 = 5a - 4$. Add 4 to both sides to get $-5 = 5a$. Divide both sides to get $-1 = a$. The correct answer is (A).

4. **D**   The question asks for the value of a variable in a system of inequalities. There are variables in the answer choices, so plug in. Find a value of *y* that works in the first equation, such as $y = 2$. Plug this in to the second inequality to get $x < 3(2) + 4$, which is $x < 10$. Use this inequality to plug in for *x*. Make $x = 9$. Next, plug in this value for *x* into each answer choice and eliminate any choice that is not true when $x = 9$. Choice (A) becomes $9 < \frac{7}{3}$. This is false; eliminate (A). Choice (B) becomes $9 < 3$; eliminate (B). Choice (C) becomes $9 < \frac{19}{3}$; eliminate (C). Choice (D) becomes $9 < 11$; keep (D). The correct answer is (D).

5. **B**   The question asks for the value of an angle on a figure. Use the geometry basic approach. Start by labeling the figure with the given information. Because *O* is the center of the circle, *BO* and *CO* are both radii, so $BO = CO$, and triangle *BOC* is an isosceles triangle. Therefore, angle *CBO* is also equal to 36°; mark this in the figure. The angles in a triangle add up to 180°, so the third angle in the triangle with angles 28° and 36° must equal $180 - 28 - 36 = 116$°. Label this angle in the diagram:

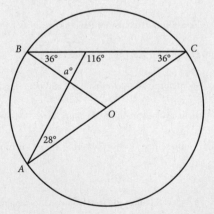

A straight angle has 180°, so the angle adjacent to the 116° must be $180 - 116 = 64$°; label this in the diagram. Finally, the triangle containing the angle with measure *a*° has 180°, so *a* must be $180 - 36 - 64 = 80$°. The correct answer is (B).

6. **C** The question asks for the perimeter of the traffic island. Use the geometry basic approach. Start by drawing an isosceles triangle. Next, label the figure. Because there are variables for the side lengths, plug in. Make $s = 6$. Label the two equal sides as having a length of 6. The third side is *4 meters shorter than the equal sides*, so the third side must be $6 - 4 = 2$ meters. Label that side. The perimeter is the sum of the sides: $6 + 6 + 2 = 14$. This is the target value; circle it. Next, make $s = 6$ in each answer and eliminate any answer that does not equal the target value. Choice (A) becomes $2(6) - 4$, which is $12 - 4$ or 8. This does not equal the target value; eliminate (A). Choice (B) becomes $\dfrac{(6)^2 - 4(6)}{2}$, which is $\dfrac{36 - 24}{2}$ or $\dfrac{12}{2}$, which is 6. Eliminate (B). Choice (C) becomes $3(6) - 4$, which is $18 - 4$ or 14. Keep (C), but check (D) just in case. Choice (D) becomes $\dfrac{6 - 4}{2}$, which is $\dfrac{2}{2}$ or 1. Eliminate (D). The correct answer is (C).

7. **D** The question asks for the equation of a circle given the endpoints of the diameter. The equation of a circle in standard form is $(x - h)^2 + (y - k)^2 = r^2$, where (h, k) is the center and r is the radius. Since the endpoints have the same x-coordinate, the length of the diameter is the difference in the y-coordinates. Therefore, the diameter is $7 - 1 = 6$, and the radius is 3. This means that $r^2 = 9$. Eliminate (B) and (C), which have $r^2 = 36$. Be careful of sign changes with the coordinates of the center of the circle. In this circle equation, the h is -11, so the first part of the equation is $[x - (-11)]^2$, or $(x + 11)^2$. Eliminate (A). The correct answer is (D).

8. **C** The question asks for the solution set of the equation. Since the question asks for a specific value and the answers contain numbers, plug in the answers. Begin by labeling the answers as a and start with (B). If $a = 1$, the equation becomes $1 - 6 = \sqrt{8(1) - 7} - 4$, which is $-5 = \sqrt{1} - 4$ or $-5 = -3$. This is false; eliminate (B) and (D) because both answers include 1. There must be a positive number or 0 under the square root; eliminate (A) because if $a = 0$, there would be a negative number under the radical. Only one choice remains, but test it to be sure. If $a = 11$, then the equation becomes $11 - 6 = \sqrt{8(11) - 7} - 4$, which is $5 = \sqrt{81} - 4$ or $5 = 9 - 4$. This is true. The correct answer is (C).

9. **A** The question asks for an equivalent form of an expression when one function is divided by another. There are variables in the answer choices, so plug in. Make $a = 5$. The first function becomes $h(5) = 5^2 + 5 - 20 = 25 + 5 - 20 = 10$. The second function becomes $k(5) = 5^3 - 16(5)$ $= 125 - 80 = 45$. The question asks for $\dfrac{h(a)}{k(a)}$, so plug these values in to get $\dfrac{10}{45}$. This is the target

value; circle it. Now plug $a = 5$ into the answer choices to see which one matches the target value. Choice (A) becomes $\frac{5 + 5}{5(5 + 4)} = \frac{10}{5(9)} = \frac{10}{45}$. This matches the target, so keep (A) but check the remaining answers just in case. Choice (B) becomes $\frac{5 + 5}{5(5 - 4)} = \frac{10}{5(1)} = \frac{10}{5}$. Eliminate (B). Choice (C) becomes $\frac{5 + 5}{5 + 4} = \frac{10}{9}$. Eliminate (C). Choice (D) becomes $5 + 5 = 10$. Eliminate (D). The correct answer is (A).

10. **C** The question asks for an equation that represents a graph. One option would be to pick a point that is on the graph and plug it into the answer choices to see which ones are true. The answers are all in factored form, however, which shows the roots or solutions of a function. If $(x - a)$ is a factor of a polynomial, then a is a solution, and the graph will cross the x-axis at a. This graph crosses the x-axis at -2, 0, and 1, so the factors must include $(x + 2)$, x, and $(x - 1)$. Eliminate (B) and (D) because they do not contain these factors. Compare the remaining answers, (A) and (C). They have the same factors, so plugging in the points will result in true statements for both. Instead, pick an x-value that is not a root, such as $x = -1$. The exact y-value is not clear, but it must be positive. Choice (A) becomes $y = -(-1)(-1 - 1)(-1 + 2)$ or $y = 1(-2)(1)$. This becomes $y = -2$, which does not match the graph. Eliminate (A). The correct answer is (C).

11. **A** The question asks for the value of an expression given an equation. Because the question includes a relationship between the variables, plug in. Start by plugging in for y and solving for x in the first equation. Make $y = 2$. The equation becomes $\frac{x}{3(2)} = 3$, which is $\frac{x}{6} = 3$. Multiply both sides by 6 to get $x = 18$. Next, plug $y = 2$ and $x = 18$ into $\frac{y}{x}$ to get $\frac{2}{18}$, which is $\frac{1}{9}$. The correct answer is (A).

12. **B** The question asks for the number of jars that hold 3 tomatoes. Since the question asks for a specific value and the answers contain numbers in increasing order, plug in the answers. Begin by labeling the answers as "jars with 3 tomatoes" and start with (B), 52. If 52 jars hold 3 tomatoes each, then these jars hold a total of $52 \times 3 = 156$ tomatoes. Because there are 80 jars, there are $80 - 52 = 28$ jars that hold 5 tomatoes each, for a total of $28 \times 5 = 140$ tomatoes in these jars. This gives a total of $156 + 140 = 296$ tomatoes, which matches the value given in the question, so stop here. The correct answer is (B).

13. **A** The question asks for the value of a function. In function notation, the number inside the parentheses is the x-value that goes into the function, and the value that comes out of the function is the y-value. Plug $x = 0$ into the f function to get $f(0) = 2 - [g(0)]^2$. Now plug $x = 0$ into the g function to get $g(0) = 3(0) - 3 = 0 - 3 = -3$. Plug this value into the f function for $g(0)$ to get $f(0) = 2 - [-3]^2 = 2 - (9) = -7$. The correct answer is (A).

14. **B**   The question asks for an equation that models a specific situation. Translate the question in bite-sized pieces and eliminate after each piece. One piece of information says that the population of Bulgaria is decreasing. This will translate to a negative slope, so eliminate (C) and (D), which have positive slopes. Compare the remaining answers. The difference between (A) and (B) is the slope, so calculate slope using the formula $slope = \dfrac{y_2 - y_1}{x_2 - x_1}$. The question states that the population was *approximately 9 million people in 1989* and *7.4 million people in 2011*. Because x is *years after the year 1989* and $P(x)$ is in *millions of people*, the points are $(0, 9)$ and $(22, 7.4)$. Use the slope formula to get $slope = \dfrac{7.4 - 9}{22 - 0}$, which is $-\dfrac{1.6}{22}$. Both answers have slopes with a denominator of 220, so multiply by $\dfrac{10}{10}$ to get a slope of $-\dfrac{16}{220}$. The correct answer is (B).

15. **B**   The question asks for the value of k in the system of equations. Since the question asks for a specific value, plug in the answers. With two equations, it may be hard to tell if a value that doesn't work is too big or too small, so start with any of the answers. Since 0 is an easy number to work with, start with (B). If $k = 0$, the first equation becomes $y = x^2 + 2x + 0$ or $y = x^2 + 2x$. The second equation states that $y = 2x$, so the right sides of the two equations can be set equal to get $2x = x^2 + 2x$. Subtract $2x$ from both sides to get $x^2 = 0$. Take the square root of both sides to get $x = 0$. There is only one solution when $k = 0$. The correct answer is (B).

16. **17**   The question asks for the sum of y and z, which are two of the coefficients in the expression $xa^2 + ya + z$. This expression comes from subtracting the first polynomial ($a^2 + 2a + 4$) from the second polynomial ($3a^2 - 4a + 27$), so the resulting expression is $(3a^2 - 4a + 27) - (a^2 + 2a + 4)$. Work in bite-sized pieces. It is unnecessary to know what x is to solve the question, so ignore the a^2 terms. Subtracting the a terms gives $-4a - 2a = -6a$, so $y = -6$. Subtracting the constants gives $27 - 4 = 23$, so $z = 23$. Therefore, $y + z = -6 + 23$, which is 17. The correct answer is 17.

17. **6**   The question asks for the positive solution of a quadratic. When given a quadratic in standard form, which is $ax^2 + bx + c$, it is often necessary to factor it to solve the question. Find two numbers that add to -1 and multiply to -30. These are -6 and 5. Therefore, the equation factors to $(n - 6)(n + 5) = 0$. Set each factor equal to 0 and solve to find the solutions. If $n - 6 = 0$, then $n = 6$. If $n + 5 = 0$, then $n = -5$. The question asks for the positive solution, so $n = 6$. The correct answer is 6.

18. **3**   The question asks for the value of a variable in the context of a model. In the form $y = mx + b$, m is the slope and b is the y-intercept. Therefore, this question asks for the slope of the equation, so calculate slope using the formula $slope = \dfrac{y_2 - y_1}{x_2 - x_1}$. The question states that *at the start of the month she has completed 12 assignments* and x is *the number of weeks since the start of the month*, so when

$x = 0$, $y = 12$. Additionally, the question states that *she completes 3 assignments per week*, so when $x = 1$, $y = 12 + 3$, or 15. Therefore, two points are (0, 12) and (1, 15). The slope formula gives *slope* = $\frac{15 - 12}{1 - 0}$, which is $\frac{3}{1}$ or 3. The correct answer is 3.

19. **22**   The question asks for the area of a sector of the circle. The parts of a circle have a proportional relationship, so the fraction of the degrees in the shaded region is the same as the fraction of the sector area out of the total area. Set up the proportion $\frac{degrees}{360} = \frac{sector\ area}{total\ area}$, then plug in the given information to get $\frac{110}{360} = \frac{sector\ area}{72}$. Since calculator use is not allowed, reduce the fraction on the left to $\frac{11}{36}$ before cross-multiplying to get 11(72) = 36(*sector area*). Rather than doing the awkward multiplication on the left, divide both sides by 36 first to get 11(2) = *sector area*. Therefore, the shaded region has an area of 22. The correct answer is 22.

20. $\frac{14}{8}$, $\frac{7}{4}$**, or 1.75**

The question asks for the value of a variable given a system of equations. Try to make the other variable disappear. Because the unwanted variable has the same coefficient in both equations, stack the equations and subtract:

$$
\begin{array}{r}
9x + 2y = 17.75 \\
- [x + 2y = 3.75] \\
\hline
8x\qquad\ = 14
\end{array}
$$

Divide both sides by 8 to get $x = \frac{14}{8}$. Since this answer fits in the grid, there is no need to reduce. The correct answer is $\frac{14}{8}$, $\frac{7}{4}$, or 1.75.

Section 4: Math (Calculator)

1.   **B**   The question asks for the year when the number of tenants in the building increased the fastest. Use ballparking and estimation to eliminate incorrect answers. The graph represents the total number of tenants on the y-axis and years on the x-axis. For the number of tenants to increase the fastest, the line should have a great positive slope. In 2005 and 2007, the slope is negative; eliminate (A) and (C). In 2006, the slope of the line is steeper than in 2009; eliminate (D). The correct answer is (B).

2. **D** The question asks about population based on information about a study of a sample from that population. Since the residents were randomly selected, the incidence of the gene mutation found in the study should match that of the larger population. To extrapolate the study results, set up a proportion. In this case, the proportion is based on the number of mutations out of the total of each group: $\frac{4}{500} = \frac{x}{15,000}$. Cross-multiply to get $500x = 60,000$. Divide both sides by 500 to get $x = 120$. The correct answer is (D).

3. **C** The question asks for an algebraic expression to represent a situation. There are variables in the answer choices, so plug in. Make $n = 2$. If each box of cookies costs \$2, then 4 boxes of cookies will cost $2 \times 4 = \$8$. This is the target value; circle it. Now plug $n = 2$ into the answer choices to see which one matches the target value. Choice (A) becomes $\frac{2}{4}$, which reduces to $\frac{1}{2}$. This does not match the target, so eliminate (A). Choice (B) becomes $\frac{4}{2}$, which reduces to 2. Eliminate (B). Choice (C) becomes $4(2) = 8$. Keep (C), but check (D) just in case. Choice (D) becomes $2 + 4 = 6$. Eliminate (D). The correct answer is (C).

4. **A** The question asks for the value of an angle on a figure. Use the geometry basic approach. Start by labeling the figure with the given information. Mark lines l_1 and l_2 as parallel and the angle marked $a°$ as 110. It may not be immediately obvious how to get the value of b, so see what else can be determined. There are 180° in a triangle, so the angle to the right of a is $180 - 110 - 30 = 40°$. When two parallel lines like l_1 and l_2 are cut by a third line, like the one to the right of the 40° angle and the angle marked $b°$, two kinds of angles are created: big and small. All small angles are equal, and both these angles are small angles. Therefore, $b = 40$. The correct answer is (A).

5. **B** The question asks for a system of equations that models a specific situation. Translate the question in bite-sized pieces and eliminate after each piece. One piece of information says that the total number of digital and paper subscriptions was 1,800, so one of the equations must be $d + p = 1,800$. Eliminate (C), which does not contain this equation. Compare the remaining answer choices. All are equal to 20,760, which is the total revenue from the sale of subscriptions. Find the other information related to money. Digital subscriptions cost \$8, so $8d$ must be part of the equation. This does not appear in (A), so eliminate it. The revenue from the digital subscriptions must be added to the revenue from the paper subscriptions to get the total revenue, but (D) multiplies the values. Eliminate (D). The correct answer is (B).

6. **A** The question asks for the predicted value given a graph. This specific value will be based on the line of best fit, but the maximum heart rate of a 60-year-old runner is not on the graph. Use either the equation or the graph of the line of best fit to determine the value. In the equation, the x-value is

the age and the y-value is the heart rate. The equation becomes $y = -0.84(60) + 216.9$ or $y = -50.4 + 216.9 = 166.5$. To use the graph instead, continue the line of best fit off the right side of the graph a bit, then estimate where an age of 60 years would fall along the horizontal axis. From this point, trace up to find the intersection with the line of best fit, using the answer sheet as a straight edge if necessary. It is between the horizontal gridlines for 160 and 170 on the maximum heart rate axis. Only the value in (A) falls between 160 and 170. The correct answer is (A).

7. **C** The question asks for the value of $c - 2$ in the given equation. Since the question asks for a specific value and the answers contain numbers in increasing order, plug in the answers. Begin by labeling the answers as "$c - 2$" and start with (B), 3. If $c - 2 = 3$, then the equation becomes $\frac{3}{3} = 3$ or $1 = 3$. This is not true, so eliminate (B). A smaller value of $c - 2$ is needed to make the two sides of the equation closer to the same value, so try (C) next. If $c - 2 = \sqrt{3}$, the equation becomes $\frac{3}{\sqrt{3}} = \sqrt{3}$. Multiply both sides by $\sqrt{3}$ to get $3 = \sqrt{3} \times \sqrt{3}$ or $3 = 3$. This is true. The correct answer is (C).

8. **B** The question asks for an equation with a y-intercept of -1. To find the equation, look for the y-intercept in each answer choice. Each answer choice is already in slope-intercept form: $y = mx + b$, where m represents the slope and b represents the y-intercept. Therefore, the correct answer must have a b term of -1. Choices (A), (C), and (D) have y-intercepts of $-\frac{1}{2}$, 0, and 1, respectively; eliminate them. The correct answer is (B).

9. **D** The question asks for a system of inequalities that models a specific situation. Translate the question in bite-sized pieces and eliminate after each piece. One piece of information says that Sarah purchases *more than 360 items*. The items she purchases are canvases (a) and paint bottles (b), so one inequality must be $a + b > 360$. Eliminate (B) and (C) because they do not contain this inequality. Compare the remaining answer choices. The difference between (A) and (D) is which way the inequality sign is pointing. The question states that Sarah *goes over-budget*, so she spent more than \$1,700. The expression on the left is therefore greater than the cost. This does not fit (A), so eliminate it. The correct answer is (D).

10. **C** The question asks for the number of beakers needed to hold 4 liters of solution. Since the question asks for a specific value and the answers contain numbers in increasing order, plug in the answers. Begin by labeling the answers as "number of beakers" and start with (B), 4. If there are 4 beakers each holding 800 milliliters, they can hold a total of $4 \times 800 = 3,200$ milliliters. There are 1,000 milliliters in a liter, so 3,200 milliliters is equivalent to 3.2 liters. There are 4 liters of solution, so there are not enough beakers. Eliminate (B) and (A), which are too small. Try (C) next. If there are 5 beakers, they can hold $5 \times 800 = 4,000$ milliliters or 4 liters. This matches the question. The correct answer is (C).

11.　**A**　The question asks for the radius of the beaker, in inches. Since the question asks for a specific value and the answers contain numbers in increasing order, plug in the answers. Begin by labeling the answers as "radius" and start with (B), 2.28 inches. If n = 2.28, the volume becomes $\frac{21\pi(2.28)^3}{12} \approx \frac{21\pi(11.85)}{12} \approx \frac{782}{12} \approx 65$ cubic inches. The question states that the volume of 800 milliliters is 13.2 cubic inches, so this is much too large. Eliminate (B), (C), and (D). The correct answer is (A).

12.　**A**　The question asks for the graph that models a specific situation. To find the best graph, read the question carefully and compare features of the graphs in the answer choices, then use Process of Elimination. The question states that the beaker was full of a solution which then evaporated over time. Therefore, the height of the solution in the beaker must be decreasing. Choice (C) shows a constant height over time. Eliminate (C). Choice (D) shows a linear decrease over time. Although the solution evaporates at a constant rate, the odd shape of the beaker would make the height of the solution change in a non-linear way. Eliminate (D). Since the beaker is narrower at the top, the height of the solution will decrease quickly at first then more slowly near the wide base of the beaker. Eliminate (B), which shows the height decreasing more quickly near the end of the evaporation period. The correct answer is (A).

13.　**A**　The question asks for the power rating of a machine given that power is work per unit time. Set up the power equation: $power = \frac{work}{time}$. Now find the information about work and time. Work is defined as *the product of the mass of the object, in kilograms; the distance the object moves, in meters; and the gravitational constant of 9.8 meters per second squared*. Put this into the power formula to get $power = \frac{(mass)(distance)\left(9.8\,\frac{m}{s^2}\right)}{time}$. The time is given as 18 seconds, the mass as 100 kilograms, and the distance as 3.6 meters. Plug these values into the formula to get $\frac{(100\text{ kg})(3.6\text{ m})\left(9.8\,\frac{m}{s^2}\right)}{18\text{ s}} = \frac{3,528}{18} = 196$. The correct answer is (A).

14.　**B**　The question asks for one variable in terms of another. There are variables in the answer choices, so plug in. Make x = 2. This is the target value; circle it. Use this to find the value of y: $y = \frac{1}{2^3} = \frac{1}{8}$. Now plug $y = \frac{1}{8}$ into the answer choices to see which one matches the target value. Use a calculator if needed to find the values. Choice (A) becomes $\left(\frac{1}{8}\right)^{\frac{1}{3}} = \sqrt[3]{\frac{1}{8}} = \frac{1}{2}$. This does not match the target value, so eliminate (A). A negative exponent flips the base to its reciprocal, so (B) becomes $\left(\frac{1}{8}\right)^{-\frac{1}{3}} = (8)^{\frac{1}{3}} = \sqrt[3]{8} = 2$. Keep (B), but check the remaining answer choices just in case. Choice (C) becomes $-\left(\frac{1}{8}\right)^3 = -\left(\frac{1}{512}\right)$, and (D) becomes $\left(\frac{1}{8}\right)^3 = \left(\frac{1}{512}\right)$. Eliminate (C) and (D).

The correct answer is (B).

15. **C** The question asks for the value of x that is not in the domain of $f(x)$, which is a value of x that does not work in the equation. Since the question asks for a specific value and the answers contain numbers in increasing order, plug in the answers. Begin by labeling the answers as x and start with (B), 0. If $x = 0$, the function becomes $f(0) = \frac{5}{0^2 - 5(0) + 4}$, which is $\frac{5}{4}$. This is a value for $f(x)$ that works, so $x = 0$ is in the domain of $f(x)$; eliminate (B). It can be tricky to determine whether a larger or smaller number is needed when working with quadratics, so just pick a direction. Try (C). If $x = 1$, the function becomes $f(1) = \frac{5}{1^2 - 5(1) + 4}$, which is $\frac{5}{1 - 5 + 4}$ or $\frac{5}{0}$. This is undefined, so $x = 1$ must not be in the domain of $f(x)$. The correct answer is (C).

16. **B** The question asks about the mean, median, and mode of a set of data. The mean or average is defined as $\frac{total}{\# \ of \ things}$. The number of things is 24, since the farmer took the total for each of the 24 chickens for the week. To find the total, take each number of eggs times the frequency for that number, then add all the results together. The total is $8(1) + 7(3) + 6(8) + 5(5) + 4(2) + 2(5) = 8 + 21 + 48 + 25 + 8 + 10 = 120$. Therefore, the mean is $\frac{120}{24} = 5$. The median of a list of numbers is the middle number when all values are arranged in order. In lists with an even number of items, the median is the average of the middle two numbers. There are 24 chickens, so the median number of eggs will be the average of the eggs laid by the 12th and 13th chickens. The number of eggs are already listed in order, so start counting from the 1st chicken, which laid 8 eggs. The 2nd, 3rd, and 4th chickens laid 7 eggs each. The next 8 chickens, the 5th through the 12th, laid 6 eggs and the 13th chicken laid 5 eggs. Therefore, the median number of eggs is $\frac{6+5}{2} = 5.5$. This is greater than the mean, so eliminate (A) and (D). Now find the mode, which is the most common number in a

set of data. In this set, the number of eggs with the highest frequency is 6, so the mode is 6. This is also greater than the mean, so eliminate (C). The correct answer is (B).

17. **B** The question asks for a certain value on a graph. *Hours* are listed along the horizontal axis, so find 12 on that axis. From this point, trace up to find the intersection with the line of best fit, using the answer sheet as a straight edge if necessary. It is between the horizontal gridlines for 70% and 80% on the *Job Satisfaction* axis. Only the value in (B) falls between 70% and 80%. The correct answer is (B).

18. **A** The question asks for a proportion, which is defined as $\frac{part}{whole}$. Read the table carefully to find the numbers to make the proportion. There were 250 participants who watched the new ad, so that is the *whole*. Of these participants, 120 had a favorable opinion, so that is the *part*. Therefore, the proportion is $\frac{120}{250} = \frac{12}{25}$. The correct answer is (A).

19. **B** The question asks for a percent decrease based on data. Percent change is defined as $\frac{difference}{original} \times 100$. Set it up, then find the numbers on the table. The question asks *for the percent decrease...from January 1ˢᵗ, 2010, to January 1ˢᵗ, 2011*. The graph lists time as *Months since January 1ˢᵗ 2008*. There are two years or 24 months from January 1ˢᵗ, 2008 to January 1ˢᵗ, 2010, so the crime rate for January 1ˢᵗ, 2010 is at 24 months on the horizontal axis. From this point, trace up to find the intersection with the line of best fit, using the answer sheet as a straight edge if necessary. It is at a crime rate of 1,000. There is one more year or an additional 12 months between January 1ˢᵗ, 2010 and January 1ˢᵗ, 2011, so the crime rate for January 1ˢᵗ, 2011 is at 36 months on the vertical axis. This intersects the line of best fit at a crime rate of 800. Therefore, the percent decrease is $\frac{1,000 - 800}{1,000} \times 100 = \frac{200}{1,000} \times 100 = 0.2 \times 100 = 20\%$. The correct answer is (B).

20. **C** The question asks for the meaning of a coefficient in context. Start by reading the full question, which asks for the meaning of the number 16.8. Then label the parts of the equation with the information given. The question states that y is the violent crime rate in the city and x is the number of months since the crime prevention program began. The number 16.8 is multiplied by months and subtracted from 1,412, so it must have something to do with the decrease in the crime rate over time. Next, use Process of Elimination to get rid of answer choices that are not consistent with the labels. Choice (A) refers to the number of months, but x represents time in the equation, so eliminate (A). Choice (B) refers to the average crime rate, but y represents the crime rate in the equation, so eliminate (B) also. Choice (C) refers to a *reduction* in the crime rate over time, so keep (C). Choice (D) refers to the exact crime rate in 2008, when the program began. To check this,

plug in $x = 0$. The equation becomes $y = 1,412 - 16.8(0) = 1,412 - 0 = 1,412$. Therefore, the crime rate at the start of the program in January 2008 was 1,412. Eliminate (D). The correct answer is (C).

21. **A** The question asks for an inequality that models a specific situation. Translate the question in bite-sized pieces and eliminate after each piece. One piece of information says that Samuel's salary will increase from \$49,500 to \$64,500 once he completes the MBA program. Therefore, the *additional income* each year will be (64,500 – 49,500), so eliminate (C) and (D), which do not include this term. Compare the remaining answer choices. The difference between (A) and (B) is the direction of the inequality symbol. The question states that the *total additional income* should *exceed the cost of tuition*. Therefore, the additional income per year times the number of years will be greater than the tuition. This translates to $(64,500 – 49,500)n > 73,320$. The answer choices isolate n, so divide both sides by (64,500 – 49,500) to get $n > \dfrac{73,320}{(64,500 – 49,500)}$. The correct answer is (A).

22. **C** The question asks for the graph of a function given a description of that function. The *zeroes* of a polynomial are the points where it crosses the x-axis, or where $y = 0$. Therefore, the graph of this polynomial will contain the points (–4, 0) and (2, 0). Look at the graphs and eliminate any that do not include these points. Choice (A) has zeroes at (–4, 0), (–1, 0), and (2, 0). Choice (A) also has a third zero not mentioned in the question, so check the remaining answers. Choice (B) has zeroes at (–4, 0) and (2, 0). Keep (B) as well. Choice (C) has zeroes at (–4, 0) and (2, 0). Keep (C) as well. Choice (D) has zeroes at (–2, 0) and (4, 0). Eliminate (D). The question also states that the graph should only contain values for y that are greater than or equal to –3. Choices (A) and (B) contain values of y less than –3. Eliminate (A) and (B). The correct answer is (C).

23. **C** The question asks for a statement that is supported based on the results of a poll that was conducted. Read each answer carefully and use Process of Elimination. Choice (A) refers to high voter turnout on Election Day. It is impossible to know whether additional voters will be for or against the proposition, since only one poll was conducted. Furthermore, no information is given regarding the number of people polled or how they were selected. The poll sample may be too small or too biased to draw conclusions about the larger population. Eliminate (A). Choice (B) refers to the ages of voters. No information was given about the ages of the poll participants, so no conclusion can be drawn about voters based on age. Eliminate (B). Choice (C) refers to the method in which the poll participants were reached. This applies directly to the poll, so it could contain a reasonable conclusion. The percent of participants contacted by cell phone who supported the proposition was 30%, whereas 55% of all participants contacted by landline supported it. Since the percent is higher for landline participants, (C) is true. Keep it, but check (D) just in case. Choice (D) refers to only the landline users, but it has the same problem as (A) in that no information is given to determine if these participants make up a representative sample. Eliminate (D). The correct answer is (C).

24. **D** The question asks for an equation that models a specific situation. There are variables in the answer choices, so plug in. Make $n = 14$ days in the original equation, so $x = 2$ weeks in the answer choices. The original equation becomes $w = 109(1.12)^{14} \approx 109(4.887) \approx 532.7$. This is the target value; circle it. Now plug $x = 2$ into the answer choices to see which one matches the target value. Choice (A) becomes $w = 109(2.21)^{\frac{2}{7}} \approx 109(1.254) \approx 137$. This does not match the target, so eliminate (A). Choice (B) becomes $w = 109(1.12)^{\frac{2}{7}}$, which will be even smaller than (A). Eliminate (B). Choice (C) becomes $w = 109(1.84)^2 = 109(3.3856) \approx 369$. Eliminate (C). Choice (D) becomes $w = 109(1.12)^{7(2)} \approx 109(4.887) \approx 532.7$. The correct answer is (D).

25. **D** The question asks for a true statement regarding the results of a study that was conducted. Read each answer carefully and use Process of Elimination. Choice (A) refers to the size of the sample. Generally, the larger the sample, the more reliable the study results. No numbers are given regarding the sample size or number of residents, so this is difficult to determine. Keep (A) for now, but check the other answers. Choice (B) refers to the days that the study was conducted. While doing the study two days instead of one would improve the results, there is no way to tell if that will make the result completely reliable. Again, keep (B) but see if there is a better answer. Choice (C) refers to the location of the study. Again, a busier location may help get more respondents, but it is unclear if that will make the study reliable. Eliminate (C). Choice (D) refers to bias in the study, which means that the group involved might be more inclined to a certain outcome. Since the study only involved people entering the library, the results are likely to favor library-use more than if randomly selected people had participated. Since exact numbers were not given, the sample size is less of a problem than the bias in the sample. Eliminate (A). The correct answer is (D).

26. **A** The question asks for the value of d in point (c, d). Start by determining the value of c in terms of d. The question states that $\frac{c}{d} = \frac{3}{2}$. Cross-multiply to get $2c = 3d$. Divide both sides by 2 to get $c = \frac{3d}{2}$. Next, use the given information to determine the equation of the lines. Use slope-intercept form: $y = mx + b$, where (x, y) is a point on the line, m is the slope, and b is the y-intercept. The first line contains point (c, d) and has a slope of 2, so its equation is $d = 2c + b$. Substitute $\frac{3d}{2}$ for c to get $d = 2\left(\frac{3d}{2}\right) + b$, which becomes $d = 3d + b$ or $-2d = b$. The second line contains the point $(3, 2d)$, has a slope of -3, and the same y-intercept as the first equation, so its equation is $2d = -3(3) + b$, or $2d = -9 + b$. Substitute $-2d$ for b to get $2d = -9 - 2d$. Add $2d$ to both sides to get $4d = -9$. Divide both sides by 4 to get $d = -\frac{9}{4}$. The correct answer is (A).

27. **C** The question asks for the relationship between two variables. When given a table of values and asked for the correct equation, plug values from the table into the answer choices to see which one

works. In the answers, *n* is *years after 2010*. Therefore, according to the table, $n = 3$ when the unemployment rate was 13%. Choice (A) becomes 1.5(3) + 11.5, which is 4.5 + 11.5 or 16. This does not match the unemployment rate; eliminate (A). Choice (B) becomes 0.5(3 – 2,010) + 11.5, which is 0.5(–2,007) + 11.5 or –1,003.5 + 11.5, which is –992. Eliminate (B). Choice (C) becomes 0.5(3) + 11.5, which is 1.5 + 11.5 or 13. Keep (C), but check (D) just in case. Choice (D) becomes –1.5(3) + 11.5, which is –4.5 + 11.5 or 7. Eliminate (D). The correct answer is (C).

28. **A**   The question asks for the model that best fits the data. The question states that water is added *at a constant rate*. Therefore, the rate of increase is linear rather than exponential. Eliminate (C) and (D), which are equations for exponential growth. Next, find a value from the data to plug in to the remaining answers. The pool *contains 60% more water after the hose has run for 5 hours*. The pool initially contained 750 gallons, so after 5 hours it contains $750 + 750 \times \dfrac{60}{100} = 1,200$ gallons. Therefore, when $t = 5$, the answer should equal 1,200. Choice (A) becomes 750 + 90(5), which is 750 + 450 or 1,200. This is true, so the correct answer is (A).

29. **D**   The question asks for the value of a function. In function notation, the number inside the parentheses is the *x*-value that goes into the function, and the value that comes out of the function is the *y*-value. The vertex of the graph of function *h* is at (–1, –3), so $a = -1$ and $h(a) = h(-1) = -3$. Substitute to get $f(h(a)) = f(-3)$. Use the table to determine that $f(-3) = 11$. The correct answer is (D).

30. **B**   The question asks for a true statement based on the data. Consider each answer and use Process of Elimination. Choice (A) compares the ranges of Group A and Group B. The range of a list of values is the greatest value minus the least value. In Group A, the greatest value is 9 and the least value is 3, so the range is 9 – 3, which is 6. In Group B, the greatest value is 13 and the least value is 8, so the range is 13 – 8 = 5. Eliminate (A), which says the range of Group B is larger. Also eliminate (D), which says the ranges are equal. Choices (B) and (C) compare the standard deviation of the two groups. Standard deviation is a measure of how close together the data points are in a group of numbers; a list with numbers close together has a small standard deviation, whereas a list with numbers spread out has a large standard deviation. In Group A, the data points are evenly distributed, whereas in Group B most of the data points are around 12. Therefore, the standard deviation of Group B must be less than the standard deviation of Group A. Eliminate (C). The correct answer is (B).

31. **14**   The question asks for the value of *n* if the two equations represent the same line. Make the second equation equal to the first by multiplying the second equation by 2 to get $14x - 8y = 18$. Both equations are equal, so *n* must equal 14. The correct answer is 14.

32. **66**   The question asks for a measurement and gives conflicting units. When dealing with scale maps or models, make a proportion, being sure to match up units. The proportion is $\dfrac{1 \text{ liter}}{3 \text{ milligrams}} = \dfrac{22 \text{ liters}}{x \text{ milligrams}}$. Cross-multiply to get $x = 66$. The correct answer is 66.

33. **9**   The question asks for the value of c in the equation. Start by substituting –3 for x to get $\frac{1}{3}c + (-3)$ = 0. Add 3 to both sides of the equation to get $\frac{1}{3}c = 3$. Multiply both sides by 3 to get $c = 9$. The correct answer is 9.

34. **6**   The question asks for the value of a variable in a system of equations. Since $p(x) = q(x)$ where the two functions intersect, one way to solve this would be to graph both functions on a graphing calculator and trace to find the intersections. Another method is to solve algebraically by setting the equations equal to one another. This gives $15 - 5x = \frac{1}{3}(x - 9)^2 - 18$. Add 18 to both sides to get $33 - 5x = \frac{1}{3}(x - 9)^2$. Clear the fraction by multiplying both sides by 3 to get $99 - 15x = (x - 9)^2$. FOIL the right side to get $99 - 15x = x^2 - 9x - 9x + 81$, which is $99 - 15x = x^2 - 18x + 81$. Add $15x$ to both sides to get $99 = x^2 - 3x + 81$. Subtract 99 from both sides to get $0 = x^2 - 3x - 18$. Factor by finding two numbers that add to –3 and multiply to –18. Those numbers are –6 and 3, so the equation becomes $0 = (x - 6)(x + 3)$. Set each factor equal to 0 and solve to get $x - 6 = 0$ or $x = 6$ and $x + 3 = 0$ or $x = -3$. The question asks for the positive x value. The correct answer is 6.

35. **0.6**   The question asks for the value of the sum of two trigonometric functions. The functions of sine and cosine usually apply to right angles and give the ratio of the side opposite or adjacent the angle, respectively, to the hypotenuse. This question has a right angle, but the angles in question are not the other two angles of triangle ABC. The angles $\angle DBA$ and $\angle DBC$ add together to make the right angle, so use the fact that $\sin(x°) = \cos(90° - x°)$. If $\angle DBC$ is $x°$, then $\angle DBA$ is $(90° - x°)$ and $\sin(\angle DBC) = \cos(\angle DBA) = 0.3$. Therefore, $\cos(\angle DBA) + \sin(\angle DBC) = 0.3 + 0.3 = 0.6$. The correct answer is 0.6.

36. **0.11**   The question asks for a rate in terms of points per minute. Begin by reading the question to find information on the average number of points lost. The question states that *during two days of trading the Dow Jones Industrial Average lost 68.9 points* and that *there were 5 hours of trading during each of the two days combined.* Therefore, there were $2 \times 5 = 10$ hours of trading. There are 60 minutes in an hour, so 10 hours is $60 \times 10 = 600$ minutes. To determine rate, divide amount by time: $\frac{68.9 \text{ points}}{600 \text{ minutes}} \approx 0.1148$ points per minute. The question asks for the rate to the nearest hundredth of a point per minute, so round to 0.11. The correct answer is 0.11.

37. **1.3**   The question asks for the value of r in the function. Use the table to fill in the other variables and solve. Choose a point that makes the math easier. Because the exponent is divided by 2 in the function,

choose 2 days. At 2 days after germination, the plants weighed 6.6 grams, so $d = 2$ and $H(2) = 6.6$. The function becomes $6.6 = 5.0r^{\frac{2}{2}}$, which is $6.6 = 5.0r^1$ or $6.6 = 5.0r$. Divide both sides by 5.0 to get $r = 1.32$. The question asks for the value of r rounded to the nearest tenth, so round 1.32 to 1.3. The correct answer is 1.3.

38. **9.6** The question asks for the difference between the masses of two groups of plants. Start by determining the mass of the 4 plants that germinated 4 days ago. According to the table, plants that germinated 4 days ago have a mass of 8.4 grams per plant, so 4 plants would have a mass of 4×8.4 = 33.6 grams. Next, find the mass of the 3 plants that germinated 8 days ago. These plants have an average mass of 14.4 grams, so their total mass is 3×14.4 = 43.2 grams. To find the difference, subtract: $43.2 - 33.6 = 9.6$ grams. The correct answer is 9.6.

Section 5: Experimental

1. **A** Note the question! The question asks whether the phrase should be added, so it's testing consistency of ideas and precision. If the phrase is consistent with the first part of the sentence and it plays a precise role, then it should be added. The first part of the sentence states that the Orbiter crashed on Mars. The new phrase states that it should have gone *into orbit around the planet to collect and transmit data*. This explains what the Orbiter's mission was supposed to be, so it's consistent and plays a precise role. The phrase should be added, so eliminate (C) and (D). The phrase does *give details that clarify that the crash was unexpected*, so keep (A). The phrase does not *establish an important shift in focus*, so eliminate (B). The correct answer is (A).

2. **A** The change in the answer choices is from a noun to different pronouns, so the question is testing precision. Determine the subject of the pronoun, and choose an answer that makes the meaning consistent and precise. The underlined portion must establish who is *against adopting the metric system*. At this point in the passage, no specific party has been established, so the most precise answer will be the specific noun, not the general pronoun. *People* is a specific noun, so keep (A). *They, them*, and *those* are general pronouns, so eliminate (B), (C), and (D). The correct answer is (A).

3. **C** Verbs are changing in the answer choices, so the question is testing consistency of verbs. A verb must be consistent with its subject and with the other verbs in the sentence. All the answer choices are consistent with the subject of the verb, *the other group*, so look for other verbs. The first part of the sentence states that *one group used*, so the underlined portion must be consistent with that verb. Only *used* is consistent. Eliminate (A), (B), and (D). The correct answer is (C).

4. **D** Note the question! The question asks where sentence 2 should be placed, so it's testing consistency. Determine the subject matter of the sentence, and find the other sentence that also discusses that information. Sentence 2 states that *neither group realized*, so it should be placed after the sentence that mentions the two groups. Only sentence 5 mentions *one group... and the other group*, so sentence 2 should be placed after sentence 5. The correct answer is (D).

5. **B** Note the question! The question asks for the best combination, so it's testing concision. Select the shortest choice that eliminates the redundancy present in the original sentences. Evaluate (B) first because it's the shortest. The pronoun *which* refers to the *replacement of Roman numerals with the base-ten Arabic numbering* in the first part of the sentence. Because *which* replaces that same phrase in the second part of the sentence, the redundancy has been eliminated and the answer is concise. The correct answer is (B).

6. **B** The number and placement of the commas is changing in the answer choices, so the question is testing comma usage. The commas are changing in two places (and there's a dash), so check for unnecessary information. Because *decimal* and *base-ten* mean the same thing, it is unnecessary to say it twice. Therefore, there should be either commas or dashes before and after the phrase *or base-ten*. The comma and the dash cannot be used together, so eliminate (D). Eliminate (A) and (C) because the commas are in the wrong place. The correct answer is (B).

7. **D** The number and placement of the commas is changing in the answer choices, so the question is testing comma usage. The sentence does not contain a list, so check for unnecessary information. Removing any of the phrases between the commas creates an incomplete sentence. Therefore, all the phrases are necessary, and there is no reason to use a comma. The correct answer is (D).

8. **C** Note the question! The question asks for the explanation of how the metric system was important for trade over long distances, so it's testing consistency of ideas. Select the choice that is consistent with *important for trade over long distances*. *Cheating* is not consistent with *long distances*, so eliminate (A). Although (B) mentions *long-distance*, *different currencies* is not consistent with the *metric system*; eliminate (B). The *buyers and sellers* not being *from the same place* is consistent with *trade over long distances*, so keep (C). The type of *goods* is not consistent, so eliminate (D). The correct answer is (C).

9. **C** First, the pronouns are changing in the answer choices, so the question is testing consistency. The pronoun must be consistent in number with the noun it is replacing. The noun is *France*, which is singular. Thus, the pronoun must also be singular. Eliminate (A) and (B), which are plural. Next, the verbs are changing, so the question is testing consistency. A verb must be consistent with its subject and with the other verbs in the sentence. The sentence states that *France was*, which is the simple past tense. Thus, the underlined portion must also be in the simple past tense. *Organized* is the simple past, so keep (C). *Had organized* includes the unnecessary helping verb *had*, so eliminate (D). The correct answer is (C).

10. **C** Note the question! The question asks for the choice that maintains the style and tone of the passage, so it's testing consistency. The overall tone of the passage is semi-formal and educational, so the correct answer should be consistent with this tone. Choices (A), (B), and (D) are too informal. The correct answer is (C).

11. **A** The transition phrase is changing in the answer choices, so the question is testing consistency of ideas. The sentence contains two phrases separated by a comma, so evaluate those two ideas to

determine how they should be connected. The first part states that *the American colonies were part of the British Empire*, and the second part states that *they used the British Imperial System of measurement*. These ideas are similar, so eliminate (B) and (D) because they indicate opposite ideas. Using *therefore* would create two complete ideas separated by a comma. GO punctuation cannot separate two complete ideas, so eliminate (C). The correct answer is (A).

12. **D**   The vocabulary is changing in the answer choices, so this question is testing word choice. Look for a word whose definition is consistent with the other ideas in the sentence. The sentence is trying to state that both Jefferson and Franklin were proponents of "getting rid of" the British system, so the correct answer must be consistent with this idea. *Sacrificing* means "to kill or destroy something as an offering," so eliminate (A). *Ducking* means "to get out of the way of something," so eliminate (B). *Evading* means "to avoid something," so eliminate (C). *Abandoning* means to "give something up" or to "leave something behind." This is consistent with the rest of the sentence. The correct answer is (D).

13. **D**   The transition phrase is changing in the answer choices, so the question is testing consistency of ideas. Evaluate the ideas that come before and after the transition to determine how they should be connected. The prior idea is that both Jefferson and Franklin were proponents of adopting the metric system. The next idea is that there were *insurmountable roadblocks to adopting the metric system*. These are opposite ideas, so a transition that changes direction is needed. *For example, moreover*, and *thus* all indicate the same direction, so eliminate (A), (B), and (C). *However* indicates a change in direction. The correct answer is (D).

14. **B**   The punctuation is changing in the answer choices, so the question is testing STOP and GO punctuation. Use the vertical line test, and identify the ideas as complete or incomplete. Draw the vertical line between the words *War* and *it*. The first phrase is an incomplete idea, and the second phrase is a complete idea. STOP punctuation can only come between two complete ideas, so eliminate (A) and (C), which both contain STOP punctuation. HALF-STOP punctuation must come after a complete idea, so eliminate the colon in (D). A comma is GO punctuation, which can separate an incomplete idea from a complete idea. The correct answer is (B).

15. **B**   The vocabulary is changing in the answer choices, so the question is testing word choice. The correct choice will match the idea of *sending a delegation to France* to the purpose of the trip. The purpose was not *by learn* or *of learn*, so eliminate (C) and (D). If the word *for* is used, the phrase should say *for learning*, so eliminate (A). The purpose was *to learn about the metric system*. The correct answer is (B).

16. **A**   Note the question! The question asks for the best introduction to this paragraph, so it's testing consistency of ideas. The previous paragraph ends by stating that the U.S. kept the British system. This paragraph discusses a few times that the U.S. tried and failed to convert to the metric system. The correct answer will be consistent with this idea. *Multiple attempts...to establish the metric system* is consistent, so keep (A). Discussing *France* is not consistent, so eliminate (B). Eliminate (C) because

it does not mention the metric system. The topic of *political upheaval* is not consistent, so eliminate (D). The correct answer is (A).

17. **C**   The phrases are changing in the answer choices, so the question is testing concision and precision. Select the shortest choice whose meaning is precise. The terms *enthusiasts* and *admirers* mean the same thing, so that idea should not be repeated. Eliminate (A) and (D) because they are redundant. Choices (B) and (C) mean the same thing, so select the more concise choice. The correct answer is (C).

18. **A**   Note the question! The question asks for the conclusion of the essay, so it's testing consistency of ideas. The essay started by stating that some people believe the metric system caused the Mars Climate Orbiter to crash, and it ended by stating that the United States had been unable to make the metric system mandatory. The correct answer must be consistent with these ideas. Choice (A) states that our *speed limit signs are* not in *kilometers per hour* and revisits the *Mars Climate Orbiter crash*, so keep it. Stating what *school children learn* is not consistent, so eliminate (B). Discussing *businesses* in relation to *government agencies* is not consistent, so eliminate (C). Stating that *no one is motivated to make the change* is not consistent, so eliminate (D). The correct answer is (A).

RAW SCORE CONVERSION TABLE SECTION AND TEST SCORES

Raw Score (# of correct answers)	Math Section Score	Reading Test Score	Writing and Language Test Score	Raw Score (# of correct answers)	Math Section Score	Reading Test Score	Writing and Language Test Score
0	200	10	10	30	530	28	29
1	200	10	10	31	540	28	30
2	210	10	10	32	550	29	30
3	230	11	10	33	560	29	31
4	240	12	11	34	560	30	32
5	260	13	12	35	570	30	32
6	280	14	13	36	580	31	33
7	290	15	13	37	590	31	34
8	310	15	14	38	600	32	34
9	320	16	15	39	600	32	35
10	330	17	16	40	610	33	36
11	340	17	16	41	620	33	37
12	360	18	17	42	630	34	38
13	370	19	18	43	640	35	39
14	380	19	19	44	650	35	40
15	390	20	19	45	660	36	
16	410	20	20	46	670	37	
17	420	21	21	47	670	37	
18	430	21	21	48	680	38	
19	440	22	22	49	690	38	
20	450	22	23	50	700	39	
21	460	23	23	51	710	40	
22	470	23	24	52	730	40	
23	480	24	25	53	740		
24	480	24	25	54	750		
25	490	25	26	55	760		
26	500	25	26	56	780		
27	510	26	27	57	790		
28	520	26	28	58	800		
29	520	27	28				

*Please note that these scores are best approximations and that actual scores on the SAT may slightly vary, depending on individual adaptations made by the College Board.

CONVERSION EQUATION 1   SECTION AND TEST SCORES

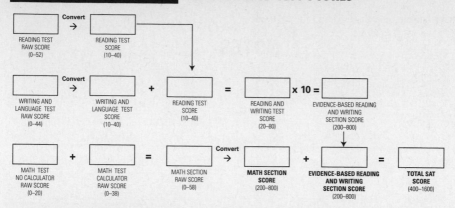

CONVERSION EQUATION 2   SECTION AND TEST SCORES

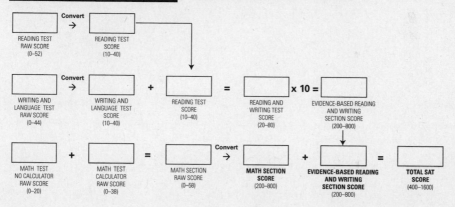

NOTES

NOTES